PROTECTION
OF
Computer Systems
and Software

New Approaches for Combating Theft of Software and Unauthorized Intrusion

PROTECTION
OF
Computer Systems and Software

New Approaches for Combating Theft of Software and Unauthorized Intrusion

Edited by
Frank L. Huband
and
R.D. Shelton

Law & Business, Inc.

Library of Congress Cataloging-in-Publication Data

Protection of computer systems and software.

Papers presented at a workshop sponsored by the
National Science Foundation.
Bibliography: p.
Includes index.
1. Computer crimes—United States. 2. Copyright—
Computer programs—United States. 3. Computers—
United States—Access control. 4. Computer crimes—
United States—Prevention. I. Huband, Frank L.
II. Shelton, R.D. III. National Science Foundation
(U.S.)
KF9350.P76 1985   345.73'0268   86–10271
ISBN 0-1500-4393-7   347.305268

CONTENTS

Chapter 3: Legal Approaches to Software Protection: Federal Protection of Proprietary Rights 47

by Jon A. Baumgarten

Chapter 4: Technical Approaches to Software Protection 95

by Neil Iscoe

Chapter 5: Electronic Bulletin Boards: A New Threat to Computer Systems 123

by Donn B. Parker and John F. Maxfield

Chapter 6: Legal and Managerial Approaches to Intrusion Protection 147

by Susan H. Nycum and Daniel L. Appelman

Chapter 7: Technical Solutions to the Computer Security Intrusion Problem 179

by Eugene F. Troy, Stuart W. Katzke, and Dennis D. Steinauer

Chapter 8: Summary and Conclusions ...241

by Frank L. Huband

PREFACE AND ACKNOWLEDGMENTS

Combating the growing problems of computer crime requires an unusual variety of talents. Lawyers can advise client organizations of how best to protect themselves under existing laws. Engineers and computer scientists can devise technical protection methods. Educators can help instill a more appropriate sense of the ethics and legalities of computer use. Federal, State, and local government officials can help strengthen legislation and prosecute existing violations. Because none of these efforts have been adequate to allay concerns about computer crime, it is desirable to open the lines of communication between these groups to permit more unified approaches. This book is the first combined treatment of the various countermeasures to two of the most disturbing kinds of computer crime: the theft of computer software and the unauthorized intrusion into computer systems by telephone.

The authors are some of the leading authorities in the field. Michael Tyler, who has written on many facets of computers for *Datamation,* researched the extent of the software piracy problem, primarily by interviewing many of the leaders of the microcomputer software industry. Jon Baumgarten is an attorney with an extensive practice in the protection of intellectual property and, as former general counsel for the U.S. Copyright Office, was instrumental in drafting legislation that extended copyright protection to computer software. His chapter surveys the current state of copyright and patent protection. Neil Iscoe is president of a software firm, Statcom Corporation, and director of a task force of the Association of Data Processing Service Organizations (ADAPSO) that is evaluating current technical protection methods. His chapter explains those methods in terms that are understandable by all. Donn Parker and John Maxfield, who are information security consultants, help define the extent of the computer intrusion problem, particularly the growing use of computer bulletin boards as a means of exchanging the necessary information. Mr. Parker has written six books on aspects of computer crime, while John Maxfield has intimate knowledge of the culture of the intruders from his infiltration of their society. Susan Nycum and Daniel Appelman are currently surveying the state of legal protection against computer crime for the U.S. Department of Justice. Their chapter pays particular attention to the coverage of the various State statutes that have the primary role in the area. Gene Troy, Stuart Katzke, and Dennis Steinauer work at the National Bureau of Standards to improve protection of computer systems against intrusion, and their chapter surveys the types of intrusion and their technical countermeasures.

The chapters include formal reviews by the following experts: Stanley Besen, Michael Keplinger, Stephen Morse, Joseph Tompkins, Daniel Burk, and Marvin Schaefer. About 40 invited participants attended oral presentations of the chapters at a workshop sponsored by the National Science Foundation. Highlights of the discussion are appended to each chapter.

Among the many other people who made the workshop and this subsequent book a success were the staff of The MAXIMA Corporation who assisted in workshop logistics and chapter editing: Richard Scarino, Meta de Coquereaumont, and Michael Hayes. Lynn S. Glasser and Stephen W. Seemer at Law and Business, Inc., also provided invaluable support.

LIST OF CONTRIBUTORS

Daniel Appelman
Gaston, Snow and Ely Bartlett
Palo Alto, CA

Jon A. Baumgarten
Paskus, Gordon & Hyman
Washington, DC

Stanley Besen
The Rand Corporation
Washington, DC

John Bjork
Office of the Inspector
   General
Small Business Administration
Washington, DC

Eric Bloch
National Science Foundation
Washington, DC

Jane Bortnick
Congressional Research
   Service
Library of Congress
Washington, DC

Daniel Burk, Esq.
Thomas & Fiske
Alexandria, VA

Frank J. Carr
Information Resources
   Management
General Services
   Administration
Washington, DC

Belle Cummins
Office of Congressman Barney
   Frank
Washington, DC

Robert Entman
National Telecommunications
  and Information
  Administration
Policy Analysis and
  Development
Washington, DC

Carol Erlebach
National Science Foundation
Washington, DC

Bonnie Fisher
Office of the Inspector
  General
Department of Health and
  Human Services
Washington, DC

Linda Garcia
Office of Technology
  Assessment
Washington, DC

E. Ric Giardina
MicroPro International
San Rafael, CA

Charles Goldfarb
Office of Management and
  Budget
New Executive Office Building
Washington, DC

Alan Greenberg
State Department
Washington, DC

Joe Grunfest
Council of Economic Advisors
Old Executive Office Building
Washington, DC

George A. Hazelrigg, Jr.
Division of Policy Research
  and Analysis
National Science Foundation
Washington, DC

Peter W. House
Division of Policy Research
  and Analysis
National Science Foundation
Washington, DC

Frank L. Huband
Division of Policy Research
  and Analysis
National Science Foundation
Washington, DC

Neil Iscoe
STATCOM Corporation
Austin, TX

Jan Jancin
IBM Corporation
Arlington, VA

Stuart Katzke
Institute for Computer Science
  and Technology
National Bureau of Standards
Gaithersburg, MD

Wayne Kay
Telecommunication Consultant
Arlington, VA

Michael S. Keplinger
U.S. Patent and Trademark
  Office
Arlington, VA

Carole Kitti
Office of Management and
  Budget
Washington, DC

Richard Klafter
Electrical Engineering
  Department
Temple University
Philadelphia, PA

Deborah Leavy
House Subcommittee on
  Courts, Civil Liberties, and
  the Administration of
  Justice
Washington, DC

David Leibowitz
Copyright Office
Washington, DC

A. M. Long
IBM Corporation
Gaithersburg, MD

Larry Martin
Office of ADP Management
Department of Energy
Washington, DC

John Maxfield
BOARDSCAN
Detroit, MI

Mark McCarthy
House Energy and Commerce
  Committee
Washington, DC

Steven Metalitz
Senate Subcommittee on
  Patents, Copyrights, and
  Trademarks
Washington, DC

Stephen Morse
Altos Computer Systems
San Jose, CA

Edward H. O'Connell
Office of Rep. William J.
  Hughes
Washington, DC

Lawrence Oliver
Division of Computer
  Research
National Science Foundation
Washington, DC

Thomas P. Olsen
Senate Subcommittee on
  Patents, Copyrights, and
  Trademarks
Washington, DC

Ralph Oman
Senate Subcommittee on
  Patents, Copyrights, and
  Trademarks
Washington, DC

Donn Parker
SRI International
Menlo Park, CA

David Peyton
Information Industry
  Association
Washington, DC

Roger K. Salaman
NTIA/ITS
Boulder, CO

Richard Scarino
The MAXIMA Corporation
Bethesda, MD

Marvin Schaefer
Computer Security Evaluation
  Center
Department of Defense
Ft. Meade, MD

Stephen Seemer
Law and Business, Inc.
Clifton, NJ

R. D. Shelton
Division of Policy Research
  and Analysis
National Science Foundation
Washington, DC

Robert S. Shriver
Wolfensohn Ventures, Inc.
New York, NY

Oliver R. Smoot
Computer and Business
  Equipment Manufacturers
  Association
Washington, DC

Dr. George Sponsler
IEEE Committee on Computer
  Privacy
Bethesda, MD

Dennis Steinauer
Institute for Computer Science
  and Technology
National Bureau of Standards
Gaithersburg, MD

William S. Taylor
Abrams, Westermeier, &
  Goldberg
Washington, DC

Gail Thackeray
District Attorney's Office
Philadelphia, PA

Joseph B. Tompkins, Jr.
Sidley and Austin
Washington, DC

Michael Tyler
Datamation
Philadelphia, PA

one

INTRODUCTION

R. D. Shelton*

I. BACKGROUND

The Computer Crime Task Force of the American Bar Association recently estimated that computer crime rivals conventional white-collar crime in cost and impact. Their report,[1] based on a survey of 283 large corporations and government agencies, concludes that there is "disturbing and undeniable evidence that the scope and significance of computer crime and its potentially devastating effects are broad and deep." The most significant forms of computer crime reported are thefts of assets, including software, embezzlement of funds, defrauding of consumers and investors, and destruction or alteration of data and

---

* R. D. Shelton is Professor of Electrical Engineering and Computer Science at the University of Louisville. He is currently on assignment to the National Science Foundation where he is performing research on Federal policies in the information sciences area.

[1] Joseph B. Tompkins, Jr., James R. Jorgenson, Nathaniel E. Kossack, and Marcia L. Proctor, *Report on Computer Crime* (Washington, D.C.: American Bar Association, 1984).

software. The report concludes that "the need for Federal crime legislation is unmistakable."

Although there are current Federal statutes that bear on computer crime, the increase in the extent of these problems calls for consideration of whether additional measures are needed. Based on a workshop sponsored by the National Science Foundation in October 1984, this book addresses two of the most troubling computer crime issues: (1) unauthorized duplication or use of software and (2) unauthorized intrusion or access to computer systems. Each chapter represents a paper presented at that workshop, followed by a critique by workshop participants.

Industry leaders estimate that at least one unauthorized copy of each business software diskette is produced for every one that is legitimately purchased. Protection of such property can be enhanced by both legal and technical means. The Federal role in the legal area currently includes the copyright system (which has come to be the primary legal protection method), the issuance of trademarks and patents, and the prosecution of violations under these laws and customs regulations.

Unauthorized access to computer systems has become an area of increasing concern. A popular movie has focused on this subject, and news articles of hobbyists with inexpensive home equipment improperly obtaining access to computer systems containing sensitive information are becoming more common. The Federal legal countermeasures in this area can include prosecution of intruders into Federal, financial, and national security computer systems under provisions of the Hughes Bill (18 U.S. Code 1030) enacted in October 1984. Additional statutes extending Federal responsibility in this area are likely to be considered in the U.S. Congress in coming years.

Although State and Federal Governments could take further legal countermeasures to reduce computer-related crime, these countermeasures could represent intrusion into private activities, and this intrusion might not be socially acceptable. However, technical countermeasures such as devices that attach to the user's computer hardware and encryption of diskette lock codes may minimize the need for more legislation by providing effective protection. A principal theme of this book is the interplay between technical and legal countermeasures and the quest for a balance between the two.

Although copyright laws should be sufficient for the protection of software, technical protection is still necessary to deter those who disregard the law. But the technology will need continual refinement, because protection schemes in the past were quickly defeated by more sophisticated copying methods.

Legai countermeasures for protecting computer systems from intrusion primarily are based on a wide variety of state laws that have not been effective deterrents, as discussed in Chapter 6. The technical protection methods presented in Chapter 7 seem to be sufficient to stop all but the most sophisticated penetrations. However, these methods are not as widely used as they might be, so more widespread use is a viable solution.

Although the two areas of computer crime addressed might appear to be unrelated, they have many features in common. Often the same individuals are engaged in both unauthorized copying and access, and sometimes for the same reasons. Computer bulletin boards are frequently key vehicles for the exchange of information necessary to conduct both activities. Both activities are generally conceded to cause serious harm to their victims, although there is little known about the exact extent of harm. A minority view, however, holds that a certain amount of both activities may actually have beneficial results. Penetrations by amateurs, for example, may not do much harm but may expose vulnerabilities that could be exploited by professional criminals. Similarly, a certain amount of unauthorized copying may increase the market for software by the increased exposure of the product. Both activities are considered by many to be mere mischief, and the perpetrators are sometimes admired instead of denigrated. Education of the public on the ethics and legalities of the activities is a priority solution for both.

2. PREVIEW

This book presents parallel treatments of unauthorized copying and intrusions. There is a chapter for each treatment which defines the scope of the problem, and additional chapters discuss the legal and technical solutions that are available.

Michael Tyler of *Datamation* defines the scope of one software piracy problem—the unauthorized copying of commercial microcomputer software—in Chapter 2. The computer industry is currently the third largest industry in the United States, and innovative software is an important component in making computer products competitive. Anecdotal evidence indicates that there is substantial piracy of home software, particularly among teenage hobbyists. Some observers fear that teenage computer pirates will develop a contempt for the legal system, resulting in increased white-collar crime.

Although business software is copied for resale by some professional pirates, amateur "softlifters" are much more numerous. These are ordinary business users who duplicate a single purchased (or pirated) disk for use on many machines. Software vendors believe that they suffer substantial revenue losses from such piracy, but the precise economic impact of illegal software copying is currently unknown. However, in his ensuing critique, Stanley Besen of the Rand Corporation describes a study he conducted whose outcome indicates that some unauthorized copying can actually produce benefits for vendors. Mr. Tyler, he argues, is insufficiently critical of loss estimates given him by vendor executives.

In Chapter 3, Jon Baumgarten of Paskus, Gordon, and Hyman reviews the legal countermeasures available to deter software piracy. Although trade secret, patent, and trademark approaches have some value, the 1976 Copyright Act as amended and interpreted by the courts has become the principal basis for protection of computer software. It provides automatic legal protection for the newly created applications and operating system software in any tangible medium; also registration with the U.S. Copyright Office confers additional advantages.

There are still areas of disagreement in the interpretation and application of the Act, including the right of users to make archival copies of copyrighted software they have purchased. This provision was inserted because the process of loading a program into a computer for execution can be interpreted as copying, and it was felt that the users must logically have the right to do whatever copying was essential to properly use their purchase. Companies who advertise devices to "make archival copies, make archival copies for your friends, sell archival copies, and flat out get in the archival copy business" use this provision as a loophole. Michael Keplinger, in the critique section of Chapter 3, amplifies Jon Baumgarten's remarks and provides information on the activities of other countries to protect computer software.

Neil Iscoe of STATCOM Corporation discusses in Chapter 4 the technical schemes available to deter unauthorized copying of computer software and discusses some of the methods used to defeat the schemes. Not only do most microcomputer software vendors use some type of diskette protection method, but more than 30 firms specialize in the marketing of technical protection. The Association of Data Processing Service Organizations (ADAPSO) is pursuing several approaches to reduce the theft of software from its member organizations, including educating the public that theft is wrong, proposing additional legislation, and testing and standardizing technical means of protection. However, improved protection is seen as a challenge to be overcome by a legion of amateur pirates, so that there is a continuing cycle of advancements in protection and advancements in copying.

In his critique, Stephen Morse of Altos Computer Systems adds a taxonomy of technical protection methods. He also amplifies the issue of the tradeoff between greater protection and greater inconvenience to the legitimate user and points out that many of the schemes require the cooperation of hardware vendors, who have no incentive to help.

Donn Parker of SRI International and John Maxfield of Boardscan, Inc. define the extent of the problem of unauthorized access by telephone into computer systems in Chapter 5. Studies indicate that the problem is serious and growing, but overall measures of its extent are not available. It is clear that expensive countermeasures have been necessary at many companies and Government agencies. Illicit computer-telephone activities are the outgrowth of abuse of the public telephone system by the phone "phreaks" of the 1950s and 1960s. The computer bulletin board, itself a combination of telecommunication and computer techniques, has come to be an important vehicle for the exchange of the information necessary to penetrate computer systems.

In his critique, Joseph Tompkins of Sidley & Austin notes that he recently served as chairman of a task force of the American Bar Association (ABA) which surveyed the extent of computer crime. He defends the ABA findings, which Donn Parker considered to be typical of overstatements of the quantification of the extent of computer crime.

In Chapter 6, Susan Nycum and Daniel Appelman of Gaston Snow and Ely Bartlett discuss some of the legal and managerial approaches that are available to combat intrusion. Legal jurisdiction resides primarily in the 50 States, and the diversity of State approaches has left gaps in the legal basis for countermeasures. Many States have taken no action at all, and many statutes seem to be inadequate to deter and prosecute intrusion. The Federal Government could assist by coordinating, for example, the development of a model State statute. Management has the obligation to provide at least a barrier to intrusions so that deliberate malicious intent is needed to penetrate it.

Daniel Burk of Thomas & Fiske, in his critique, agrees with the call for additional uniformity in State statutes and points out additional advantages to such an approach, such as the wider applicability of the case law as it is developed.

In Chapter 7, Eugene Troy, Stuart Katzke, and Dennis Steinauer of the National Bureau of Standards review the methods available for erecting intrusion barriers. The types of protection include physical, emanations control, threat monitoring, communications port protection, resource access control mechanisms, and cryptography. The wide variety of controls available can protect against all but the most sophisticated threats, but they have not been used to their potential. One reason is that computer vendors and service providers like to make their systems "user-friendly," and this ease of access is incompatible with the erection of security barriers. In his critique, Marvin Schaefer of the Computer Security Evaluation Center discusses the means by which password access controls and other technical countermeasures can be defeated.

two

THE EXTENT OF
SOFTWARE PIRACY

Michael A. Tyler*

I. THE IMPORTANCE OF SOFTWARE PIRACY

The rapid growth of the computer industry in the past two decades is transforming the nature of offices in the United States. Yet we, as a society, have at times been unable to adapt our life- and work-styles to the Information Age—or, alternatively, computer and software vendors have been unable to adapt their products to the ways of our society. The twin problems of software piracy and computer systems intrusions arise in large part from this imperfect human-machine interface. This paper examines the origins, scope, and economic consequences of software piracy in the United States.

At first glance, the problem may not seem severe. The issue does not rival the national deficit or the arms race in importance, and publicized instances of alleged piracy seem less frequent than similar instances of unauthorized entry into computer

---

* Michael A. Tyler is the former Assistant News Editor of *Datamation* Magazine. He has written news and feature articles on computers, telecommunications, and software.

systems. First impressions can be deceiving, however, and the software piracy problem is both deeper and more dangerous than has so far been recognized. Computer software is one of the few strategically important areas in which the United States holds a clear and significant lead over all other nations in the world, including Japan. Many industry experts believe that piracy today will jeopardize our ability to maintain that lead tomorrow. If the Nation loses its lead, observers say, the economic and political costs may ultimately be greater than the costs of Japanese intrusions into other industries or Soviet advances into high-technology areas.

To understand why software is so important, and hence why software piracy is so important, it is helpful to maintain a perspective of the computer industry's position in American business. Currently, the computer industry is the United States' third largest, behind petroleum and automobiles, according to John F. Akers, president of International Business Machines (IBM) Corp. By 1990, however, the industry will be the United States' largest, he says. "The auto and oil industries are inherently limited by the nature of their products because there are only so many drivers in the world and they can only drive so many miles. But our industry has unlimited potential because society will always want more information."[1]

Although it is impossible to calculate industry revenues exactly, estimates vary from $150 billion to $250 billion in 1983, or 5 to 8 percent of the Gross National Product. Revenues from the 100 largest industry vendors, as listed in *Datamation* magazine, totaled $98.1 billion in 1983, of which IBM alone contributed $35.6 billion.[2] Total industry software revenues are equally difficult to calculate, but they are estimated at about $16 billion. Software revenues from the 100 largest industry vendors—many of whom sell hardware almost exclusively— topped $10 billion in 1983.[3] Some segments within the software

---

[1] Address by John F. Akers, president of IBM Corporation, National Computer Conference, Las Vegas, NV (July 9, 1984).

[2] Pamela Archbold, "The Datamation 100: Fathoming the Industry," *Datamation* 30, no. 8 (1984): 52–144.

[3] Archbold, pp. 52–144.

industry are doubling annually, and microcomputer software vendors, most of whom are too small to be listed in *Datamation's* Top 100, are in many cases tripling or quadrupling every year.[4] The microcomputer business software segment alone is expected to generate $2.2 billion in 1984, up from $1.4 billion in 1983.[5] That figure will probably reach $9 billion by 1987.[6] The software industry is one that will play an increasingly central role in this Nation's development into a postindustrial society.

In that context, any problem that poses a significant threat to the software industry can be considered a matter of national concern. Piracy is currently one of the most frequent and troublesome problems facing the software industry, and it is one that is likely to escalate as the industry grows, if it is not checked.

2. BACKGROUND

2.1 What Is Software Piracy?

In the past five years, several different forms of software piracy have developed, some more malicious—and malignant— than others. Perhaps the most dramatic type is the piracy associated with high-level international corporate intrigue, such as the IBM-Hitachi trade secrets case. In that case, IBM had suspected that Hitachi was stealing trade secrets relating to IBM's advanced mainframe computers and operating systems. IBM cooperated with the Federal Bureau of Investigation in a "sting" operation that caught Hitachi in the act of purchasing illegally-

---

[4] For example, Lotus Development Corp., in Cambridge, MA, reported revenues of $53 million in its first year. Ashton-Tate Inc., in Culver City, CA, doubled its 1982 sales and topped $40 million in 1983. Microsoft Inc., in Bellevue, WA, reported similar revenues in 1983 and had predicted it would top $100 million in 1984. If so, it would have become the first microcomputer software firm to be listed in *Datamation's* Top 100.

[5] Telephone interview with Ron Ward, executive vice president of Future Computing Inc., Dallas, TX (September 26, 1984).

[6] Ward, telephone interview.

obtained, confidential IBM documents. That kind of piracy—
of software for highly advanced systems by competitors who
know the illegality of their actions—is rare, with at most a
handful of cases being publicly known.[7] Moreover, the effects
of this kind of piracy may indeed hurt victim software vendors,
but the purloined knowledge may still benefit the industry as
a whole, by spurring competition and thus new product development.

Another form of mainframe software piracy is the theft or
illegal purchase of software by Communist Bloc countries. Digital Equipment Corp. was fined $1.5 million for selling its
"superminicomputer" VAX systems to a company in the Federal
Republic of Germany known to have ties with the Soviet Union,
in violation of laws restraining U.S. companies from doing
business with firms that have been known to sell militarily-
sensitive equipment to the Warsaw Pact nations.[8] Along with
the hardware, one can presume, the software that tells the
computer how to function also changed hands improperly.
Again, this type of piracy is rare, and although it may have an
effect on the Soviet Union's efforts to catch up to Western
technology, it has little effect on U.S. industry.

A third form of software piracy at the mainframe level, at
least theoretically, is the unauthorized duplication of software
by corporations that do not pay for it. Mainframe computer
sites are extremely complex, however, and in most cases the
customer pays to have a full-time vendor engineer on the
premises to help maintain the system. The likelihood of getting
caught by a vendor engineer is high. Moreover, any company
big enough to have such sophisticated computers and software
is also an attractive target for litigation because of the visibility
and potentially lucrative damage awards such a suit might
generate. Because of the probability of getting caught and the
specter of litigation, this form of software piracy is not a significant factor in the economics of the industry.

---

[7] D. B. Tinnin, "How IBM Stung Hitachi," *Fortune* 107 (March 7,
1983): 50–56.

[8] "Fines DEC," *Datamation* 30, no. 16 (1984): 64.

The unauthorized duplication of microcomputer software, however, is probably the most virulent form of software piracy in the United States today. This paper focuses primarily on its extent and the damage it inflicts on American industry. Many variations of this form of piracy have developed as the industry has grown.

2.2 Evolution of Microcomputer Software Piracy

2.2.1 Legal Pirates

At the dawn of the microcomputer industry in the mid-1970s, there was little software available. The few firms in the industry provided hardware and a few simple software utilities to help users develop their own programs. The first users were hobbyists who read *Popular Mechanics* and *Byte* and who used computers to play games more than anything else. By the end of the 1970s, these hobbyists had developed a large number of programs, and they formed user groups to share them. Few users took the trouble to protect their programs, since doing so might have meant that they would not have been able to trade for other users' programs. As a consequence, the majority of these early software programs were considered to be in the public domain. Users who swapped programs were acting to fill a market void, and their actions were entirely legal and ethical.

As the microcomputer industry grew, these software programmers became a cottage industry and began copyrighting and selling their programs. Some firms, like Microsoft Inc., of Bellevue, Washington, were established specifically to develop and market microcomputer software. Users continued to trade these programs, but now the trading cost the new vendors money. The high cost of developing software, when compared with the cost of duplicating it, created this black market. At the time, a typical program might have cost $150, whereas users could buy blank diskettes for $4. While copying of audio or video tapes required two tape players, software copying could be done with only one computer and one disk drive. Moreover, the copying procedure was so easy that virtually anyone could do it. A person simply had to place the original diskette in the disk drive, type a few characters that tell the computer to store the program in its memory, switch diskettes, and then type a few more characters that tell the computer to write the program onto the new diskette. Because the program consisted entirely of ones and zeros, the copy was an exact duplicate of the original.

Software vendors feared that pirates, heretofore individuals trading with each other, would become more entrepreneurial, and no wonder. Nothing stopped a pirate from buying a product, copying it, and reselling it without absorbing any of the original development costs. *Byte* magazine noted in May, 1981, that the practice of "hobbyists copying commercial programs for a few friends . . . [is] obviously a serious matter for those who sell software to the home market, [but] its relative economic significance is fairly small. The real problem is the commercial duplication—often entirely legal—of software."[9] For example, a Florida company called Data Cash Systems developed a microcomputer chess game that it sold for $169 in 1977. A year later, JS & A Group of Chicago brought the identical program to market and sold it for $99. Data Cash sued for copyright infringement, but lost in both district court and the U.S. Court of Appeals on the grounds that the copyright law, as it stood then, did not cover "object code," the program's stream of ones and zeros that only the machine could understand.[10]

2.2.2 Software Licenses

The software vendors believed they had no legal recourse under the Copyright Act, so they began to develop licensing practices designed to protect their products from being copied. They hoped they could then monitor their licensees carefully and prosecute pirates under contract law. Thus was born the so-called "shrink-wrap" license, a legal document that was inserted face-up inside the cellophane coverings of unopened

---

[9] Christopher Kern, "Washington Tackles the Software Problem," *Byte* (May 1981): 128–183.

[10] Kern, pp. 128–183.

software packages. The license specified that the software vendor retained title to the product and that by opening the package customers agreed to a contract forbidding them from selling or giving the product to others. In the ensuing years, several variations on this theme have been employed, although the legality of the shrink-wrap license has still not been decided by the courts. Even if courts affirm its validity, however, users who acquire the package without agreeing to the license are not bound by the license, according to the Data Cash suit. The vendors' efforts thus concentrated on ensuring that users could only acquire software by agreeing to abide by the shrink-wrap license.

2.2.3 Copy Protection

In addition to new licensing procedures, the vendors also developed technological schemes to prevent software from being copied at all. At first, these were fairly simple techniques, but they engendered a new form of piracy: people, usually teenagers, began breaking encryption schemes just for the fun of it. Vendors began making their schemes more and more complex, and pirates continued rising to the challenge. Steven P. Jobs, formerly chairman of Apple Computer, told *Time* magazine, "I've never seen a software protection scheme that someone around here couldn't break in 24 hours."[11] These pirates rarely sold the copies they made, however, and were most often treated as a nuisance—albeit a potentially dangerous nuisance.[12]

Because software was still scarcer than hardware, this kind of piracy was often encouraged by hobbyist magazines and computer clubs.[13] "It's fun to break programs," one club member told *Esquire* magazine. "Some groups, they promote it. What

---

[11] "Roaming Hi-Tech Pirates," *Time* (February 8, 1982): 61.

[12] Lee Gomes, "Secrets of the Software Pirates," *Esquire* (January 1982): 58–63.

[13] Gomes, pp. 58–63, in which typical club trading activities are described. Neil Shapiro, "Yo Ho Ho Computing," *Popular Mechanics* (July 1982): p. 8, in which readers are advised how to copy software. There is also *Hardcore Computing*, a small magazine based in Tacoma, WA. Its sole purpose is to aid readers in combating software protection devices.

happens is that one person in the group buys it and everyone copies it at a meeting. I have some friends who have a computer store and they don't stock software because the problem is so great."[14]

Pirates considered themselves a new breed of romantic heroes and even set up nationwide electronic bulletin boards to purvey the programs they purloined. One in New York, dubbed the Pirate's Cove, advertised, "Feel free to exchange messages (or whatever)."[15] Some of the more successful ways of getting around protected software were turned into products like Locksmith, a $99 program from Omega MicroWare in Chicago that decoded protection schemes developed for Apple computer software.

2.2.4 CONTU and the Software Copyright Act

The war between the pirates and the software vendors escalated. Vendors, believing that piracy—particularly the sort using electronic bulletin boards and other methods of mass distribution—would ultimately ruin their businesses, began pressing for changes in the laws, and their efforts succeeded. In 1980, the Advisory Commission on New Technological Uses of Copyrighted Works (CONTU) recommended changes in the copyright law that marked the first time any group associated with the Federal Government had recognized the problem of software copying.[16] Congress followed CONTU's advice, and in December 1980, President Carter signed into law the Computer Software Copyright Act.[17]

The law said that computer software was copyrightable material and that all reproduction or duplication of any copyrighted software without the approval of the copyright holder was a violation of the copyright. The law had two essential provisos, however. The first said that a copyrighted software program could be duplicated if the duplication was necessary for the

---

[14] Gomes, pp. 58–63.

[15] "Roaming Hi-Tech Pirates," p. 61.

[16] National Commission on New Technological Uses of Copyrighted Works, *Final Report,* stock no. 030–020–00143–8 (Washington, D.C.: U.S. Government Printing Office).

[17] 17 U.S.C. Sections 106–117.

product's use. Since software on a disk must be copied from the disk into the computer's memory before it will operate, some felt that all use of software would have been outlawed without this provision. The second provided that users could make one archival copy of any copyrighted program to protect themselves from the danger of electrical or mechanical failure of the original. It did not require a customer to show the need for a backup, however, which may imply that customers can copy software even if the vendor provides an archival backup copy as part of the product. According to Michael Keplinger, an attorney with the U.S. Patent and Trademark Office who was instrumental in the drafting of the law, "Anytime you try to legislate a rapidly moving technology you are likely to cause more problems than you solve."

The Computer Software Copyright Act cut down significantly on organized unauthorized copying. The trading of copyrighted software at clubs or over bulletin boards, and the passing of a program to a friend, were all forbidden under the new law. In a sense, the software cottage industry had taken its first steps as a legitimate segment of U.S. business enterprise. The trade press reacted by performing an abrupt about-face, defending the software vendors and condemning piracy for profit in its editorial pages, and refusing to run advertisements for products like Locksmith.[18]

Vendors of products like Locksmith still thought they had a legitimate market, however, because they enabled game customers to make the one archival copy permitted under the Computer Software Copyright Act. A series of lawsuits, most notably *Atari Inc. v. JS & A Group Inc.*,[19] substantially limited that niche. In that case, JS & A sold a product called Prom Blaster for $119. It enabled users to copy software cartridges for the Atari Model 2600 home computers. The company claimed that the product was sold only to let users copy JS & A's own software, which would certainly be legal under the "archival exemption" of the copyright law. Although copying other products was possible, JS & A argued, it was not the primary use

---

[18] Gomes, pp. 58–63.
[19] No. 83 C 8333 (Northern District of Illinois, 6 December 1983).

of the product. The court ruled that, "It strains credulity that consumers would spend that much for a machine that could only copy JS & A's games," and enjoined JS & A from selling the device.

2.3 New Directions

At the same time, the direction of the industry started to change. Although hobbyists and their games were still the largest segment of the microcomputer market, Apple and later IBM models began infiltrating corporate ranks. Programs for word processing, spread sheets, data management, and other business functions were introduced, and copying spread to the business user.

"When the market moved from the hobbyists to the general business consumers, it also began to follow the normal mechanisms of society," says Ron Ward, executive vice president of Future Computing Inc., a Dallas-based market researcher.

"General consumers are used to copying. It's acceptable to photocopy pages from a book, or articles from a magazine, whether it's to keep for your file in the office or to provide a ready reference in school in pursuit of your degree." Similarly, he says, people don't think twice about taping records for their portable cassette players or their friends. "Our environment trains us to think it's acceptable to copy copyrighted material."[20] This attitude and these business microcomputer users are the primary targets of current efforts to restrict software piracy.

3. SOFTWARE PIRACY TODAY

3.1 A Split Market

In the past four years, the division of the microcomputer industry into two sectors, home/games and business, has ex-

---

[20] Ward, telephone interview.

panded into a chasm. The vast majority of both hardware and software vendors now concentrate exclusively on one area or the other. Those that have tried to bridge the widening gap have failed, often spectacularly. Atari's move into business computers with its Model 1200 in part precipitated its downfall. Tandy has tried on several occasions to parlay its success in the home market into success in the business market, but its share of both markets has fallen from over 20 percent four years ago, before the markets split, to less than five percent now.[21] Texas Instruments successfully expanded from home computers to business computers, but within weeks its home computer effort disintegrated.[22] Even mighty IBM flopped when it tried to enter the home market. Its personal computer (PC) had captured a third of the business market in its first year and a half, and a dozen competitors offered machines that were plug-compatible with the IBM model.[23] Yet, its PCjr for the home never lived up to expectations, and IBM has since discontinued it.[24]

The same division has taken place in software, for which home software vendors like Sierra On-Line and Tandy have failed to bridge the growing chasm. To date, only two major business software vendors have attempted to sell game software: IBM, for its PCjr, and Microsoft, whose Flight Simulator only runs on business machines.

---

[21] *Datamation Brand Preference Survey* (New York, NY: Technical Publishing Co., 1984).

[22] "Texas Instruments Cleans Up Its Act," *Business Week* (September 19, 1983): 56–64.

[23] A plug-compatible machine is one that can run the same software without modification as the IBM model. One of the plug-compatible devices, from Compaq Computer Corp. of Houston, enabled its manufacturer to record $111 million in revenues in its first year, a record in American industry, according to Archbold (pp. 52–144). Market share data for IBM from *Datamation Brand Preference Survey* (New York, NY: Technical Publishing Co., 1983 and 1984 editions).

[24] Dennis Kneale, "IBM Is Expected to Announce Changes Designed to Increase Sales of its PCjr," *The Wall Street Journal* (July 30, 1984): 2.

3.2 The Home Market

3.2.1 Scope

On both sides of the market, piracy is thought to be rampant today. No firm statistics exist, although estimates range from 1 to 30 illegal copies for each program sold legitimately. In the home software industry, the pirates are almost entirely teenagers, an outgrowth of the hobbyists who invented software piracy. One 16-year-old boy from a Boston suburb told *Time* magazine that he frequently copies Atari games that would otherwise cost $13 to $50 and distributes them among friends. "This is illegal, but we're basically honest people," he said. "I don't know anyone who doesn't pirate software."[25] As *Esquire* noted after a club meeting, "Hundreds of dollars had illicitly changed hands that night. All the copyright laws, all the inveighing by software houses, all the antipiracy editorials in computer magazines, only make the fruit taste sweeter."[26]

Because of that attitude, piracy is probably most common in the market for home software games, for which 20 to 30 copies of some programs are made, most often for trading.[27] "These do not represent lost revenue for software developers, however, because the purchasers are probably kids without much money," says Don Devine, chairman of the Software Protection Committee of the Association of Data Processing Service Organizations (ADAPSO), a trade association representing 700 software vendors. "They couldn't go out and buy them, so they use little programs to break the copy protection and then trade them. The only effect on the vendors is that the games will have a very short life cycle."[28]

---

[25] "Roaming Hi-Tech Pirates,"p. 61.

[26] Gomes, pp. 58–63.

[27] Telephone interview with David Sturtevant, director of public communications, ADAPSO, Arlington, VA (September 18, 1984).

[28] Telephone interview with Don Devine, chairman of Software Protection Committee of ADAPSO (September 24, 1984) (all attributions).

3.2.2 Economic Effects

Of course, vendors see those short life cycles as having a significant economic impact on them. Jerry Jewell, president of Sirius Software in Sacramento, CA, says, "We have to introduce three or four new products per month just to stay ahead of the pirates."[29] Shorter life cycles mean that more products must be developed and that product development expenses must be amortized over a shorter period of time, both of which raise costs. Moreover, even though they admit that most copying is informal, vendors feel they must support larger legal staffs to deter commercial copying infringement lawsuits against organized pirates,[30] and that clearly costs money.

Although vendors agree that shorter life cycles and larger legal departments do not reduce revenue, and although they admit that even 20 to 30 copies of each legitimate sale do not indicate 20 to 30 lost sales, they also point out that a rise in costs has the same net effect as a drop in revenue. Their profits suffer severely from piracy. This appears to be one reason that business software vendors do not venture into the home computer software market.

3.2.3 Social Effects

In addition to its economic impact on vendors of home computer software, piracy has important social effects. The teenagers of today, after all, are the leaders of tomorrow. To an extent, their piracy antics have either been ignored or rewarded by society, which either considers piracy no worse than photocopying or calls youths "creative" if they break copy protection schemes and share the wealth. Some software publishers have turned a new variation on the old saw, telling youthful pirates, "if we can't beat you, join us." Many former pirates are, ironically, now gainfully employed developing new software protection schemes for home vendors.[31]

---

[29] "Roaming Hi-Tech Pirates," p. 61.
[30] "Roaming Hi-Tech Pirates," p. 61.
[31] Gomes, pp. 58–63.

Some observers claim that teenage software piracy may actually be good for society because it helps youngsters develop computer literacy and interest in careers in the computer industry, thereby ensuring that the United States will have trained computer specialists ready to lead the country into the next century. This argument, however, does not take into account what may be a darker side of software piracy. Many fear that today's software pirates may turn out to be tomorrow's white-collar criminals.

3.3 The Business Market

3.3.1 Evolution

As the market for business software has grown, so too have the possibilities for software piracy. From the start, the informal copying of programs for friends or colleagues existed, although its impact was masked by another, more malicious scheme: software rentals. A company called United Computer Corp. discovered that many business microcomputer purchasers were unhappy with the high cost of software—typically $150 to $600 per program—and started renting the programs to users for one to three weeks. The company charged 15 to 25 percent of the retail cost of the software for the rental and allowed customers to convert a rental into a purchase (at a 20 percent discount) if they liked the package. If not, United rerented it over and over again to different users. The company stated that 80 percent of its revenues came from rentals.[32]

The software vendors exploded in anger, believing that the rental operation was a thinly veiled scheme to promote software piracy. Two vendors, MicroPro International Corp. of San Rafael, CA, and Peachtree Software Inc. of Atlanta, GA, filed $10 million copyright infringement and breach of contract suits

---

[32] "Software Rentals: Piracy Is The Hot New Issue," *Business Week* (August 1, 1983): 90–91.

against United Computer,[33] charging that the firm opened sealed
software packages, removed the license documents, and then
resealed the packages, leading customers to believe that they
were not doing anything wrong by renting the software and
copying it onto blank diskettes. The two vendors also charged
that United Computer's price structure encouraged customers
to copy the software themselves and return the rented diskettes,
rather than purchasing the rental copies from United Computer.
"The commercial success of [United Computer's] software rental
business is predicated upon the unlawful copying [of MicroPro's]
and others' copyrighted software" because the discount on the
sales price precluded United Computer from making a profit
on any sales, MicroPro alleged in its suit.

The main legal test in the case was that of the validity of
the shrink-wrap license, says ADAPSO general counsel Ron
Polenski.[34] The Peachtree suit was settled out of court, he adds,
whereas United filed for bankruptcy before the MicroPro suit
could be adjudicated. The suits intimidated other rental operations, but the lack of judicial comment left the license untested;
as a result, software producers still assume it is valid.

With the decline in software rentals, the vast majority of
software piracy in the business market now appears to be the
sharing of programs among colleagues in offices or schools. Two
factors have seemingly invited more software piracy in those
environments. First, the tremendous influx of personal computers into corporations has resulted in a situation in which
the nearest fellow user is no longer half a mile away, but a few
footsteps away. In many cases, work groups have been set up
in which several employees all work alongside one another on
personal computers. "The industry has caused some of its own
problems. When a small work group of three or four people is
working together as a unit, if you ask each of them to pay the

---

[33] *MicroPro International Corp. v. United Computer Corp.*, No. C 83
3019WWS (Northern District of California, June 17, 1983); *Peachtree Software Inc. v. United Computer Corp.*, No. C 83 2082A (Northern District
of Georgia, 1983).
[34] Telephone interview with Ron Polenski, general counsel of ADAPSO
(September 18, 1984) (all attributions).

full price of the software you're almost challenging them to steal it," Devine says. "The industry has been slow to develop pricing strategies to accommodate multiple purchases despite the fact that those are becoming the most common sort."

The second factor has been the development and rapid market acceptance of microcomputers, such as IBM's PC XT, that have so-called Winchester hard disk drives. These devices, which seal the disk inside the disk drive to make it less susceptible to dirt or jostling, can hold more than 20 times the capacity of a typical floppy disk drive. Many users, encouraged by the hardware makers, load the software into the hard disk and then keep it there, using the original floppy diskette as the backup copy. In most cases, all of that is within the letter and spirit of the law.

Some users, however, have discovered that the same diskette can be loaded into more than one hard disk. One user describes a typical situation:

> We have one area in our company where there are four IBM XTs doing nothing but Lotus 1–2–3. These four employees discovered that the Lotus copy protection program lets you load 1–2–3 into the hard disk and then remove the floppy disk. This group would work it out so that each person would load Lotus into his XT, then pass it on to the next person, and so on. We had four versions of 1–2–3 running from the same package, and the users found nothing wrong with that. We did, and we bought three new copies. They thought it was like passing a magazine around, with all four of them reading the same article.

3.3.2 Scope

No one really knows how much piracy exists in the business microcomputer software market. It is, after all, difficult to quantify: asking businessmen whether they steal software is about as likely to elicite an honest answer as asking them whether they steal office supplies. Some will acknowledge their actions; many will deny them.

The best that one can do, then, is to guess. Here are some vendor and consultant estimates:

David Cole, former chairman of Ashton-Tate Inc., the California publisher of the popular dBASE II data base management software: "Between 2 and 10 unauthorized copies are made for every package sold."[35]

Alan Dziejma, president of the now-bankrupt Business Solutions Inc. on Long Island, NY, the publisher of the Jack2 integrated software package: "There are about two and one-half times as many Jack2s in use as we have sold. I hear about people who buy one copy and ask for 29 more manuals as backups."[36]

Kenneth Scott, vice president of Microrim Inc., a Bellevue, WA, firm that sells the leading contender to dBASE II, R-base 4000: "Upwards of 40 percent of all micro software is pirated. Networks especially scare the hell out of me because you can then get 25 illegal users borrowing that one copy."

Don Devine, chairman of the Software Protection Committee of ADAPSO, of Arlington, VA the trade organization: "I can't be scientific, but I would say that for the popular business software between two and three illegal copies are made for every legitimate copy sold."

Michael Gallup, vice president of product marketing for Datapoint Corp., an office automation vendor in San Antonio, TX: "Large companies don't cheat. There will always be someone somewhere, of course, but it's really not a problem."[37]

Daniel Fylstra, chairman of VisiCorp, the San Jose, CA marketer recently acquired by Paladin: "For every authentic version of VisiCalc, there are 1½ illegal, copied ones."[38]

Bob Leff, president of Softsel Inc., the Nation's largest software distributor, in Inglewood, CA: "I was hearing numbers like three, four, five illegitimate copies for every legitimate one. If someone

[35] All attributions to David Cole, former chairman of Ashton-Tate, Culver City, CA, are from Michael Tyler, "Software Piracy: Only One Per Customer," *Datamation* 30, no. 5 (1984): 49–55.

[36] All attributions to Alan Dziejma, president of Business Solutions, Inc., Kings Park, NY, and to Kenneth Scott, vice president of Microrim Inc., Beaverton, OR, are from *Datamation* 30, no. 5 (1984): 49–55.

[37] Interview with Michael Gallup, vice president of Product Marketing, Datapoint Corp., San Antonio, TX (September 25, 1984) (all attributions).

[38] "Roaming Hi-Tech Pirates," p. 61.

did a study and said it was 10 to 1, I probably would raise an eyebrow, but I could certainly believe it. Part of the scary aspect of it is that we don't really know what the numbers are."[39]

3.3.3 A New Methodology

As the issue of piracy has become more prominent, some market researchers are beginning to consider ways of quantifying its extent and effects. The most notable effort to date is being undertaken by ADAPSO, which has contracted with Future Computing to develop a survey that could address the issue. "You can develop a nonthreatening, nonconfrontational survey of a small segment of the population and then extrapolate," ADAPSO's Devine explains. "We'd have to determine how many floppy diskettes are sold, and then subtract known uses, such as originals, legitimate backups, data diskettes, and so on. Then, what's left over would apparently have no legitimate use and would be considered pirated software."

The survey has already been mailed to 70,000 users of four software packages, including Lotus 1–2–3, dBASE II, and WordStar, the most popular word processing package. Some 40,000 responses had been returned by the end of September 1984, but no data analysis has been performed yet. "We know the sales of these packages, and by the questions we ask and the way we ask them, we will be able to determine who the users are," Future Computing's Ward says. "We can tell exactly what the ratio between number of users and number of sold copies will be, taking into account the legitimate multiple user licenses and potential hard disk pirated copies. The data will be very accurate."

3.3.4 Who Are the Pirates?

"The pirates are probably not the mafioso type that invaded the record industry a few years back,"*Forbes* magazine opines. "They tend to be regular folks, people who think nothing of photocopying a few pages of *Forbes* or taping a favorite film

---

[39] Gomes, pp. 58–63.

on their Betamax."[40] Most industry experts—vendors, consultants, and users— agree that the vast majority of illicit software duplication today is performed by generally honest white-collar workers. "The everyday user is our biggest problem," Cole says. "It's so easy to do, and most people don't know they are committing a crime when they copy a software program for a friend or a co-worker."

Not all white-collar workers are the same, however, a point that some industry participants seem to miss. The most important distinction is among three types of users: those who are simply ignorant, those whom Cole calls "softlifters," and those who are "plain and simple thieves, because pirates is too romantic a word," according to Marv Goldschmitt, vice president of business development at Lotus Development Corp., the Cambridge, MA, publisher of the best-selling Lotus 1–2–3 and Symphony financial analysis products.[41] No one knows, however, the relative amount of illegal software duplication committed by each group, any more than the total amount of piracy is known.

When microcomputers first began appearing in large numbers in corporations two years ago, those corporations could legitimately claim that their employees were ignorant about software licensing and copyright laws. After all, most of the early software had been in the public domain, and some users may not have noticed that software was increasingly being copyrighted.[42] Today, however, that class of pirates is fast disappearing, vendors believe. However, Goldschmitt says that sometimes schools are still ignorant of the laws and often condone "copy days" on which they let students copy and trade programs simply because they do not know it is illegal.

The second class of corporate pirates, softlifters, also consists of otherwise honest people who are the heart of the business

---

[40] Kathleen K. Wiegner, "Pirates versus Piranhas," *Forbes* (August 15, 1983): 35–36.

[41] Telephone interview with Marv Goldschmitt, vice president of business development, Lotus Development Corp., Cambridge, MA, (October 2, 1984) (all attributions).

[42] Gomes, pp. 58–63.

software marketplace. "The softlifters [know] that it is wrong and illegal to copy software," Goldschmitt says, "but they are frustrated by our copy protection techniques because they want to use the products unfettered on their hard disks, or they want to make more backups, or they want to use the product at home on a different machine." These users, he says, pirate software because it is too frustrating or inconvenient not to pirate it. They will stop pirating software once the technology is developed to make it more convenient not to cheat, he adds.

Finally, there are the true white-collar criminals. "The software thief is masked by the softlifters, which gives him the cloak of legitimacy," Goldschmitt says. "He is stealing software simply for economic or political gain. He does not want to buy 10 packages for 10 computers if he can buy one and copy it nine times," especially if he is under a budget constraint. Many other forms of this type of software theft are visible, Goldschmitt says. He adds that dealers make copies of programs and give them away in order to encourage users to buy hardware; accounting firms, which encourage employees to use microcomputers because the machines provide better audit trails, often give employees free copies of software and documentation; and individuals who cannot afford to buy a package or who cannot list a purchase on their expense accounts may simply copy from someone else.

3.3.5 Why Pirate?

In some cases, users are ignorant of the rules of the game; in other cases, the piracy rules, as detailed in license agreements, are unnecessarily restrictive. One office worker at a New Jersey Fortune Service 500 firm proudly says his company abides by the rules, but then notes that he has modified Lotus 1-2-3 to make it easier to operate directly from a hard disk. A strict interpretation of Lotus's license agreement would indicate that his modification is questionable at best, but even Lotus's Goldschmitt says his firm "would have no quarrel with that as long as he is the only user with that particular package."

These "ignorant" users appear to be a shrinking minority as publicity concerning piracy continues. Why do more informed people pirate when they know it is illegal? "It's an attitudinal problem," ADAPSO's Devine says. They see signs on public photocopying machines in the library that warn against infringing on copyrights of authors and publishers, and believe that copying software is no more wrong and that they are no more likely to be caught committing the act.

"Copying is normal, and as long as the duplication is both relatively straightforward and easy, people will continue to do it," says Ron Ward, executive vice president at Future Computing. He describes one company he has surveyed, whose name he would not divulge, where employees reasoned that because Lotus 1-2-3 came with two diskettes (the system disk and the backup disk, both of which are copy protected to discourage copying altogether), it was perfectly acceptable to use both disks at the same time. "We had to convince the employee of that company that it was the vendor's intent that you run only one copy at a time," Ward adds.

Users, particularly of the "plain and simple thief" category, also steal software because they see immediate gain for themselves with little or no impact on the "big business" software vendors. Although not a victimless crime, unauthorized duplication is at least an impersonal crime, whose victims are not likely to engender much public sympathy. After all, what's $500 here or there to a company like Lotus, whose revenues in 1983 were $53 million? The rationale, these users say, is the same one they use in making personal long-distance telephone calls from work—and over the course of a two-year cycle for a software product, many white-collar employees certainly run up $500 personal long-distance bills at work.

A variation of this rationale emerges among users who believe that software is overpriced in the first place. "Software is intangible, so customers don't always see what they are paying for," Goldschmitt says. "They aren't just getting a program. They're getting a broader service."

Individuals may also pirate software because they are told to do so. Dr. Stanley Besen of the Rand Corp. in Washington, DC, draws the distinction between corporate piracy and individual piracy within corporations.[43] Copying in many firms is limited to individuals sharing programs in the absence of any corporate policy to the contrary, but many firms actively encourage piracy. Some have gone so far as to hire temporary workers to copy the diskettes and manuals and distribute them to many users across the country, according to Lotus chief executive Mitchell Kapor.[44] *Business Week* tells of some companies that encourage their employees to save the firm money by copying software. Some, with more integrity and legitimate concerns such as the inconvenience of buying from retail outlets, have asked software vendors to allow them to duplicate software on company premises strictly for company business. Although some firms now offer such "corporate licenses," they are in the minority. Donald R. Hollis, senior vice president of First Chicago Corp., says that he has approached vendors, claiming that he could not acquire enough software legitimately to meet the growing demands of his company's microcomputer users. So far, he says, "We've gotten a cold shoulder."[45]

4. THE EFFECTS OF SOFTWARE PIRACY

4.1 Lost Revenue

The reason that business software vendors object to any form of illegal duplication is that they believe their revenues have already suffered from piracy and most likely will continue to do so. The precise economic impact that piracy has on vendors is, however, currently incalculable. If the number of illegal copies is unknown, it follows that the total economic cost of piracy in the business market is also unknown. Nonetheless, estimates abound, including the following:

---

[43] Telephone interview with Stanley Besen, the Rand Corp., Washington, DC (October 2, 1984) (all attributions).

[44] Tyler, "Software Piracy: Only One Per Customer," pp. 49–55.

[45] "Can Software Makers Win the War Against Piracy?" *Business Week* (April 30, 1984): 108–109.

Nigel A. Smith, vice president of product marketing for Microsoft Inc., estimates that half of Microsoft's sales are lost to pirates.[46]

Fylstra of VisiCorp admits, "We're not sure how much we're losing in sales, but it is probably millions."[47]

Jean Yates, president of Yates Ventures, a California market research and consulting firm, last year speculated that informal copying of personal computer programs could drain as much as $500 million in annual sales from software companies in 1983.[48]

Goldschmitt of Lotus says, "The most conservative estimate that I have heard, and I have to emphasize that it is an estimate, is that there is a 30 percent revenue loss industry-wide." Using Future Computing's estimate of $2.2 billion in 1984 revenues, that comes to a loss of almost a billion dollars.

Cole suggests that a maximum of 10 illegal copies for every legitimate copy could mean a loss to the industry of up to $20 billion per year.

Clearly, there is a great deal of speculation and variation, and very little data. Revenue losses for each incident of piracy are much higher in the business market than they are in the home market. According to ADAPSO's Don Devine, "Not every pirated copy is a lost sale, since there are people, especially in small businesses, who will find a product useful if it is free but not worth the cost if they have to pay $500 for it. Still, two-thirds to three-quarters of pirated copies represent lost sales. These are users who like the product enough to have bought it."

The number of lost sales resulting from piracy, multiplied by the price of the product, might seem to be the most appropriate methodology for calculating the economic impact of piracy on the software vendors. Such an estimate would be inaccurate, however, according to Rand's Besen. He notes that software vendors have already implicitly taken piracy into account when setting their prices; if their legitimate sales were

---

[46] "Getting Tough on Software Theft," *Business Week* (May 31, 1982): 28–29.

[47] "Roaming Hi-Tech Pirates," p. 61.

[48] "Software Rentals," pp. 90–91.

significantly higher, they would charge less money for each product.

Besen believes that a better way to gauge the effect of piracy on revenue would be to determine the total number of units sold, if copying were to be eliminated, multiply that value by the expected lower per-unit prices, and then subtract the vendor's current revenues to derive the amount lost to piracy. No such analysis has ever been done, Besen says, although he expects to begin one in the fall of 1984 based on the results of the ADAPSO/Future Computing study.

4.2 Other Economic Factors

Just as the shorter life cycle of software has hidden costs to home software vendors, so the loss of revenue to business software vendors has several hidden effects, and they can be more severe than the obvious impact on revenue. As was the case with home software, there is the cost of protecting products in the courts. Bringing a lawsuit against a corporation suspected of illicitly duplicating software can cost $50,000 in a matter of months, [49] but it is one of the few ways to fight piracy through the legal system. Firms without that kind of ready cash—and many microcomputer software firms would have trouble coming up with that amount—simply cannot enforce their licensing agreements.

A more important effect of a revenue drain is on all of the ancillary activities that the customer does not always recognize. The $500 Lotus charges for 1–2–3 certainly covers the traditional costs of bringing a product to market and selling it, such as development costs of software and documentation, manufacturing costs, marketing and distribution costs, corporate overhead, and distributor and dealer markup. Yet, it also pays for Lotus's consumer-advice telephone hotline, updates to the program, development of new products (some of which, as in all industries, never make it to market), and dealer training pro-

---

[49] Gervaise Davis III, general counsel of Digital Research Inc., Pacific Grove, CA, in "Getting Tough on Software Theft," pp. 28–29.

grams. All of these are considered part of the Lotus 1-2-3 product, Goldschmitt says, but none of them come inside the box customers take home from the store. As a result, people who use pirated software do not get the full product and service, and hence the reputation and effectiveness of the product may be diluted.

Moreover, the added services make software prices, if anything, too low rather than too high, vendors say. "Software is totally unregulated. In free enterprise, if someone were able to develop a product similar to one on the market and make a profit selling it for less money, they would do so. That hasn't happened in this industry," Goldschmitt says. Moreover, he adds, "look at all the software companies that have a respectable market share, one that in any other industry would enable them to be profitable and that are struggling in this industry."

Indeed, the arena is strewn with wounded or defeated major competitors. Sorcim Inc. and Information Unlimited Software Inc., companies that ranked near the top of the financial analysis and word processing markets, respectively, both were unable to maintain a profit and were purchased by a mainframe software house, Computer Associates International.[50] Similarly, MicroPro, despite a 45 percent share of the word processing market, ran into trouble in 1983 and was forced to lay off hundreds of workers.[51] Clearly, piracy is not the only cause, but "if they had 30 percent more revenue they'd be in much better shape," Goldschmitt notes.

4.3 Effects on New or Small Companies

Few software vendors have been able to market more than one successful product. Many observers, therefore, pin their hopes for the future of the industry on new companies bringing fresh new ideas to the market. "There are a lot of people who have very creative and good software ideas who never take them

---

[50] Michael Tyler, "CA Goes Shopping Again," *Datamation* 30, no. 12 (1984): 50–54.

[51] "MicroPro Says Profit Fell in Third Quarter, Cuts Work Force 20%," *The Wall Street Journal* (June 11, 1984): 16.

to market because they can't figure out a way to sell the product without pirates compromising their investment," Devine at ADAPSO says. "The ideas never come to fruition, because the developers are intimidated by piracy."

Even if a new company has an idea it has turned into a product, it still must market the product in an increasingly competitive environment. Although several hundred firms have entered the business software market, and doubtless many more would enter were there less piracy, only a handful have emerged as industry leaders. The vast majority continue to struggle to find some niche and remain alive, and piracy represents the possible final, fatal straw to many in such an overcrowded, competitive market. Moreover, the barriers to entry that face new firms are astronomical: to get any attention above the din of competition, firms must now spend from $2 million to $8 million to introduce new business software, and few, if any, start-ups have that kind of capital.[52] Thus, they rely on venture capital.

The venture capitalists, however, have not been happy with the current piracy situation, and they have paid more attention to how potential clients protect their software. As a result, they have become less inclined to back software start-ups. "The growth of the industry is dependent on innovative new companies backed by venture money, but these people are increasingly concerned that the rip-off factor is too high," Goldschmitt says. "The risks are higher with newer firms that can't cut back on secondary services because there aren't any. They are the firms who are hurt the most and who can afford it the least." Says Mark W. Pelczarski, president of Penguin Software in Illinois, "A lot of the smaller software companies won't be around next year because of piracy."[53]

The indirect effect of software piracy on the ability of new companies to get started may be, in the long term, the most devastating aspect of the problem; Lotus, Ashton-Tate, and other established firms will survive piracy, even if it means being

---

[52] Michael Tyler, "Finding New Ways to Sell," *Datamation* 30, no. 11 (1984): 51–54.

[53] "Software Rentals," pp. 90–91.

unable to remain independent. Yet, in an industry in which new faces represent the key to the future, their successors may never have the chance to make their marks.

4.4 Social Effects

Software vendors find themselves in a difficult public relations position in that their best customers are also their worst enemies. "We don't want to be punitive to our customers," Lotus's Goldschmitt says, "but at the same time we have to develop ways to protect ourselves. Unfortunately, the technological methods we are using today are simply archaic, and customers are frustrated because the copy protection techniques make it more difficult to use the software."

The result is that both sides are uneasy. "The customer feels distrusted by the vendor. The vendor feels it's taking risks for which it is not being compensated, because the customer betrays him," Goldschmitt adds. These feelings lead to an atmosphere in which "there is a decrease in trust between the vendor and the customer. Because we are a new industry, we can almost afford to lose money more than we can afford to lose that trust." At ADAPSO, Devine says, "if we're not careful, we are going to lose the goodwill of our customers. Then we're really in trouble."

5. COMBATING SOFTWARE PIRACY

5.1 Technology

5.1.1 Copy Protection

Both vendors and users would be happy to see a software protection system that works. "The ones we have now are neither fish nor fowl, in that they don't give us the security of knowing that users aren't stealing software and they don't give the users the freedom to work legitimately without inconvenience," Goldschmitt says. Many techniques have been developed[54] (see Chapter 4).

Goldschmidt notes that Lotus is working with Quadram Corp. (an Atlanta hardware peripherals manufacturer), Microsoft, and ADAPSO's Software Protection Committee to develop a standard technology that will benefit both legitimate users and vendors. "It is not done yet, but I think we will be able to demonstrate it in the very near future," he says. "It's not perfect, but in our society we just have to live with stealing. Our standard will be no more inconvenient than the cameras that watch you in a department store."

Until then, says Ron Stegall, Tandy vice president of computer marketing, "It's a trade-off: How much you want to stop piracy versus how much you are willing to inconvenience your honest customers."[55] So far, virtually every major firm has some form of copy protection, and some observers say that firms who do not protect their software are only bringing piracy upon themselves. "Such publishers deserve getting copied, because they could easily avoid the problem," according to Maureen Fleming of International Resource Development, a Norwalk, CT, market research firm.[56] By contrast, says Donn Parker of SRI International in Menlo Park, CA, "Apple Computer says it can't sell a computer system if it looks harsh or threatening. You have to balance friendliness with stridency."

Of course, developing or buying software protection schemes costs money, and no one is certain that the cost is justified by how much piracy it deters. Nor can anyone say whether the protection schemes deter customers from buying one brand when another is not copy protected and therefore somewhat easier to use. Goldschmitt says that when the Lotus-Quadram scheme is put into production, it will eliminate inconveniences caused by other protection schemes and will neither deter sales nor encourage copying out of convenience.

---

[54] Tyler, "Software Piracy," pp. 49–55, and Gina Kolata, "Scheme to Foil Software Pirates," *Science* (September 23, 1983): 1279 describe some current technological methods of protecting software.

[55] "Can Software Makers Win the War Against Piracy?" pp. 108–109.

[56] "Can Software Makers Win the War Against Piracy?" pp. 108–109.

5.1.2 Serial Numbers

Another potential solution is for software vendors to work with hardware vendors to develop a system whereby the software program would read a serial number electronically from the machine on which it runs. If the hardware serial number did not match the one imprinted on that copy of the software package, the program would not operate.[57] Hewlett-Packard (HP) and Lotus have developed, for example, one such arrangement, for the HP model 110 portable computer and Lotus 1-2-3. Most hardware vendors, however, have so far resisted the idea, perhaps because they feel that the availability of software, even if it is illegally obtained, encourages hardware sales.

5.2 Price

Some vendors have found that new price structures can be created to discourage piracy, particularly with the advent of multiple-user and network systems. Dawna L. Travis, manager of client services for Management Decision Systems in Waltham, MA, says, "You try to have a discount volume pricing strategy, so that it is in the buyer's interest to buy five copies of a program rather than to buy one and make four duplicates."[58]

Scott of Microrim believes that such strategies are needed but do not exist. "We as an industry just don't know how to price or license software, especially for multiple-user and networked systems. And corporate users are moving toward such systems, which makes the problem more critical."

At the Rand Corp., Besen notes that pricing can be adjusted either higher or lower. "Sometimes the optimal strategy will be to raise the price to take into account the number of illegal copies that will be made, while sometimes the optimal solution will be to lower the price to discourage people from copying"

---

[57] Tyler, "Software Piracy," pp. 49–55.

[58] All attributions to Dawna L. Travis, manager of client services for Management Decision Systems, Waltham, MA, are from Tyler, "Software Piracy," pp. 49–55.

by reducing the difference in cost between buying legitimate software and copying it.

5.3 Lawsuits

Vendors have begun taking their cases against corporate pirates to the courts. The U.S. Copyright Office notes an "obvious increase" in the number of software copyright infringement lawsuits over the past year, but it says that the increase is proportionate to the growth in the industry as measured by the number of copyrights issued.[59] These suits are primarily against corporations that have actively encouraged widespread copying, because such cases are generally much easier to discover and litigate than cases against individuals within corporations, Lotus's Goldschmitt says. Indeed, his firm has taken the lead, filing two suits against big customers: a $10 million suit claiming that Rixon Inc., a Schlumberger subsidiary in Silver Spring, MD, had made illegal copies of Lotus 1-2-3 and shipped them to 13 branch offices around the country, and a $1 million suit claiming that Health Group Inc., a Nashville health care management concern, had copied Lotus 1-2-3 and distributed it among hospitals and nursing homes in the South. Both suits were settled out of court for undisclosed amounts of money and promises from the defendants to destroy unauthorized copies and refrain from similar actions in the future, ADAPSO's Ronald J. Polenski, associated general counsel, says.

Reaction to the Lotus suits has been mixed throughout the industry. "I think they and we should be aggressive and sue when we have the information," Microrim's Scott says. "Software publishers should get together and pool some money to litigate against flagrant and not-so-flagrant users. I think we're prepared to take on the copiers."

David Saykally, president of Context Management Systems, the Torrance, CA publisher of the MBA package, holds an opposite view. "The worst thing you can do is to get embroiled

---

[59] Telephone interview with Patrice Lyons, senior attorney, U.S. Copyright Office, Washington, DC (August 28, 1984).

in a lawsuit. It will slow your business and wrap up your management. Lotus's suit is consuming lots of its management's time. Besides, I don't think it's positive press."[60]

Nonetheless, the suits have been effective. "The Lotus suits caused us to put out a strong communication to employees not to go around any roadblocks in the software or to copy the software," Gallup of Datapoint says. "As a vendor we especially have to take care to uphold the contract."

The same sentiment is beginning to ripple through the industry. *Business Week* reported two cases in which companies have changed their policies in reaction to the Lotus suits.[61] Travelers Corp. now keeps track of which computers are authorized to run which software and sends auditors around the company to make spot checks, according to Thomas M. Ottman, second vice president for data processing.

"Everybody knows that copying is grounds for termination," he adds. Henry L. Kee, vice president of Chemical Bank, says he does not sign any requisitions for personal computers unless they are accompanied by requests for software. Many other firms and users say that the Lotus suits have been instrumental in changing their attitudes toward copying. "People all over the industry are scared stiff," says an actuary at Prudential, who keeps close contact with microcomputer users in other firms. "These companies are making sure they buy one copy of Lotus for every personal computer, just to be safe."

Saykally at Context explains, "It's too damaging not to be honest. Major corporations don't want to be subjects of lawsuits. They will start policing usage internally. The central purchasing facility will have [that] responsibility."

Mitchell Kapor, Lotus's chief executive, agrees. "We sent a mailing to two firms telling them we had evidence they were copying. We said we were prepared to sue and asked them what they would do. Within 15 minutes of receiving that letter, executives at the two firms called to say they would stop."

---

[60] All attributions to David Saykally, president of Context Management Systems, are from Tyler, "Software Piracy," pp. 49–55.

[61] "Can Software Makers Win the War Against Piracy?" pp. 108–109.

5.4 The Software Protection Fund[62]

Combating piracy does take time and money away from other aspects of a publisher's business, and for that reason early in 1984 Cole of Ashton-Tate set up the Microcomputer Software Protection Fund with a proposed $500,000 budget. The Fund, supported by member software publishers, is working with the Microcomputer Software Association of ADAPSO to investigate corporate abuses, to set up an advertising and public relations campaign, and "to vigorously pursue prosecution in cases of corporate infringement," Cole says.

The Fund's purpose, like the Lotus suits, may sound like a cannon blast across the pirates' bow, but that is somewhat misleading. It is not so much that publishers want to intimidate customers into honesty as they want to maintain an amicable and profitable relationship. The investigation of corporate abuses, for instance, so far consists more of behind-the-scenes detective work than of any overt actions. "When someone calls our 800 number, we check to see if that person has actually bought our product," says Saykally. "If not, we've caught an unauthorized copy."

Lotus's Kapor admits that both the Rixon and Group Health cases were discovered because people at those firms turned in their employers. "A Good Samaritan told us," he quips.

Similarly, the Fund suggested some guidelines for consumer advertising that manifest a more benign attitude than the bluster of some of its members. "These ads are aimed at our customers, people who are basically honest and who must be treated with respect," the guidelines read. "We can expect [them], in many cases, to participate with us in their own education."

5.5 Education

ADAPSO is attempting to educate corporate users in other ways as well. The trade association is developing a direct mail

---

[62] All material for this section is excerpted from Tyler, "Software Piracy," pp. 49–55.

kit that it intends to send to dealers, distributors, corporate lawyers and executives, school superintendents, and others. "We want to get them to consider the implications of stealing software, but we can't take a heavy-handed approach or people will just turn us off," says David Sturtevant, director of public communications for ADAPSO. "It's similar to a lot of drunk driving campaigns, which have made a lot of progress in the past five years in changing the way we think about drunk driving."[63] Goldschmitt at Lotus notes, "We can demotivate softlifting and eliminate copying out of ignorance with effective education. Then we would know that the only piracy is done by people who are absolutely, knowingly stealing."

Goldschmitt reports that the educational process is already working. "We have had a significant amount of positive press educating companies, and I'm encouraged. People call us frequently to tell us that they know of others in their organizations who are copying, or to tell us that they have discovered a problem and corrected it, but now want to compensate us for it." He says that in most cases, "We've been able to resolve the problem simply by opening a dialogue." So far, neither Lotus nor other firms have encouraged customers to report abuses with anything more than appeals to fair play and honesty. Some in the industry have suggested offering rewards to informants, but the vendors are concerned that such an approach would alienate customers by implying that they are criminals.

Part of the education process is the development and implementation of corporate policies against software piracy. In 1983, such policies were virtually unknown, but today more companies are following the examples of Travelers and Chemical Bank in setting up guidelines. "Some executives have said that of course they have policies, but they're not written down," ADAPSO's Devine says. "We need these policies, and we need the corporations to communicate them to their users. We've developed and are distributing a model, a sample policy, that fits on half of a regular sheet of paper to explain what piracy is, that it is illegal, that the corporation forbids it, and that the corporation will buy whatever software is needed."

---

[63] Sturtevant, telephone conversation.

5.6 Legislation

The software industry, led by ADAPSO, has begun lobbying for legislative action on both the Federal and State levels to prohibit and punish piracy. The legislation at the State level to a large degree overlaps the Computer Software Copyright Act, but it is more explicit in defining piracy and in determining punishments. So far, bills have been introduced in three States, although none has passed yet.[64]

At the Federal level, ADAPSO has focused on two issues. First, it is working to establish a first-use doctrine for computer software to append to the copyright law, which would give legislative support to the "shrink-wrap" license and drive the final nails into the coffins of software rental firms. Second, it is working with book publishers, movie and television producers, and record studios to ask Congress to increase the maximum penalty for each instance of willful copyright infringement in any medium from $50,000 to $250,000. ADAPSO introduced the bills in 1984 to garner early support but says it has no expectation that either will pass any time soon.[65]

"You need both Federal and uniform State legislation," says Daniel Burk, a lawyer with Thomas & Fiske in Alexandria, VA. "Piracy can be within or between States. Moreover, we have nothing close to good case law precedent yet, and more legislation would help as well."

6. CONCLUSION

Many people agree that the illicit duplication of microcomputer business software is a widespread problem of the software industry. Its causes run deep, and its effects are both broad in scope and potentially devastating in impact. Yet, given the lack of hard data, some in the industry remain skeptical. "To a real business customer, $500 is not much to spend to get the package

---

[64] Tyler, "Software Piracy," pp. 49–55.
[65] Sturtevant, telephone conversation.

in its legal state rather than to copy the disk and the manual," says Dziejma of Business Solutions. Travis, of Management Decision Systems, says, "There is a psychology of each user wanting to have his very own Lotus with the Lotus label and the Lotus manual and so on. It's much less of a concern than other issues that don't get as much attention."

There are even some iconoclasts who believe that a little piracy is good for the industry. Says one, "If they copy one of our programs, that's one more potential customer to buy our next program."[66] Richard P. Rumelt, associate professor of business strategy at the University of California, Los Angeles, argues that pirates hold down prices and spread word-of-mouth advertising. "A program that is widely pirated can become more successful than one that is not."[67]

That is clearly a minority view. Most vendors—and even users—believe that action needs to be taken to eliminate piracy, or more realistically at least to eliminate piracy among honest people and confine it to the same white-collar criminals who may embezzle from their employers. Still, computer software piracy is a more recent social phenomenon than other forms of white-collar crime, and it may therefore be somewhat easier to reduce.

All of the actions so far taken by the software industry, individually as well as collectively, have begun to do the job. Burk notes, "There is an incredible interdependence between the legal and managerial and technology issues. You need the technological devices to justify the need for corporate policies, lawsuits, or legislation, and you need legal support before these devices will pose any deterrent."

The software industry is growing, and it will continue to grow with or without piracy, although perhaps at different rates. Its success is clearly in the national interest. As ADAPSO's Devine says, "Microcomputer software is the greatest hope the United States has in increasing worker productivity across the board, which in turn boosts the entire economy."

---

[66] Tyler, "Software Piracy," pp. 49–55.
[67] "Can Software Makers Win the War Against Piracy?" pp. 108–109.

—————————— **DISCUSSION** ——————————

Stanley Besen:* Michael Tyler's paper accurately reflects the views of the computer software industry on the subject of software copying. Most of my criticisms, therefore, are not directed at the paper, but rather are aimed at the claims made by the industry that Tyler reports. I wish, however, that Tyler were as skeptical in the inferences that he draws from the "evidence" about the effects of copying as he is about the evidence itself. Moreover, I do not accept his view that the "shakeout" presently occurring in the computer software industry is significantly affected by unauthorized copying. Rather, I am inclined to attribute these developments to the newness of the industry and to the ease of entry into it. In such circumstances, high turnover of firms can be expected, as is occurring in the computer hardware industry, for which copying clearly cannot be blamed.

I agree with Tyler that the "extent and effects" of computer software copying are largely unknown. By contrast with the data on the extent of copying of records, tapes, books, and journals, no such data exist for computer software. Thus, even the lowest estimates reported by Tyler should probably not be given much credence because, although they are low, they do not seem to be based on any systematic examination of the copying that is actually taking place. Perhaps the Future Computing survey to which Tyler refers will remedy this problem, but, at the moment, no evidence appears to be available.

On the subject of the effects of copying computer software, it is not always recognized how difficult it is to assess these effects, even if the extent of copying were known completely. Some estimates of the revenue loss from copying simply take an estimate of the number of copies that are made and multiply it by the existing market price, a procedure that is clearly inappropriate. However, even when it is recognized that the price of originals is likely to be affected by the extent of copying, it is seldom recognized how difficult it is to determine the prices

————————

* Participants in this workshop are listed in the Appendix.

that would have been charged for originals in the absence of copying. If estimates of these prices are inaccurate, so will the associated estimates of harm. I hope to generate my own estimates of harm, but I am painfully aware of the shortcomings that these estimates will have (in this connection, it is interesting to note an article that recently appeared in *The Economist* [September 8, 1984, p. 72] that suggests that industry estimates of harm from the copying of computer software in Great Britain may be greatly exaggerated).

The reason that it is so difficult to assess the harm to producers that results from copying is that producers can be expected to modify their behavior to mitigate the adverse effects of copying. Among the types of "self help" that are available are changes in the price of originals, the adoption of technical "fixes" to make copying more difficult, changes in marketing strategies, and shifting to the production of products for which copying is unattractive (a detailed analysis of pricing responses is contained in S. M. Besen, "Private Copying, Copying Costs, and the Supply of Intellectual Property," Rand Corporation, N–2007–NSF, in press). Moreover, these modifications are interdependent. For example, it may be possible to lower the price of originals if copying can be limited by technical means.

Why do we care about correctly assessing the harm that results from copying? If producers of intellectual property desired only that copying be held to be an infringement, with enforcement through the civil courts, it probably would not be important to determine whether copying caused great harm. Presumably, a producer who is harmed greatly by copying would be willing to employ the judicial process to enjoin copying, or to obtain damages, and one who suffers little harm would not. However, producers generally want more than the right to bring private actions against infringers. They want governmental assistance in detecting and punishing violators, and, when that is not possible, they have asked that royalties be imposed on copying media or machines, with the proceeds to be paid to copyright holders. However, such approaches involve the use of scarce resources and create their own inefficiencies, so that before adopting them there should be an expectation that they will do more good than harm. That is why it is so important to estimate the harm from copying with some precision.

In order that I not be misunderstood, I believe that the piracy of computer software may be a serious problem, worthy of substantial public efforts to control it. However, it may not be. Only when the "extent and effects" of copying are better understood will we know.

Jon Baumgarten: One thing that has troubled me frequently is the notion that pricing self-help is the answer to all of the problems of copyright owners. All they have to do is raise their prices and they've solved their problems. . . . Isn't it arguable that the more you raise prices to try to offset losses by unauthorized duplication, the more you give the public impetus to try?

Rick Giardina: I've probably spent somewhere between 20 and 30 hours over the last six weeks sitting in executive committee meetings at MicroPro dealing with pricing of a new product that the company is going to put out within the next 6 to 8 weeks.

At no time, either at those meetings or in the 4 years of meetings I've had on other products, have we ever discussed as a potential element the cost of pirating as a price consideration. Increasingly, this industry is being market driven by price. We have experienced price denigration to an incredible extent over a short period of time. . . .

I don't know of anyone, in my own personal experience, who has taken piracy into account when they do their pricing. It's impossible.

Jon Baumgarten: Are you saying you don't or you can't?

Rick Giardina: We don't because we can't.

Stanley Besen: I don't want to be misunderstood as suggesting that raising prices solves all the problems. I'm just saying that it is one of a number of tools that a firm can use to mitigate the effects of copying.

It may be correct that no one explicitly takes into account the extent of piracy, although I must say I'm surprised about that. It is nevertheless the case that presumably there are market studies which ask the question: If we set the price at a certain level, how many would we sell?

To the extent that the demand for originals reflects the demands of more than one user of that original . . . copying is taken into account in market studies.

Still, another reason why worrying about price is important here gets back to the question of estimating the harm. If one is going to make estimates of harm which assume that the price of originals is independent of whether copying is occurring, one can easily get a very misleading picture of the harm to the industry caused by copying. Estimates of harm that pre-price, as if it's a variable independent of the extent of copying, tend to be very misleading.

Michael Tyler: There's a lot of value to both sides, and I think that when you develop pricing . . . part of the decision that goes into what price you're going to charge for your next product is how many you think you're going to sell.

Presumably, the more you're going to sell, the less you would charge per unit. However, what your expected market is . . . implicitly does depend on what the piracy factor is going to be. If you're going to price the product very expensively, there will be few legitimate purchases, but you may wind up with the same installed base.

If you take the total number of copies out there, both sold and pirated copies, that number may be more constant than we realize. Therefore, to some extent, the higher the price on those who do copy will mean that there's a higher amount of piracy among [them]. The higher price among those who buy it legitimately may also engender a higher rate of piracy among those who would otherwise buy it.

Rick Giardina: At this point in the market's history, we have not been able to make a determination with respect to price on whether or not it's going to contribute to piracy. The sole determination is whether we can sell the product at that price, given the competition and given the other issues that are involved with respect to getting a product out to market.

Mike Keplinger: Presumably, if piracy does result in increased costs for the product that's out there, then that means the legitimate person subsidizes the pirate; that is, by paying a higher price for the product that you buy and don't copy, as you're supposed to, you are, in effect, paying for the unauthorized copies that are made.

Dennis Steinauer: I'm curious as to why the only pricing solution that's been discussed here has been raising the price. I believe that sometimes you can make more by lowering the price. It seems that a number of vendors are doing that very successfully. It is now easier for me to write a check for $50 and to buy a diskette than to try to find a pirated copy.

Michael Tyler: There are companies who are discovering that lowering prices does discourage piracy because it lowers the difference between the cost of a legitimate copy and the cost of a pirated copy. It is no longer worth it to copy, and that's part of the idea of pricing it to be in the buyer's interest to buy more and copy less. There will always be some copying. You have to recognize that and then you have to say, "How do we control the number of illicit copies"?

—————————— **three** ——————————
LEGAL APPROACHES TO SOFTWARE PROTECTION: FEDERAL PROTECTION OF PROPRIETARY RIGHTS

Jon A. Baumgarten*

I. INTRODUCTION

Historically, the protection of software against unauthorized reproduction and use developed in the mainframe environment. It focused on privity of relationships among developers, employees, licensees, and customers, and hence relied principally on common law notions of contract, fiduciary and confidential dealings, and trade secrets.

More recently, however, several factors have combined to focus attention on Federal legislation—the copyright and patent laws[1]—as an important source of software protection. These

———————————
* Mr. Jon A. Baumgarten is a former General Counsel of the U.S. Copyright Office and partner in the law firm of Proskauer, Rose, Goetz & Mendelson. He is the author of various articles, and a book, dealing with copyright in the communications, computer, entertainment, arts and publishing communities.

The assistance of William F. Patry of Paskus, Gordon & Hyman in preparing the copyright section of this paper is gratefully acknowledged. Mr. Patry is also the author of the patent section.

[1] Trademark laws, including the Federal trademark statute—the Lanham

factors include the unbundling of hardware and software packages, the emergence of independent software publishers, the transformation of software into a consumer good brought on by the success of the personal computer in home, school, and business markets, the ease and inexpensiveness of software duplication, and fundamental legal changes made by the Copyright Revision Act of 1976 (effective January 1, 1978). The first half of this chapter reviews the nature and sufficiency of software protection available under the Copyright Act, while the second half explores the patentability of computer programs and related issues.

2. COPYRIGHT

The Copyright Act[2] accords to authors and their successors certain exclusive rights in "original works of authorship."[3] There are two fundamental requirements of copyrightable subject matter:

> *The work must be "fixed."* The work must be embodied in some tangible form with sufficient stability to be "perceived, reproduced, or otherwise communicated for a period of more than transitory duration."[4] Computer programs written on paper or embodied in punched cards, magnetic tape, floppy or hard disks, and semiconductor chips meet this standard.[5]

Act (Trademark Act of 1946), 15 U.S.C. §1051 et. seq—offer substantial protection to software publishers. But since these laws are directed at the publishers' trade indicia and reputation, rather than software as a work per se, they are not treated in this paper.

[2] 17 U.S.C. §101 et seq. (1978, as amended).

[3] 17 U.S.C. §102(a) (1978).

[4] See 117 U.S.C §101 (1978) (definitions of "fixed" and "copies").

[5] The House Report accompanying the 1976 Copyright Act notes that purely evanescent or transient reproductions such as those "captured momentarily in the 'memory' of a computer" are not fixed. H.R. Rep. No. 94–1476, 94th Cong., 2d Sess. 52 (1976). This invites interesting debate over RAM and similarly volatile storage and the impact of NOVRAM and CMOS technology, but has little significance to marketed programs that are the focus of this paper.

The work must be "original." The work must be the product of individual creative effort rather than copying. The copyright standard of "originality" does not require patent standards of uniqueness, invention, comparison with prior art, or any particular degree of technological, literary, or aesthetic merit.[6] It amounts to little more than a proscription on copying the work of others.[7]

A third requirement of copyrightable subject matter is categorical: it must be a "work of authorship." However, this is an expansive category encompassing most products of intellectual endeavor.[8]

The exclusive rights accorded by copyright are essentially to reproduce, adapt or revise, distribute (only until the first sale of a particular copy), publicly perform, and publicly display the

---

[6] *Financial Information, Inc. v. Moody's Investors Service, Inc.,* No. 84–7110 (2d Cir. filed December 18, 1984); *L. Batlin & Son v. Snyder,* 536 F. 2d 486, 490 (2d Cir.) (en banc) (1976); *Alfred Bell, Inc. v. Catalda Fine Arts,* 191 F. 2d 99 (2d Cir. 1971).

[7] *See,* for example, *Alfred Bell, Inc. v. Catalda Fine Arts* 191 F. 2d 99 (2d Cir. 1971); *Hubco Data Products Corporation v. Mat. Assistance Inc.,* 219 U.S.P.A. 450 (D. Idaho 1983). The courts have, however, required that works evidence more than a de minimis quantum of authorship. *See,* for example, *Laskowitz v. Marie Designer, Inc.,* 119 F. Supp. 541, 552 (S.D. Cal. 1954) (phrase "This is nature's most restful posture" found not to satisfy originality requirement). *See also* Copyright Office Circular R34 (catch-words, catch phrases, mottoes, slogans, or short advertising expressions not subject to protection).The National Commission on New Technological Uses of Copyrighted Works (CONTU) noted this requirement as applied to computer programs, stating that a program "consisting of a very few obvious steps could not be a subject of copyright." CONTU Final Report at 20.

[8] *See* 17 U.S.C. §102 (1978): "§102. Subject matter of copyright: In general (a) Copyright protection subsists, in accordance with this title, in original works of authorship fixed in any tangible medium of expression, now known or later developed, from which they can be perceived, reproduced, or otherwise communicated, either directly or with the aid of a machine or device. Works of authorship include the following categories: (1) literary works; (2) musical works, including any accompanying words; (3) dramatic works, including any accompanying music; (4) pantomimes and choreographic works; (5) pictorial, graphics, and sculptural works; (6) motion pictures and other audiovisual works; (7) sound recordings."

work.[9] These broad rights are subject to a number of specific limitations and exceptions set forth in Sections 107 through 118 of the Act. Two basic limitations, however, must be particularly noted:

Copyright protects only the "expression" reflected in the work, not its underlying idea or any principle, discovery, or method of operation described.[10] This is of great importance to software copyright as will be noted more fully below; it also marks a fundamental distinction between the scope of copyright and patent protection.

Copyright only precludes copying; it does not preclude independent creation of the same or similar work; as stated by Judge Learned Hand: "[I]f by some magic a man who had never known it were to compose anew Keats's Ode on a Grecian Urn, he would be an 'author,' and if he copyrighted it, others might not copy that poem, though they might of course copy Keats's."[11] This same principle does not, however, apply to patented works.[12]

Under the Copyright Act of 1976 copyright protection is automatic—that is, as soon as copyrightable work is fixed, it is copyrighted. The use of a certain notice of copyright is important to avoid forfeiture of protection upon publication, and registration of claim to copyright with the Copyright Office is desirable for certain remedial, evidentiary, and enforcement purposes (but is quite inexpensive); however, neither notice nor registration is, generally, a condition of securing copyright protection.[13]

Owing to the fact that copyright is readily and cheaply available and offers meaningful protection against copiers, its

---

[9] 17 U.S.C. §106 (1978).

[10] 17 U.S.C. §102(b) (1978).

[11] *Sheldon v. Metro-Goldwyn Pictures Corp.*, 81 F. 2d 49, 54 (2d Cir. 1936).

[12] *Eastern Oil Well Survey Co. v. Sperry-Sun Well Survey Co.*, 131 F. 2d 884 (5th Cir. 1943).

[13] *See generally*, J. Baumgarten, *Copyright Protection for Computer Software* in Fifth Annual Computer Law Institute (New York: Law & Business Inc./Harcourt Brace Jovanovich, Inc., Course Handbook, 1984).

attraction to program developers in the new environment is apparent.

2.1 Current Status of Copyright Protection

Before January 1, 1978, the Copyright Office registered claims to copyright in published computer programs as "books";[14] however, this practice was not tested in the courts and hence no clear law emerged.[15] Additionally, many programs were arguably "unpublished," a desirable posture for trade secret purposes, and hence ineligible for registration.[16]

The Copyright Act of 1976, although governing all published and unpublished works, did not expressly enumerate computer programs as copyrightable subject matter; but certain definitional references and legislative history indicate that Congress intended such works to be protectable as "literary works,"[17] an enumerated species of "works of authorship."

The Software Copyright Amendments of 1980,[18] following the recommendations (as revised) of the National Commission on New Technological Uses of Copyrighted Works (CONTU), also did not expressly enumerate computer programs as copyrightable subject matter, but in adding a definition of "computer

---

[14] See Copyright Office Circular 61 (1964).

[15] See, however, Harcourt Brace & World, Inc. v. Graphic Controls Corp., 329 F. Supp. 517 (S.D.N.Y. 1971) (prior law) (Copyright Office practice approved in non-program case) (dictum).

[16] However, some took the position that programs could be unpublished for general purposes but sufficiently published for investive copyright purposes and made registrations under this theory.

[17] See, for example, 17 U.S.C. §101 (definition of "literary works"); H.R. Rep. No. 94–1476, 94th Congress, 2d Sess. 51, 54, 56–57, 151–152 (1976); S. Rep. No. 94–473, 94th Congress, 1st Sess. 50–51, 52, 54–134 (1975). Accord: Final Report of the National Commission on New Technological Uses of Copyrighted Works 16 (1978) (". . . it was clearly the intent of Congress to include computer programs within the scope of copyrightable subject matter in the Act of 1976."); Tandy Corporation v. Personal Micro Computers, Inc., 524 F. Supp. 171 (N.D. Cal. 1981).

[18] P.L. 96–517, 96th Congress, 2d Sess. (1980).

program" to Section 101 of the Act[19] and establishing certain limitations on exclusive rights in computer programs,[20] these amendments demonstrated Congress' understanding that programs were covered by the Act.[21]

The amendments did not, however, expressly refer to the object code or object form of the program, or to operating system programs, leading defendants in infringement suits to argue, based in part on CONTU Commissioner John Hersey's dissent,[22] that copyright was designed to extend only to the source code form of applications programs, i.e., that copyright protection is predicated on the existence of interpersonal communication. Further uncertainty in this regard was added by the Copyright Office's decision to register object code deposits only under its "rule of doubt."[23] Defendants also alleged that programs lost protection when embodied in read-only memory (ROM) (based apparently on the argument that the program thereby became a purely utilitarian object and as such was disqualified from protection), or, alternatively, that reproduction of the program as embodied in ROM was not a reproduction of the work in a "copy" within the meaning of the Act.[24]

---

[19] 17 U.S.C. §101 (1980), ("A computer program is a set of statements or instructions to be used directly or indirectly in a computer in order to bring about a certain result.")

[20] 17 U.S.C. §117 (1980), discussed below. See also H.R. Rep. No. 96–1307, Part I, 96th Congress, 2d Sess. 23–24 (1980).

[21] *See*, for example, *Williams Electronics, Inc. v. Artic International Inc.*, 685 F. 2d 870 (3d Cir. 1982) (". . . copyrightability of computer programs is firmly established under the 1980 amendments to the Copyright Act [and] we need not consider the scope of prior acts."); *Apple Computer, Inc. v. Formula International, Inc.*, 724 F. 2d 521 (9th Cir. 1984).

[22] See CONTU Final Report at 27–37. *See also Taylor Instrument Co. v. Fawley-Brost Co.*, 139 F. 2d 98 (7th Cir. 1943), *cert. denied*, 321 U.S. 785 (1944); *Brown Instrument Co. v. Warner*, 161 F. 2d 910 (D.C. Cir.), *cert. denied*, 332 U.S. 801 (1947) ("machine parts" doctrine).

[23] *See* Copr. Off. Guide Letter (Lit.) R–70 (July 1981). Note, however, that the Office's "doubt" may be based only on its inability to examine— i.e., "read"—object code deposits to determine whether they reflect appreciable authorship; not on a "doubt" as to the copyrightability of object code per se.

[24] 17 U.S.C. §106(1) (1978) (copyright owner given exclusive right to reproduce the work in "copies"); see also idem. at §101 (definition of

Although not all courts (including the United States Supreme Court) have addressed these arguments, those that have have rejected them,[25] and it therefore appears relatively safe (subject to the possibility of contrary decisions in other circuits or by the United States Supreme Court) to conclude that (1) computer

---

"copies"). A related and third argument was that embodiment in ROM was not a "fixation" in a "copy." *See*, id., definition of "fixed."

[25] *See*, for example, *Williams Electronics, Inc. v. Artic International,* 685 F. 2d 870, 877 (3d Cir. 1982) (ROM duplication as "copy" within definitional provisions: "We cannot accept defendant's suggestion that would afford an unlimited loophole by which infringement of a computer program is limited to copying of the program text but not to duplication of a computer program fixed on a silicon chip"); *Apple Computer, Inc. v. Franklin Computer Corp.,* 714 F. 2d 1240, 1248 (3d Cir. 1983), cert. dismissed per stip. January 4, 1984 (rejecting alleged human-to-human communication requirement, holding that computer programs are infringed when embodied in ROM and copied without authorization, sustaining protection of object code, and confirming copyrightability of both operating systems and applications programs); *Apple Computer, Inc., v. Formula International Inc.,* 725 F. 2d 521 (9th Cir. 1984); (following *Franklin* opinion); *see also GCA Corp. v. Chance,* 217 U.S.P.Q. 718 (N.D. Cal. 1982) ("[b]ecause the object code is the encryption of the copyrighted source code, the two are to be treated as one work; therefore, copyright of the source code protects the object code as well"); *Tandy Corp. v. Personal Micro Computers,* 524 F. Supp. 171 (N.D. Cal. 1981) (ROM as infringing "copy" under definitional provisions— alternative holding); *Hubco Data Products Corp. v. Mgt. Assistance, Inc.,* 219 U.S.P.Q. 450 (D. Idaho 1983); *Midway Mfg. Co. v. Strohon,* 564 F. Supp. 741 (N.D. Ill. 1983); *Midway Mfg. Co. v. Artic International,* 704 F. 2d 1009 (7th Cir.), cert. den., October 3, 1983; *Videotronics, Inc. v. Bend Electronics,* 564 F. Supp. 1471 (D. Nev. 1983); CCH Copr. L. Rep. ‖ 25,697 (D. Nev. 1984). The Seventh Circuit's decision in *Midway Mfg. Co. v. Artic International,* above, appears to have removed earlier judicial suggestions to the contrary; see *Data Cash Systems, Inc. v. JS & A Group, Inc.,* 480 F. Supp. 1063 (N.D. Ill. 1979) (ROM duplication not a "copy"—prior law, but suggestion as to similar result under 1976 Act), aff'd on other grounds, 628 F. 2d 1038 (7th Cir. 1980) (court declines to pass on lower court's rationale, but its decision, arguably, is inconsistent with it). See also *Atari, Inc. v. JS & A Group, Inc.,* CCH Copr. L. Rep. ‖ 25,613 (N.D. Ill. 1983), jurisdiction noted U.S.C.A.F.C. Nov. 8, 1984; *S & H Computer Systems, Inc. v. SAS Institute, Inc.,* 568 F. Supp. 416 (M.D. Tenn. 1983); *MicroSparc, Inc. v. Amtype Corp.,* 592 F. Supp. 53 (D. Mass. 1984); *Evans Newton, Inc. v. Chicago System Software,* No. 81–C-3564 (N.D. Ill. September 10, 1984).

programs, whether in source or object code form and whether operating or applications systems, are, as a class, proper subject matter of copyright protection; (2) embodiment of a computer program in ROM is a fixation of the program in a "copy"; and (3) the unauthorized reproduction of a computer program stored in ROM is the reproduction of a "copy" of the program that, absent defenses such as those found in Section 117 of the Act,[26] will result in infringement. (Some doubt appears to remain among commentators as to whether microcode is copyrightable subject matter.)[27]

Individual programs still, of course, must meet the copyright standards of originality and fixation discussed earlier.[28]

Computer data bases generally have been considered to be copyrightable as "compilations,"[29] and as such within the subject matter of copyright expressed in Section 103 of the Act:[30]

> . . . work[s] formed by the collection and assembling of preexisting materials or of data that are selected, coordinated, or arranged in such a way that the resulting work as a whole constitutes an original work of authorship. The term 'compilation' includes collective works.[31]

---

[26] 17 U.S.C. §117 (1980). *See* discussion of this provision below.

[27] *See* the interesting usage of and reference to microcode copyright in H.R. Rep. No. 98–781, 98th Congress, 2d Sess. 28 (1984) (Star Print) (Semiconductor Chip Protection Act). The copyrightability of microcode has been directly challenged in a suit for declaratory judgment filed by Nippon Electronics Corporation. *NEC Electronics, Inc. v. Intel Corporation*, No. C84–20799 (N.D. Cal. complaint filed December 21, 1984).

[28] *See* text at footnotes 4 through 7.

[29] *See*, for example, H.R. Rep. No. 94–1476, 94th Congress, 2d Sess. 54 (1976): "The term 'literary works' does not connote any criterion of literary merit or qualitative value; it includes . . . compilations of data. It also includes computer data bases. . . ." Because some data bases are represented in binary and hexidecimalic codes akin to object code, such issues as noted with respect to the copyrightability of object code may emerge in connection with data bases.

[30] 17 U.S.C. §103(a) (1978).

[31] 17 U.S.C. §101 (1978) (definition of "compilation") (emphasis added). Although the class "compilation" includes "collective works," collective works are a special category of compilation consisting of individual items that are themselves copyrightable, for example, poems or journal articles.

In sum, the copyrightability of computer programs and data bases has been firmly established. But, as one court has noted, "that a work is copyrighted says little about the scope of its protection."[32] It is to that more difficult question that we now turn.

2.2 The Scope of Copyright Protection

2.2.1 Idea-Expression Dichotomy

Under Section 102(b) of the Act,[33] copyright does not extend to ideas, processes, and systems, but protects only the author's "expression"—a concept easy to state in theory, but difficult to apply in practice. The legislative history of this section notes specifically that copyright protection in computer programs would not extend to the methodologies of the programs.[34] Aside from serving to deny copyright protection to ideas, principles, and methods as such, the idea-expression dichotomy also serves to deny protection whenever the idea can only be expressed in one or a limited number of ways, or the idea and the expression of the idea are "wedded" or indistinguishable,[35] a condition sometimes known as merger.

This variation of the idea-expression dichotomy has become particularly pertinent to computer program litigation. In *Apple*

As used here, the term "compilation" refers to a collection of discrete items that are not individually copyrightable, for example, a single name, telephone number, or chemical formula.

[32] *Atari, Inc. v. North American Phillips Consumer Electronics Corp.,* 672 F. 2d 607, 616–617 (7th Cir.) cert. den., October 4, 1982.

[33] *See* text at footnote 10 above.

[34] *See* S. Rep. No. 93–983, 93d Congress, 2d Sess. 107 (1974); Draft Second Supplementary Report of the Register of Copyrights on the General Revision of the U.S. Copyright Law: 1975 Revision Bill, Ch. I at 2 (1975). *See also* H.R. Rep. No. 94–1476, 94th Congress, 2d Sess. 56–57 (1976); S. Rep. No. 94–473, 94th Congress, 1st Sess. 54 (1975).

[35] *See,* for example, *Morrissey v. Procter & Gamble Co.,* 379 F. 2d 675 (1st Cir. 1967); *Herbert Rosenthal Jewelry Corp. v. Kalpakian,* 446 F. 2d 738 (9th Cir. 1971). Cf. *Herbert Rosenthal Jewelry Corp. v. Grossbardt,* 436 F. 2d 315 (2d Cir. 1970). *See also Baker v. Selden,* 101 U.S. 99 (1879); *Mazer v. Stein,* 347 U.S. 201 (1954).

Computer, Inc. v. Franklin Computer Corp.,[36] the Third Circuit addressed the dichotomy in the context of a challenge to per se protectability of the plaintiff's program and an accompanying argument that the limited number of ways to devise an operating system to achieve compatibility with applications software written to plaintiff's operating system precluded protection.

Taking what it described as a pragmatic approach based on "preserv[ing] the balance between competition and protection," the court of appeals focused on whether the idea was capable of alternate modes of expression. It held: "If other programs can be written or created which perform the same function as [plaintiff's] operating system program, then that program is an expression of the idea and hence copyrightable," and remanded for findings in this issue.[37] Although the court's definition of the "idea" of the plaintiff's program at its broadest definition of functionality does raise questions, it is likely that this approach will be refined in later litigation over discrete program segments as opposed to challenges to overall copyrightability of entire programs.

Perhaps more significant was the court's rejection of the defendant's additional argument that the idea-expression dichotomy had relevance to its desire to create an operating system capable of running Apple applications software:

> This claim has no pertinence to either the idea-expression dichotomy or merger. The idea which may merge with the expression, thus making the copyright unavailable, is the idea which is the subject of expression. . . . If other methods of expressing that idea are not foreclosed as a practical matter, then there is no merger. [Defendant] may wish to achieve total compatibility with independently developed application programs written for the Apple II, *but that is a commercial and competitive objective which does not enter into the somewhat metaphysical issue of whether particular ideas and expressions have merged.*[38]

---

[36] 714 F. 2d 1240, (3d Cir. 1983), cert. dism'd per stip.

[37] *Id.* at 1253. Remand was avoided by a stipulated settlement. *Accord: Apple Computer, Inc. v. Formula International, Inc.,* 725 F. 2d 521 (9th Cir. 1984); CONTU Final Report at 20.

[38] 714 F. 2d at 1253 (emphasis added).

2.2.2 Determining Infringing Similarity

Copyright infringement occurs when one of the copyright owner's exclusive rights is violated.[39] Infringement of the right to reproduce the work is said to result when there is "copying"[40] and "substantial appropriation," by copying, of copyrightable expression. If the only material taken is not protectible (for example, ideas, methods, processes), no infringement results.

Determinations of program copyright infringement will involve consideration of such issues as the following:

What is the protected "expression" of a programmer? Is it limited, as some suggest, to the literal code employed in the plaintiff's work, or does it include, as others assert, structurally expressive elements employed in program design, arrangement, sequence, and development?

When are the expressive elements of a program "substantially" copied? It must be noted that copyright protection is not limited to precluding verbatim or identical reproduction, but includes prohibitions on unlawful paraphrasing,[41] and that infringing substantial similarity may be measured on a qualitative, as well as quantitative, standard.[42]

Can particular elements become so common or standard as to become the equivalent of unprotectable dramatic "scenes a faire?"[43]

Because most cases that have been decided to date have involved verbatim or near verbatim copying of virtually the

---

[39] 17 U.S.C. §106, 501 (1978). Of the five rights granted, only the first— the right to reproduce the work in copies— is discussed here. *See,* however, *Midway Mfg. Co. v. Strohon,* 564 F. Supp. 741 (N.D. Ill. 1983) (alteration kit as infringement of adaptation right in program).

[40] Copying is frequently shown by inference from (1) defendant's access to plaintiff's work; and (2) a substantial similarity in the works.

[41] *Flick-Reedy Corp. v. Hydro-Line Mfg. Co.,* 351 F. 2d 546 (7th Cir. 1965), *cert. denied,* 383 U.S. 958 (1966).

[42] *Wainwright Securities, Inc. v. Wall Street Transcript Corp.,* 558 F. 2d 91 (2d Cir. 1977), *cert. denied,* 434 U.S. 1014 (1978).

[43] *See,* for example, *Alexander v. Haley,* 460 F. Supp. 40 (S.D.N.Y. 1978).

entirety of the plaintiff's program code,[44] these questions have yet to be fully explored.[45]

Additional problems arise in connection with determining infringement of data bases. Although a substantial and material taking of a data base should generally lead to a finding of infringement under copyright principles, troublesome issues may be faced owing to the varying doctrinal theories for copyright protection of compilations. If the basis for protection is, as is frequently argued, the element of editorial *selection,* what is the impact for many data bases whose essential value lies in the comprehensiveness of their content? If the basis for protection is, as is also argued, the element of *arrangement,* what is the impact for those data bases characterized by the fluidity and dynamics of their content, with any "arrangement" being more a result of the functional need to trace data to addressable locations than of artistry? And what of the impact of such a basis when the unauthorized use is by a computer with the ability to select, rearrange, restructure, and otherwise modify preexisting materials, perhaps beyond the point of recognition? And if the basis is *industriousness* or labor in compiling the

---

[44] *See Apple Computer, Inc. v. Franklin Computer Corp.* above, n.25, *Apple Computer, Inc. v. Formula International* above, n. 25. *Cf. Hubco Data Products Corp. v. Mgt. Assistance, Inc.,* 219 U.S.P.Q. 450 (D. Idaho 1983); *GCA Corp. v. Chance,* 217 U.S.P.Q. 718 (N.D. Cal. 1982); *Freedman v. Select Information Systems,* 221 U.S.P.Q. 848 (N.D. Cal. 1983); *Tandy Corp. v. Personal Micro Computers,* 524 F. Supp. 171 (N.D. Cal. 1981); *Williams Electronics, Inc. v. Artic Int'l.,* 685 F. 2d 870 (3d Cir. 1982); *Midway Mfg. Co. v. Artic Int'l.,* 704 F. 2d 1009 (7th Cir. 1983), *cert. denied,* October 3, 1983.

[45] However, *see S & H Computer Systems, Inc. v. SAS Institute, Inc.,* 568 F. Supp. 416, 423 (M.D. Tenn. 1983); *In re Certain Personal Computers & Components Thereof,* CCH Copr. L. Rep. ¶ 25,651 (USITC March 9, 1984) determination of substantial similarity); *Evans Newton, Inc. v. Chicago Software Systems,* No. 81-C-3564 (N.D. Ill. September 10, 1984). [Since the preparation of this report, several cases have concluded that the protected "expression" in a computer program goes beyond code to include structural elements. *See SAS Institute Inc. v. S & H Computer Systems, Inc.,* No. 82-3669, 70, March 8, 1985 (M.D. Tenn.); *Whelan Associates, Inc. v. Woslow Dental Laboratory, Inc.,* No. 83-4583, Jan. 22, 1985 (E.D. Pa.), appeal filed; *E.F. Johnson Co. v. Uniden Corp.,* No. 4-85-767, Dec. 13, 1985 (D. Minn.).]

data base, can this be reconciled with cases adamantly refusing copyright protection to labor, research, and the like?[46]

2.2.3 Section 117: Limitations on Rights of Copyright Owners

"Copying" plus "substantial similarity," absent defects such as lack of standing,[47] or forfeiture of protection through insufficient notice,[48] will create a prima facie showing of infringement. This showing may be rebutted by demonstrating the applicability of statutory defenses, such as fair use,[49] or other statutory limitations on the copyright owner's Section 106 rights. Principal among these other limitations on the exclusive rights of com-

---

[46] *See,* for example, *Harper & Row Publishers, Inc. v. Nation Enterprises,* 723 F. 2d 195 (2d Cir. 1983), *cert. granted,* 52 U.S.L.W. 3860 (May 29, 1984) (argued November 6, 1984); *Miller v. Universal City Studios, Inc.,* 650 F. 2d 1365 (5th Cir. 1981). However, *see Toksvig v. Bruce Publishing Co.,* 181 F. 2d 664 (7th Cir. 1950); *Rand McNally & Co. v. Fleet Mgt. Systems,* 221 U.S.P.Q. 827 (N.D. Ill. 1983); CCH Copr. L. Rep. ‖ 25,692; ‖ 25,711 (N.D. Ill. 1984); *National Business Lists, Inc. v. Dun & Bradstreet, Inc.,* 552 F. Supp. 89 (N.D. Ill. 1982). In the recent case of *Financial Information, Inc. v. Moody's Investors Service, Inc.,* No. 84–7110 (2d Cir. filed December 18, 1984), the Second Circuit, noting the conflicting theories of protection for compilations, remanded to the district court to determine whether plaintiff's compilation of daily bond redemption cards was protectible as involving selection, coordination, or arrangement, or was instead a mechanical aggregation of all information without objective judgment, suggesting, on the basis of its decision in *Eckes v. Card Prices Update,* 736 F. 2d 859 (2d Cir. 1984), that should the latter be the case, the work was not copyrightable.

[47] The Copyright Act generally permits only the legal or beneficial owner of an exclusive right to sue for infringement. 17 U.S.C. §501(b) (1978). *Cf. id.,* §501(c) [television broadcast station holding a copyright or other license to transmit or perform a work that is secondarily transmitted by a cable system treated as a legal or beneficial owner for purposes of §501(b) if such secondary transmission occurs within the local service area of the television station].

[48] *See Kramer v. Andrews,* 83–1344–3 (D. So. Car. May 29, 1984), *Videotronics, Inc. v. Bend Electronics,* 586 F. Supp. 478 (D. Nev. 1984).

[49] 17 U.S.C. §107 (1978). *See generally,* Patry, The Fair Use Privilege in Copyright Law (BNA Books 1985).

puter program copyright owners are those found in Section 117 of the Act.[50]

Section 117, as codified in the Software Copyright Amendments of 1980, provides:

> Notwithstanding the provisions of §106, it is not an infringement for the owner of a copy of a computer program to make or authorize the making of another copy or adaptation of that computer program provided:
>
> > (1) that such a new copy or adaptation is created as an essential step in the utilization of the computer program in conjunction with a machine and that it is used in no other manner, or (2) that such new copy or adaptation is for archival purposes only and that all archival copies are destroyed in the event that continued possession of the computer program should cease to be rightful.
>
> Any exact copies prepared in accordance with the provisions of this section may be leased, sold, or otherwise transferred, along with the copy from which such copies were prepared, only as part of the lease, sale, or other transfer of all rights in the program. Adaptations so prepared may be transferred only with the authorization of the copyright owner.

To date, all cases in which Section 117 has been raised as a defense have rejected it. In *Atari v. JS & A Group, Inc.*,[51] the court denied the applicability of Section 117(2) to the defendant's marketing of a device that copied computer programs contained in electronic audiovisual game cartridges. The court concluded that the defendant had not introduced evidence demonstrating that the ROM-based programs encased in the cartridges were subject to electrical or mechanical failure, which the court considered a necessary condition to the "archival" copying privilege. A similar result prevailed in *Micro-Sparc, Inc. v. Amtype Co.* (printed programs not subject to electrical or mechanical failure, and hence not subject to archival copying).[52]

---

[50] 17 U.S.C. §117 (1980).

[51] CCH Copr. L. Rep. ‖ 25,613 (N.D. Ill. 1983), jurisdiction noted U.S. Court of Appeals for the Federal Circuit, November 8, 1984.

[52] 592 F. Supp. 33 (D. Mass. 1984).

In a contempt proceeding in *Apple Computer, Inc. v. Formula International, Inc.*,[53] Section 117(1)'s "essential step" copying privilege was held inapplicable to the transfer of extracted operating systems from diskette into ROM and the distribution of such ROMs to consumers. The court concluded that Section 117 was designed to protect ultimate consumers in using programs, not to permit unauthorized reproduction and distribution by competitors,[54] and, alternatively, that it is not "essential" to embody a diskette program in a nonvolatile ROM when it could be executed through temporary RAM storage.

In these cases, the courts have strived to limit Section 117 to its perceived legislative purpose and to avoid abuse of the privileges conferred under that section. Other Section 117 issues remain to be judicially explored, however. These include the following:

What is the scope of the section's privilege for making adaptations of programs and its resultant impact on the marketing of enhancements and machine-specific revisions?

Does the reference to "a" machine in Section 117(1) permit the sequential loading of a single copy of a program into multiple computers in a single classroom, school, or business establishment? Does it permit the use of a single copy of a program in multiple-user (dumb terminal) configurations or networks (multiple personal computers)? What is the impact of these practices on the market expectations for multiple copy sales, on prices of individual copies, and on the incentive to develop software for local area networks?

Should manufacturers of devices designed to break copy protection schemes be permitted to avoid liability for contributory copyright infringement by claiming, as is common in their advertising, that their devices have substantial noninfringing uses—

---

[53] 594 F. Supp. 617 (N.D. Cal. 1984).

[54] *See also* the extension of this principle, in *Micro-Sparc, Inc. v. Amtype Corp.* (footnote 52) ("essential step" privilege limited to end user and does not permit reproduction of printed programs into diskettes by copying service even if requested by end user).

namely, enabling consumers to exercise Section 117 privileges of archival copying?[55]

Because only the "owner" of a copy of a program is entitled to Section 117 privileges, may they be exercised by purchasers of software under "shrink-wrap" or "tear-open" licenses?[56]

2.2.4 Software Rentals

Section 109(a) of the Copyright Act embodies the so-called "first sale" doctrine. Under this provision, after the first sale of a lawfully made copy, the "owner" of that copy may "sell or otherwise dispose" of it, despite the copyright owner's exclusive distribution right in Section 106(3). This privilege is utilized to permit the commercial renting of copyrighted works, including software.

Although proponents of software rentals argue that they are legitimate for "preview" purposes, software copyright owners have alleged that individuals frequently use rentals as a subterfuge to copy the programs, thereby harming sales. In the case of similar allegations regarding the rental of sound recordings, Congress recently acted to prevent such harm by precluding unauthorized commercial rentals.[57] A bill introduced late in the last session of Congress by Senator Charles Mathias[58] would have amended Section 109(a) to prohibit the rental of software, but it died at the expiration of the 98th Congress.

---

[55] Recall that this defense was denied by the trial court in *Atari v. JS & A Group, Ltd.* (footnote 51 and accompanying text). However, the applicability of that decision to high-end or business software embodied in diskettes that are subject to electromechanical failure is questionable. This particular issue has been the subject of informal Congressional inquiry to interested parties.

[56] *See below* the discussion of a related issue in connection with rentals. A "shrink-wrap" or "tear-open" license is essentially a device by which mass marketed software is provided to consumers in a form of packaging that states that by opening the package the consumer is agreeing to the terms of a license enclosed therein.

[57] The Record Rental Act of 1984, P.L. 98–450, 98th Congress, 2d Sess., October 4, 1984, amends Section 109 to prohibit the unauthorized rental of sound recordings for direct or indirect commercial advantage.

[58] S. 3074, 98th Congress, 2d Sess., October 5, 1984.

Many computer program copyright owners have marketed their software under so-called shrink-wrap or tear-open licenses, partly on the theory that these do not constitute sales or make the purchaser an owner under Section 109 (or Section 117). The validity of such arrangements as licenses rather than as sales, however, has been debated by commentators.[59]

State legislative concern over possible abuse of Sections 109(a) and 117 has been manifested in Louisiana's enactment of a "Software License Enforcement Act," governing the conditions under which a shrink-wrap license will be held enforceable as a matter of state law, and reported plans to introduce similar legislation elsewhere.[60]

2.3 Sui Generis Protection

There have been suggestions that copyright protection is an ineffective or inappropriate device for computer programs and that a unique, "sui generis," form of protection should be considered.[61] However, several factors militate against this approach.

---

[59] *See,* for example, Reynolds, *The Self-Executing License: A Legal Fiction,* 2 Computer Law Reporter 549 (1984); Davidson, *Basic Contract Questions with Respect to "Box-Top" Software Licenses,* Computer Litigation (PLI 1984); Stern and Todd, *Enforceability of Specific Provisions Contained in Box-Top Licenses,* Computer Litigation (PLI 1984). Two suits were filed by program copyright owners in 1983 against software rental outlets, based on shrink-wrap licenses and alleging violations of the Section 106(3) distribution right, contributory infringement of the Section 106(1) reproduction right, breach of license, unfair competition and unjust enrichment, *Micropro International Corp. v. United Computer Corp.* C-83-3019 WWS (N.D. Cal. 1983); *Peachtree Software, Inc. v. United Computer Corp.,* C-83-3019 (N.D. Ga. 1983). The *Peachtree* suit was settled before a decision was rendered, whereas United Computer Corp.'s institution of bankruptcy proceedings apparently ended the *Micropro* litigation.

[60] It is possible, however, that such state efforts will be questioned under the preemptive provisions of Section 301(a) of the Federal Copyright Act.

[61] *See generally,* Kinderman, *A Review of Suggested Systems for the Protection of Computer Software* in H. Brett and M. Perry (eds.), The Legal Protection of Computer Software, 1981.

First, there is no evidence that copyright is an ineffective or inappropriate form of protection for software, and, thus, calls for a sui generis approach must be considered premature at best. Although it is possible that future decisions may define the scope of protection *too narrowly* to offer meaningful protection, copyright appears to be reasonably effective against the forms of outright or wholesale duplication that currently plague the industry. (There are, of course, difficulties of enforcement and detection. These may be improved by legislative amendment—for example increased civil and criminal penalties[62]—or administrative action, such as improved customs surveillance of potentially infringing imports, and increased budgetary allocations for that purpose. Other difficulties are the result of societal factors rather than shortcomings in the copyright law itself.)[63] Of course, abandonment of the copyright system is not warranted merely because there remain open questions of judicial interpretation, or possible need for statutory adjustments (for example, in Section 109 or 117).

Viewed from another perspective, there is yet no clear demonstration that copyright offers *too much* protection to software. Even the relatively lengthy term of copyright protection, occasionally attacked as excessive for legitimate software needs, may become increasingly appropriate as valuable operating systems and applications program tools and elements acquire an increasingly useful life on their own, or as portions of other or revised works. It may also be argued that the duration issue is self-answering: if programs lose importance, they will not be copied; if they retain commercial importance, they deserve continued protection.

---

[62] *See* H.R. 4646 (B. Frank, D-Mass.), January 25, 1984, 98th Congress, 2d Sess. This bill sought to increase the penalties for unlawful appropriation of software to those currently applicable for motion picture piracy. In recognition of the potential damage arising from unauthorized accessing of financial data bases, Congress passed the Counterfeit Access Device and Computer Fraud Abuse Act of 1984 on October 12, 1984, as part of the continuing Budget Resolution, and provided for criminal penalties for unauthorized accessing of computers under certain enumerated circumstances.

[63] *See* Section 2.4.

Second, in establishing in 1984, a sui generis form of protection for semiconductor chip design, [64] Congress assured software manufacturers that such action should not be considered a precedent for limiting copyright protection for software.[65] Similarly, Congress passed a concurrent resolution introduced by Senator Lautenberg, declaring the sense of Congress that copyright is an essential form of intellectual property right protection for software and opposing any proposal by a foreign nation to withdraw copyright protection for software or to provide for a new system of protection for software incorporating compulsory licensing.[66] These proposals raise an additional point of considerable importance: any movement to depart from or diminish copyright protection for computer programs will undoubtedly be seized upon by other countries, particularly those in the Third World or by competitor nations, to avoid international copyright treaty obligations and to cloak devices for the appropriation of U.S. technology (for example, compulsory licensing, mandatory disclosure of confidential materials, unacceptable terms of protection) under the guise of some form of allegedly sui generis protection.[67]

---

[64] P.L. 98–620, 98th Congress, 2d Sess., November 8, 1984.

[65] *See* S. Rep. No. 98–425, 98th Congress, 2d Sess. 14 (1984). *See also* 130 Cong. Rec. S5836 (daily ed., May 16, 1984) (remarks of Senator Mathias).

[66] S. Con. Res. 117, passed as part of the International Trade and Investment Act of 1984, P.L. 98–573, 98th Congress, 2d Sess., October 30, 1984.

[67] The Lautenberg resolution was in fact prompted by a proposal of the Japanese Ministry of Industry and Trade (MITI) to establish a very limited form of industrial property protection, subject to compulsory licensing, for software. This proposal was not presented to the Diet during its last session, but it does not appear dead and controversy continues. Reports of South Korean, Malaysian, and Singapore's consideration of legislation modeled on the MITI proposal have been heard. A draft revision of the Korean copyright law does not expressly mention computer programs, but U.S. Government suggestions have been made that it be revised to do so in a fashion that does not adopt objectionable features of the MITI proposal. A Brazilian proposal for sui generis software protection, apparently similar to the traditionally restrictive and troublesome transfer of technology legislation, has been circulated and is apparently being followed with interest by several countries, including Columbia and Mexico, although Mexico has begun accepting computer programs for conventional copyright registration. A

Finally, it must be noted that in light of both an emerging international consensus that software is copyrightable subject matter[68] and the expressly stated position of the Executive Branch of the U.S. Government that all forms of computer programs are so protectable under the Universal Copyright Convention,[69] any substantial departure from copyright principles or diminishing of conventional copyright protection could place the United States in violation of its treaty obligations.

Canadian government White Paper, *From Gutenberg to Telidon: A Guide to Canada's Copyright Revision Proposals* (Consumer & Corporate Affairs Canada, 1984), proposed a severely reduced form of protection for machine-readable versions of software. The proposal would have left computer programs distributed in object form with little, if any, meaningful protection, and strong U.S. Government and industry objection has apparently forestalled its further consideration. Subsequent to publication of the White Paper, a trial court of the Federal Court of Canada entered a preliminary injunction against the making and distribution of copies of IBM's personal computer operating system, *IBM Corp. v. Ordinateurs Spirales, Inc.* (No. T-904-84, June 27, 1984), concluding that computer programs, including operating system programs embedded in object code form in ROM, were protected by copyright as "literary works."

[68] In addition to the Canadian decision noted in footnote 67, a lower court decision in Australia denying copyright protection for computer programs was overruled by a court of appeals on May 29, 1984. Following the full bench decision, the Australian Parliament amended its copyright law to expressly accord copyright protection to computer programs. A recent proclamation of the Hungarian government has specifically recognized that software is protected by copyright, and other decisions upholding copyright protection for software have been rendered in France, the Federal Republic of Germany, South Africa, Japan, The Netherlands, and Taiwan. The Philippine Copyright Act expressly refers to software as a protected work, and Sweden, The Netherlands, and the Federal Republic of Germany are reportedly considering express statutory confirmations of software copyright. *See generally,* J. Baumgarten, *Primer of the Principles of International Copyright,* reprinted in *Electronic Information Publishing—Old Issues in New Industries* (New York: Practising Law Institute, 1984).

[69] Universal Copyright Convention, as revised in Paris, 1971. This position was announced on behalf of the State and Commerce Departments and U.S. Trade Representative during a recent meeting with interested parties in Washington, D.C.

2.4 Other Considerations

There is little doubt that unauthorized duplication of computer programs occurs on a large scale. This includes not only outright commercial piracy, but also—and to a significant extent—amateur duplication in homes, schools, and businesses. In this context, questions concerning software protection are an aspect of larger issues faced by several copyright industries:

> To a great extent the problems of increasing unauthorized duplication of copyrighted works result from a number of related consequences of the new devices for storing, replicating, and disseminating copyrighted works. Several of these are as follows:
>
> > Reproduction of entire copyrighted works, and of substantial portions of works, has become simple and relatively inexpensive. . . .
> >
> > Unauthorized duplication has become decentralized, spread over hundreds of thousands of individuals and institutions. To recognize that such activities may impair publisher investments requires that each individual and institution withdraw from parochial self-interest and look beyond its own actions to the cumulative or aggregate impact of the activity. . . .
> >
> > The *locus* of reproduction has changed. Unauthorized copies and displays are made or downloaded at home or in the office, that is, in private and semi-private contexts in which detection is difficult at best, and enforcement efforts raise the spectre of intrusion of privacy.
>
> To a considerable extent, these three factors coalesce in a fourth: a blurring or distortion of the traditional roles that have been played by publishers and consumers. In the past these roles were easily defined: publishers created and distributed works; consumers purchased those stocks. Now, however, the consumer sees itself as capable of serving *as the publisher* —creating copies as and when needed, on demand. . . . Finally, . . . one must acknowledge the contribution of the human psyche in the post-industrial age. The societal importance of information is now given great emphasis. The enormous industrial and consumer appetite for immediate access to intellectual works and the ability of new devices to meet those demands leaves little patience for the inconvenience of dealing with proprietary rights among the

public, the technocrats who purport to serve them, and, most important, the political representatives who listen to them.[70]

The answers to these issues are not easy. Strengthening of statutory protection schemes, like the Copyright Act, is only a partial solution. Public education as to the dignity of intellectual property and the adverse effects (including, ultimately, on the public by increased prices and diminished innovation and availability) of unauthorized copying is also imperative; and examples of respect for intellectual property rights among broad interests, such as the agencies and operations of the Federal Government, must be encouraged.

3. PATENT

3.1 Introduction

Unlike the Copyright Act,[71] the Patent Act[72] does not enumerate specific subject matter eligible for protection, nor does

---

[70] J. Baumgarten, *Preserving Copyright for STM Publishers,* "Remarks Before the General Assembly of the International Group of Scientific, Technical and Medical Publishers," Frankfurt, Federal Republic of Germany, October 2, 1984. *See also* J. Baumgarten, *Copyright at the Crossroads, Billboard,* November 12, 1983 at 10.

[71] 17 U.S.C. §101 et seq. (1978). *See id.* at §102(a), which lists categories of "works of authorship." In 1980, the Copyright Act was amended to include, inter alia, a definition of a computer program as "a set of statements or instructions to be used directly or indirectly in a computer in order to bring about a certain result." 17 U.S.C. §101 (1980).

[72] 35 U.S.C. §1 et seq. (1952 and as amended). Both the Copyright and Patent Acts are based on Article I §8 cl. 8 of the Constitution, which gives Congress the power to "promote the progress of science and useful arts, by securing for limited times to authors and inventors the exclusive right to their respective writings and discoveries." Although it is not free from doubt, it appears that the term "science" refers to authors, whereas the term "useful arts" refers to inventors. *See Bleistein v. Donaldson Lithographing Co.,* 188 U.S. 239 (1903); *Graham v. John Deere Co.,* 383 U.S. 1 (1906); *Williams & Wilkins Co. v. United States,* 172 U.S.P.Q. 670 (Ct. Cl. 1972), rev'd on other grounds, 487 F. 2d 1345 (Ct. Cl. 1975), affirmed by an equally divided

it contain a definition of "computer program." Instead, the Act lists four general categories of patentable inventions or discoveries, stating:

> Whoever invents or discovers any new and useful process, machine, manufacture or composition of matter, or any new and useful improvement thereof, may obtain a patent therefor, subject to the conditions and requirements of this title.[73]

Patent protection for computer programs thus must be fit into one of these categories. To date, claims for program protection have been drawn as either a process or as a machine (commonly termed an apparatus).[74]

It has also been held that printed matter alone cannot form the basis for a patentable invention.[75] The lack of a specific designation or definition of computer programs as patentable, the requirement that computer programs fit into one of the four statutory subject matter categories, and the bar to protection of printed materials have raised the issue of whether computer programs per se are patentable. Although there is no decision squarely on point, the Court of Customs and Patent Appeals in a 1978 decision rejected an argument by the Solicitor General that under the Supreme Court's decisions in *Gottschalk v. Benson*[76] and *Parker v. Flook*,[77] computer programs were per se unpatentable, holding:[78]

---

court, 420 U.S. 376 (1975) for discussions on this point. For a suggestion that copyright protection should be subject to the same standards of novelty as patents, *see* justice Douglas' dissent from the Supreme Court's denial of the petition for certiorari in *Lee v. Runge*, 404 U.S. 887 (1971). The Douglas reasoning has not, however, been adopted by the courts. *See Alfred Bell & Co. v. Catalda Fine Arts*, 191 F. 2d 99 (2d Cir. 1951); *L. Batlin & Son, Inc. v. Snyder*, 536 F. 2d 486 (2d Cir. 1976) (en banc).

[73] 35 U.S.C. §101 (1952).

[74] However, *see* Rinkerman, *Design Patent Protection for Computer Equipment*, 3 Computer Law Reporter No. 5 (March 1984).

[75] *Guthrie v. Curlett*, 10 F. 2d 725 (2d Cir. 1926); *cf. Cincinnati Traction Co. v. Pope*, 210 F. 443 (6th Cir. 1913).

[76] 409 U.S. 63 (1972).

[77] 437 U.S. 584 (1978).

[78] *In re Johnson*, 589 F. 2d 1070, 1081–1082, n.12 (C.C.P.A. 1978).

This broad statement is not at all germane to the considerations before this court and is an erroneous statement of law. We stated in *In re Chatfield*, 545 F. 2d *supra* at 155 . . . that the mere labeling of an invention as a "computer program" does not aid in the decision making and the Supreme Court declined to decide either *Benson* or *Flook* on such broad, nonsubstantive grounds but rather considered the specific recitations in the claims. There is no reason for the Solicitor or the PTO [U.S. Patent and Trademark Office] to shortcut the analytical framework set forth in *Benson, Flook,* and the decisions of this Court by relying on unfounded generalities.

12. Very simply, our decision today recognizes that modern technology has fostered a class of inventions which are most accurately described as computer-implemented processes. Such processes are encompassed within 35 U.S.C. §101 under the same principles as other machine-implemented processes, and subject to judicially determined exceptions. . . . The overbroad analysis of the PTO errs in failing to differentiate between a computer program, i.e., a set of instructions within a computer, and computer-implemented processes wherein a computer or other automated machine performs one or more of the recited process steps. This distinction must not be overlooked because there is no reason for treating a computer differently from any other apparatus employed to perform a recited process step.

Although it may be argued that this decision precludes patent protection for computer programs as defined in the Copyright Act, viz., "a set of statements or instructions to be used directly or indirectly in a computer to bring about a certain result,"[79] subsequent decisions, reviewed below, lend support to the view that such programs as "computer-implemented processes" are protectable, provided that statutory bars or judicially created exceptions to protection applicable to noncomputer processes or apparatuses do not otherwise preclude protection.

Principal among the statutory limitations on protection are the requirements that the invention be novel[80] and nonobvi-

---

[79] *See* footnote 72.

[80] 35 U.S.C. §102. In *Diamond v. Diehr,* 450 U.S. 175, 209 U.S.P.Q. 1 (1981), the Supreme Court rejected an argument that novelty is an

ous.[81] Case law construing these provisions has held that "scientific principles and laws of nature, even when for the first time discovered, have existed throughout time, define the relationship of man to his environment, and, as a consequence, ought not to be the subject of exclusive rights of any one person."[82] Included within this bar are mathematical algorithms, which are analogs of laws of nature.[83]

The courts have also held, however, that "[a] process is not unpatentable simply because it contains a law of nature or a mathematical algorithm;" and that "an *application* of a law of nature or a mathematical formula to a known structure or process may well be deserving of patent protection."[84] It is not always an easy task, however, to neatly separate a patentable process from an unpatentable "principle."

Questions of patent protection for computer programs or computer program-related inventions accordingly have been argued primarily on the basis of whether the claim is believed to be one for a mathematical formula or for an apparatus or process that uses a computer program, containing a mathematical formula (or algorithm) in a manner that, notwithstanding such use, is nevertheless otherwise patentable.

The Supreme Court has faced such questions three times. In two of these cases the claims were rejected. In the third, the claim was upheld. An examination of those decisions, as well as decisions from the Court of Customs and Patent Appeals (CCPA; now Court of Appeals for the Federal Circuit) and other case law, will provide guidance on the current status of patent protection for computer programs.

---

appropriate consideration under the subject matter test of §101, holding that "whether a particular invention is novel 'is fully apart from whether the invention falls within a category of statutory subject matter.'" 209 U.S.P.Q. at 9.

[81] 35 U.S.C. §103 (1952).

[82] *In re Meyer*, 215 U.S.P.Q. 193, 197 (C.C.P.A. 1982).

[83] *Diamond v. Diehr*, supra, n. 4, 209 U.S.P.Q. at 8. *See also* footnotes 17 through 19; *In re Chatfield*, 545 F. 2d 152, 156 n. 5 (C.C.P.A. 1976).

[84] 209 U.S.P.Q. at 8.

3.2 Current Status of Patent Protection For Computer Programs

3.2.1 Gottschalk v. Benson[85]

In *Gottschalk,* protection was sought for "a method of programming a general purpose digital computer to convert signals from binary coded form to pure binary code." In examining this claim, the Court noted that the claim purported to cover any use of the method in all general-purpose digital computers.[86] The method itself consisted of a "generalized formulation" for programs to solve mathematical problems, viz., an algorithm. In rejecting the claim, the Court stated a fear that, if granted, it would "wholly preempt the mathematical formula and in practical effect would be a patent on the algorithm itself."[87]

3.2.2 In Re Freeman

Not all algorithms are mathematical formulae, however, and, given the uncertain application of the term in *Gottschalk v. Benson,*[88] the question of whether *Gottschalk v. Benson* held all algorithms or only mathematical algorithms unprotectable was raised.

The CCPA attempted to answer this question in *In Re Freeman*[89] by construing the *Gottschalk v. Benson* court's use of the term "algorithm" to apply only to "a procedure for solving a given type of mathematical problem," and by then

---

[85] 409 U.S. 63 (1972). For earlier decisions on patentability of software, see *Ex parte King,* 146 U.S.P.Q. 590 (Pat. Off. Bd. App. 1964) and *In re Prater,* 415 F. 2d 1393 (C.C.P.A. 1969). In 1965, a presidential commission was established to study the patent system. The following year it issued a report recommending that computer programs should not be patentable. This recommendation was introduced in a legislative proposal, S. 1042, 90th Congress, 1st Sess. §106 (1967).

[86] *Id.* at 65.

[87] *Id.* at 72.

[88] *See* discussion on this point in *In re Pardo,* 214 U.S.P.Q. 673, 676–677 (C.C.P.A. 1982); and in *Diamond v. Diehr,* 209 U.S.P.Q. 1, 8 n. 9 (1981).

[89] 573 F. 2d 1237, 197 U.S.P.Q. 464 (C.C.P.A. 1978).

creating a two-part analysis of claims believed to recite algorithms.

The first part of the analysis required a determination of whether the claim in fact either directly or indirectly recited an algorithm in the "*Benson* sense" of that term.[90] Assuming that such an algorithm was recited in the claim, the second part of the inquiry required an analysis of whether, looking at the claim in its entirety, the invention claimed only the algorithm. If so, the claim was not protectable. Since the invention in *Freeman* did recite only a mathematical algorithm, the CCPA did not need to further analyze the claim.

3.2.3 Parker v. Flook

Shortly after the CCPA's opinion in *Freeman*, the Supreme Court decided *Parker v. Flook*,[91] in which the claimed invention contained a computer program-based methodology for the updating of alarm limits on catalytic converter process variables (for example, temperature, pressure, flow rates). The claimant attempted to avoid the *Benson* holding by drawing the claim to recite a specific end use for the process, rather than claiming protection for the methodology alone. The application had been rejected by the Patent Office on the ground that the only novel element in the methodology was a mathematical formula, and thus the claim was barred under Sections 101 and 102 of the Act (the algorithm was treated as prior art and therefore was not novel).

On appeal to the CCPA,[92] the claimant's emphasis on "post-solution activity" proved successful. The victory was, however, short-lived as the Supreme Court reversed, holding:

> The notion that post-solution activity, no matter how conventional or obvious in itself, can transform an unpatentable principle process exalts form over substance. A competent draftsman

---

[90] 197 U.S.P.Q. at 471.
[91] 437 U.S. 584 (1978).
[92] 559 F. 2d 21 (C.C.P.A. 1977).

could attach some form of post-solution activity to almost any mathematical formula.[93]

The Court's decision that the process was unpatentable subject matter was, however, based on its assumption that the only novel part of claimant's process was its mathematical formula. Specifically, the Court held: "Respondent's process is unpatentable under §101, not because it contains a mathematical algorithm as one component, but because once that algorithm is assumed to be within the prior art, the application, considered as a whole, contains no patentable invention." The Court added, however, that its decision did not reflect a judgment that "patent protection of certain novel and useful computer programs will not promote the progress of science and the useful arts, or that such protection is undesirable as a matter of policy."[94]

The dissenting opinion believed that the majority was confusing the Section 101 subject matter inquiry with the novelty inquiry of Section 102.

3.2.4 In Re Walter

Following *Flook,* and in an apparent effort to narrow its negative impact, the CCPA modified the second of its two-part *In Re Freeman*[95] test as follows:

> Once a mathematical algorithm has been found, the claim as a whole must be further analyzed. If it appears that the mathematical algorithm is implemented in a specific manner to define structural relations between the physical elements of the claim (in apparatus claims) or to refine or limit claim steps (in process claims), *the claim otherwise being statutory,* the claim passes muster under §101. If, however, the mathematical algorithm is merely presented and solved by the claimed invention, as was the case in *Benson* and *Flook,* and is not applied in any manner to physical elements or process steps, no amount of post-solution activity will render the claim statutory. . . .[96]

---

[93] 437 U.S. at 590.

[94] *Id.* at 594.

[95] *See* text at footnotes 89 and 90.

[96] 205 U.S.P.Q. 397, 407 (C.C.P.A. 1980).

The key element in this test is the underscored passage that a claim that otherwise presents statutory subject matter is not rendered ineligible by the mere use of computer program.[97] Thus, in an appropriate case, the use of a computer program in a process could serve as a basis for a determination that the process was patentable.

3.2.5 Diamond v. Diehr

The CCPA position in *In Re Walter* found support in the Supreme Court's 1981 decision in *Diamond v. Diehr*,[98] which also represented a departure, in a number of respects, from the Court's earlier opinions in *Benson* and *Flook*. In *Diehr*, the claimant created a process for the accurate and continuous measurement of the proper curing time for synthetic rubber, principally through the repeated use of a well-known mathematical equation by a computer.[99]

In examining the claim, the Court stated that "the respondents here do not seek to patent a mathematical formula. Instead, they seek patent protection for a process of curing synthetic rubber. Their process admittedly employs a well-known mathematical equation, but they do not seek to preempt the use of that equation. Rather, they seek only to foreclose from others the use of that equation in conjunction with all of the other steps in their claimed process."[100]

In analyzing the effect of the use of a computer program on subject matter eligibility, the Court concluded, as the CCPA had in *In Re Walter*, that "a claim drawn to subject matter otherwise statutory does not become nonstatutory simply because it uses a mathematical formula, computer program or digital computer," and that an application of a mathematical formula "to a known structure or process may well be deserving of patent protection."[101] Although the *Diehr* Court did not

---

[97] *See* subsequent interpretation of *Walter* in *In re Abele*, 214 U.S.P.Q. 682, 686 (C.C.P.A. 1982).

[98] 450 U.S. 175, 209 U.S.P.Q. 1 (1981).

[99] 209 U.S.P.Q. at 8.

[100] *Id.*

[101] *Id.* at 9.

disagree with the holding in *Flook* that mathematical formulae must be considered to be prior art, it did hold that it is inappropriate, in determining protection under Section 101, "to dissect the claims into old and new elements and then to ignore the presence of the old elements in the analysis."[102] The Court also expressly rejected an argument that the mathematical algorithm "could not be considered at all in making the §101 determination."[103]

The Court recognized that "[a] mathematical formula as such is not accorded the protection of our patent laws," but concluded that:

> [W]hen a claim containing a mathematical formula implements or applies that formula in a structure or process which, when considered as a whole, is performing a function which the patent laws were designed to protect (e.g., transforming or reducing the article to a different state or thing), then the claim satisfies the requirements of §101.[104]

Because the Court viewed the respondent's claim as a claim for a process for molding rubber products and not for a mathematical formula, the decision of the CCPA in finding the invention to be within the scope of Section 101 was affirmed.[105]

Following *Diehr*, the Patent Office revised its "Manual of Patent Examining Procedure" as it pertained to examination of claims reciting computer programs, mathematical equations, and algorithms,[106] stating in line with *Diehr* that "a claim is not unpatentable under 35 U.S.C. §101 merely because it includes a step[s] or element[s] directed to a law of nature, mathematical algorithm, formula or computer program so long as the claim as a whole is drawn to subject matter otherwise statutory," and directing examiners to apply the two-step *Freeman-Walter* test

---

[102] *Id.* at 9 n. 12. *See also* footnote 4.

[103] *Id.* at 10.

[104] However, *cf.* dissent of Justice Stevens, the author of the *Flook* opinion. Following *Diehr*, the court affirmed by an equally divided vote a similar decision of the C.C.P.A. in *In re Bradley*, 450 U.S. 381 (1981).

[105] 209 U.S.P.Q. at 10.

[106] Manual of Patent Examining Procedure §2110 (1981).

for determining if a claim "involving mathematics and/or computer programming is in compliance with 35 U.S.C. §101."

3.2.6 In Re Taner

The CCPA's first opportunity to apply the *Diehr* opinion came in *In Re Taner*,[107] in which the CCPA reversed a decision by the Patent and Trademark Office Board of Appeals rejecting a claim for "a method for seismic exploration by which substantially plane or subtantially cylindrical seismic energy waves are simulated from substantially spherical seismic waves."[108]

The appeals board characterized the subject matter of the claim as a whole as "merely presenting and solving a mathematical algorithm"[109] and, as such, unprotectable.[110]

The CCPA's reversal of that determination illustrates the difficulty, noted at the beginning of this study, in neatly separating claims for a patentable process from those for an unpatentable "principle":

> Appellants' claims are not in our view merely directed to the solution of a mathematical algorithm. Though the claims directly recite an algorithm, summing, we cannot agree that appellants seek to patent that algorithm in the abstract. Appellants' claims are drawn to a technique of seismic exploration which simulates the response of subsurface earth formations to cylindrical or plane waves. That that technique involves the summing of signals is not in our view fatal to its patentability. Appellants' claimed process involves the taking of substantially spherical seismic signals obtained in conventional seismic exploration and *converting* ("simulating from") those signals into another form, i.e., into a form representing the earth's response to cylindrical or plane waves. Thus the claims set forth a *process* and are statutory within §101.[111]

---

[107] 214 U.S.P.Q. 678 (C.C.P.A. 1982).
[108] *Id.* at 679.
[109] *Id.* at 681.
[110] *Id.*
[111] *Id.*

3.2.7 In Re Pardo[112]

Two months after *Taner,* a claim for controlling the internal operations of a computer, including use of an "algorithm," was upheld by the CCPA. As described by the CCPA, the invention converts a computer from a sequential processor (which executes program instructions in the order in which they are presented) to a processor which is not dependent on the order in which it receives program steps.[113] The appeals board rejected the claim as reciting in its entirety an "algorithm," which it defined as an unprotectable procedure for solving a given type of mathematical program.

The CCPA examined prior decisions construing the term "algorithm" (particularly *Gottschalk v. Benson*), and drew two conclusions that it applied to the case before it: (1) the *Benson* decision used the term "algorithm" to refer solely to *mathematical* algorithms; (2) the *Pardo* claim did not recite either directly or indirectly any mathematical formula, calculation, or algorithm, but instead established rules to be followed by a data processor for its examining, compiling, storing, and executing steps.[114] The fact that the invention was "capable of handling mathematics" was held to be "irrelevant to the question of whether a mathematical algorithm is recited by the claims."[115]

3.2.8 In Re Abele[116]

On the same day as *Pardo,* the CCPA handed down a decision further refining the *Freeman-Walter* two-step analysis

---

[112] 214 U.S.P.Q. 673 (C.C.P.A. 1982). *See also* the C.C.P.A.'s pre-*Benson* decision in *In re Chatfield,* 545 F. 2d 152, 191 U.S.P.Q. 730 (C.C.P.A. 1976), *cert. denied,* 434 U.S. 875 (1977), which also involved a method for controlling the internal operations of a computer.

[113] *Id.* at 674.

[114] *Id.* at 676.

[115] *Id.* at 677. The C.C.P.A. stated that claims regarding processes, machines, or composition of matter were statutory subject matter unless they "fall within a judicially determined exception to Section 101." *Id.* No such exception was found applicable in the claim at issue. The C.C.P.A. also reversed the appeals board's holding (based on judicial notice) that the claim was obvious. *Id.* at 677–678.

[116] 214 U.S.P.Q. 682 (C.C.P.A. 1982).

of claims reciting algorithms,[117] *In Re Abele.* Appellants in *Abele* characterized the *Freeman-Walter* test as setting forth two ends of a spectrum—claims in which an algorithm is merely presented and solved by the claimed invention, and claims in which an algorithm is "implemented in a specific manner to define structural relationships between the physical elements of the claim (in an apparatus claim) or to refine or limit claim steps (in a process claim)."[118] The first type of claim was asserted to be nonprotectable; the second, protectable.

The CCPA rejected this narrow interpretation of the *Freeman-Walter* test, holding that it:

> does not limit patentable subject matter only to claims in which structural relationships or process steps are defined, limited or refined by the application of the algorithm.
>
> Rather, [it] should be read as requiring no more than that the algorithm be "applied in any manner to physical elements or process steps," provided that its application is circumscribed by more than a field of use limitation or non-essential post-solution activity. Thus, if the claim would be "otherwise statutory," . . . albeit inoperative or less useful without the algorithm, the claim likewise presents statutory subject matter when the algorithm is included.[119]

In applying this test to the claims before it (which involved image processing for computerized axial tomography or CAT scans),[120] the CCPA noted that appellants conceded that their claims implemented a mathematical algorithm and that thus the inquiry shifted to the second step of the *Freeman-Walter* analysis. Carefully examining each claim separately, the CCPA found some to be ineligible for protection as "directed solely to the mathematical algorithm portion of . . . the invention,"

---

[117] *See* text at footnotes 84, 85, 91, and 92.

[118] 214 U.S.P.Q. at 686.

[119] *Id. See also* subsequent discussion of the test in *In re Meyer,* 215 U.S.P.Q. 193, 198 n. 4 (1982).

[120] *See* description of the process, *id.* at 683–684.

whereas others in which various parts of the method[121] were otherwise protectable without application of the algorithm were held protectable even though the algorithm was applied directly to them.[122]

3.2.9 In Re Meyer

In the last CCPA decision to be reviewed, *In Re Meyer*,[123] the CCPA was faced with a claim for a data-gathering program designed to act as a memory aid for physicians during performance of neurological examinations, for example, recording the patients' response to tapping their knees or pricking their skin.[124] The program did not perform any diagnostic functions itself, aside from providing certain statistical probabilities based on use of a mathematical algorithm.

In affirming rejection of the claim, the CCPA again reviewed the *Freeman-Walter* test, holding:

> In considering a claim for compliance with 35 U.S.C. 101, it must be determined whether a scientific principle, law of nature, idea, or mental process, which may be represented by a mathematical algorithm, is included in the subject matter of the claim. If it is, it must then be determined whether such principle, law, idea, or mental process is applied in an invention of a type set forth in 35 U.S.C. 101.[125]

Citing *Abele,* the court stressed that, assuming the claim did recite a mathematical algorithm representing such principles, natural laws, ideas, or mental processes, the program must be applied to actual physical elements or process steps to qualify for protection. In examining the claim before it, the CCPA

---

[121] Appellant's apparatus claims were treated in the same manner as the method claims. *Id.* at 688. *See* subsequent comment by the C.C.P.A. on this in *In re Meyer,* 215 U.S.P.Q. 193, 198 n. 3 (1982).

[122] *Cf.* partial dissent of Judge Miller, idem. at 690, which although agreeing with the majority's formulation of the test, disagreed with its application to two claims.

[123] 215 U.S.P.Q. 193 (C.C.P.A. 1982).

[124] *See* description of the claim, *id.* at 194–196.

[125] *Idem.* at 198.

found that the program did not have such applications and was therefore "not limited to any otherwise statutory process, machine, manufacture, or composition," and as a consequence was not protectable.

3.2.10 Other Litigation

Legal disputes over patent claims involving computer programs may also occur in suits for patent infringement or declaratory judgment of patent invalidity. These suits, however, have been rare. In *Arshal v. United States,*[126] a patent for a "vectorial data processing system for extracting or prescribing directions and their rates of change from given input vectors" for use with analog computers was held invalid because, as in *Benson,* the claim recited a mathematical algorithm and was not applied to a particular technology or physical application. The court rejected the patentee's argument that the *Benson* decision's prohibition of protection for mathematical algorithms extended only to digital computers,[127] and further held that even novel and nonobvious data gathering was not protectable subject matter.[128]

In *Paine, Webber, Jackson & Curtis v. Merrill Lynch, Pierce, Fenner & Smith,*[129] an action for a declaratory judgment of noninfringement and invalidity was brought on the sole ground that the patent, a data-processing methodology combining three financial services commonly offered by financial institutions and brokerage houses, was not within the subject matter of Section 101 of the Act.

Plaintiff argued that business systems and methods could not form protectable subject matter. In a controversial[130] decision, the court held that:

---

[126] 621 F. 2d 421 (Ct. Cl. 1980).

[127] *Id.* at 428. *Cf. Gottschalk v. Benson,* 409 U.S. 63, 71 (1972).

[128] 621 F. 2d at 430.

[129] 218 U.S.P.Q. 212 (D. Del. 1983).

[130] *See* Patent Office Manual of Patent Examining Procedure §706.03(a), which states that a method of doing business is not protectable.

[t]he product of the claims of the . . . patent effectuates a highly useful business method and would be unpatentable if done by hand. The CCPA, however, has made clear that if no Benson algorithm exists, the product of a computer program is irrelevant, and the focus of analysis should be on the operation of the program on the computer.[131]

The court, however, arguably misinterpreted the CCPA's *Freeman-Walter* test, which requires the claim to be "otherwise statutory." Because the claim in *Paine Webber* may not have been otherwise statutory, it has been argued[132] that the patent should perhaps have been held invalid.

3.3 Advantages and Disadvantages of Patent Protection for Computer Programs

Given the availability of copyright protection for computer programs[133] as a class, the long term of such protection,[134] and the relatively small expense involved in securing copyright registration,[135] it may be asked what advantage there is in attempting to secure patent protection in light of the difficulty in obtaining such protection, the short term[136] of protection, and the relatively high cost of the effort.[137]

Two principal reasons emerge for seeking patent protection. First, under Section 102(b) of the Copyright Act, protection for an original work of authorship does not extend to "any idea, plan, procedure, process, system, method of operation, concept, principle, or discovery, regardless of the form in which it is

---

[131] 218 U.S.P.Q. at 220.

[132] *See* text at footnote 96.

[133] *See Apple Computer, Inc. v. Franklin Computer Corp.*, 714 F. 2d 1240 (3d Cir. 1983), pet. for cert. dismissed per settlement (January 1, 1984); *Apple Computer, Inc. v. Formula International, Inc.*, 725 F. 2d 521 (9th Cir. 1984).

[134] 17 U.S.C. §302 (1978).

[135] 17 U.S.C. §708 (1978).

[136] 35 U.S.C. §§154–155A.

[137] *See* Clark, *The Risks and Costs of Patent Litigation: A House Counsel's View*, 1973 Utah L. Rev. 618.

described, explained, illustrated, or embodied in such work."[138] Thus, although it has been held that there is no bar to obtaining both copyright and design patent protection for a single work,[139] as a practical matter, it is likely that many of the elements, indeed perhaps the most important elements,[140] of a patentable computer program would be ineligible for copyright protection under Section 102(b) of the Copyright Act.[141] In such cases, patent protection would be essential for disseminated inventions.[142]

The second principal reason for obtaining patent protection is that, notwithstanding the shorter term, during such term the patentee has the right to exclude all others from making, using, or selling the invention in the United States, even if these other parties have, subsequently, created their work independently. In contrast, however, an individual who independently creates a work of authorship[143] will not be liable to an earlier author of a copyrighted work, even though the two works are identical.[144]

For computer programs whose development involves large investment expenditures but whose commercial usefulness is relatively short, the effort in obtaining the more exclusive protection available through patent protection may well prove important.

3.4 Likelihood of Future Legislative or Judicial Changes

On October 1, 1982, the CCPA was merged with the appellate division of the United States Court of Claims to create

---

[138] 17 U.S.C. §102(b) (1978).

[139] *In re Yardley*, 493 F. 2d 1389, 1394 (C.C.P.A. 1974).

[140] For example, the process or method of operation.

[141] Although this problem would not be as likely to occur in the case of design patents, all cases to date before the Supreme Court and the CCPA have involved utility patents. However, *see* Rinkerman, footnote 74.

[142] Trade secret law provides necessary protection for undisseminated works.

[143] 17 U.S.C. §102(a) (1978).

[144] *Fred Fisher Music Co. v. Dillingham*, 298 F. 145 (S.D.N.Y. 1924).

the Court of Appeals for the Federal Circuit (CAFC).[145] This new court also has exclusive jurisdiction of appeals from United States District Courts in patent infringement suits and in actions for declaratory judgment of patent invalidity. Prior decisions of the CCPA on the patentability of computer programming are, however, binding on the CAFC, and, thus, it is unlikely that the CAFC will issue decisions in the near future dramatically liberalizing or restricting program patentability. It is also possible that, in light of the specialized nature of the CAFC, the United States Supreme Court will be less likely to review complex issues adjudicated by a lower court established specially to decide such questions.

Congressional action is also unlikely. In both *Gottschalk v. Benson* and *Parker v. Flook,* the United States Supreme Court requested congressional guidance, but none was forthcoming. In the 98th Congress, a number of bills involving new technology were introduced (but few passed),[146] and none covered issues of patent protection for computer programs.

3.5 Policy Issues Raised in Granting Patent Protection

Congressional authority to enact patent protection is found in Article I §8 cl. 8 of the United States Constitution, which states a purpose of "promot[ing] the progress of science and the useful arts." The United States Supreme Court has held that "the patent laws promote this progress by offering inventors exclusive rights for a limited period as an incentive for their inventiveness and research efforts" in the hope that "[t]he productive effort thereby fostered will have a positive effect on society through the introduction of new products and processes of manufacture into the economy, and the emanations by way of increased employment and better lives of our citizens."[147]

---

[145] P.L. 97–164, 97th Congress, 2d Sess. (1982).

[146] *See,* for example, the Semiconductor Chip Protection Act of 1984. P.L. 98–620 (November 8, 1984).

[147] *Diamond v. Chakrabarty,* 206 U.S.P.Q. 193, 196 (1980).

Given the importance of computer programs to our society, there can be little doubt that the encouragement of investment in such works fosters an important public policy. At the same time, however, the granting of a monopoly power over inventions essential to society's needs may be argued to be contrary to the public interest by vesting control in the private sector over matters affecting the citizenry. It must be noted, however, that our Founding Fathers embodied in the Constitution the system of private property and a limited grant of monopoly as the best way to further the public interest. Additionally, through the disclosure requirements of the patent act,[148] technological innovation is made available to the public. Given this benefit, as well as that from the patentable invention itself and the limited term of protection, encouragement of technological innovation through the granting of patent rights is believed, on balance, to be an effective method of achieving the constitutional goal of promoting the progress of the "useful arts."

DISCUSSION

Michael Keplinger: I am faced with a rather difficult task in reviewing Jon Baumgarten's paper because for the most part I agree with the information he has presented. However, I would like to express one point of disagreement. He stated that the law can work. I believe that the law does work, as far as the law goes.

There are open questions about how the copyright law applies to the protection of computer software. Most of these were addressed in the paper, and with regard to the development of the law related to computer software in the United States, I cannot supplement the information that was presented. Mr. Baumgarten presented an excellent summary, highlighting the salient cases that have been discussed. I agree that by and large the question of the copyrightability of computer software has been resolved. There is no question in the courts' minds that computer software is properly protectable by copyright.

---

[148] 35 U.S.C. §112 (1952).

Several things were pointed out that are worth noting. Any time you try to legislate with precision an area of rapidly moving technology, sometimes more problems will be created than will be solved. The definition of computer software established by the Commission on New Technological Uses of Copyrighted Works (CONTU) has been effective in the courts as defining the subject matter of copyright in software. However, Section 117 has turned out to be rather troublesome. Section 117 provides for input and archival copying. CONTU felt it was necessary, as a statement of policy, to make it perfectly clear and to put it on the record by making it part of the law that which the Commission thought was the state of the copyright law and how it should be worked out. The way the case law has developed in the courts has been close to what we thought it should have been, so perhaps a good job was done with the language in Section 117.

However, there are now other problems arising. In my present position in the Office of Legislation and International Affairs at the Patent and Trademark Office, we get heavily involved with trade representatives who are concerned about international trade and the promotion of American trade worldwide.

Currently, one of the most important areas of trade development is in products that embody intellectual property in some manner. One of these expanding areas is the protection of computer software, as well as the protection of high technology U.S. information products—video cassettes, audio cassettes, sound recordings, motion pictures, and broadcast programming.

Internationally, this is a real problem. How the U.S. Government approaches the international protection of computer software and, indeed how the international community approaches this question, is becoming increasingly important.

Recently, the U.S. Senate gave its advice and consent to adherence to the Brussels Satellite Convention to protect against the unauthorized interception and retransmission of satellite-transmitted, program-carrying signals, which is a first step in the right direction but which is one that probably will have little impact on the question of the protection of computer software. However, this could bring up another related concern.

Mr. Baumgarten brought up software as a service. In the future, software may become a service industry. The plans recently reported in the trade press to deliver computer software over communications links rather than selling it in copies in stores is going to be an important development; one that the law will have to cope with.

The CONTU study found that one of the more difficult things to do was to understand the technology, including its uses and its applications, and to be able to understand it in the context of the law. However, once the effort was made and once the drafters of the legislation understood what software was, in the context of the copyright and patent laws, we wondered what the confusion had been about.

As mentioned in the paper, the question of the international trade aspects of the protection of computer software is becoming increasingly important. There have been attempts in a number of countries around the world to enact special legislation for the protection of computer software. However, the more immediate trend has been to provide protection for computer software under copyright laws.

In every country where the question of computer software protection has come before the courts, they have had no problem in interpreting the provisions in their laws (many of which are drawn directly from the Bern Convention, which deals directly with literary or scientific works) that those works cover computer software. This is true in the courts in Great Britain, Canada, Japan, Hungary, France, the Federal Republic of Germany, South Africa, Taiwan, and Hong Kong and more recently in Italy.

Few countries have found it necessary to modify their copyright laws to explicitly provide for computer software protection. The United States was one of these, perhaps because we were the first to explicitly recognize it, and because of the importance of our computer industry, we felt that it was necessary.

The Australians have recently modified their copyright law to provide for the protection of computer software. It also has been reported that there is a bill making its was through the Indian Parliament to amend that country's copyright law to include computer software as copyrightable subject matter.

The point of this discussion about international protection is to highlight the fact that it is a worldwide problem. It is a question that is now facing intellectual property policymakers in other countries, and many of these countries look to the United States for leadership. My own experience in dealing with international matters verifies that actions taken in the United States have had worldwide impact on the development of copyright laws for protection of computer software.

It is necessary to keep in mind that we are dealing with the protection of a number of different kinds of intellectual properties. In the paper, this question was alluded to with respect to the relationship between a computer chip and the program that is stored in the chip and the fact that Congress has recently enacted a sui generis or specialized form of protection for microcircuit chips.

Throughout the legislative history of this provision for the protection of chips, it was made clear that that protection does not add to or detract from the copyright protection that is available for the programs that are stored in the chips. In a sense it considers chips to be equivalent to diskettes or tape cassettes as receptacles for this abstract thing called a computer program, which must be fixed into something material to obtain copyright protection. There is additional protection that is provided for in the Chip Design Act which provides protection for the layout or design of that chip, which is separate from copyright.

Another important point made in the paper was that in this area, the law is only a tool. It is a tool that is needed to help resolve the problems, but the law does not provide all of the answers, nor can the Federal Government. The Government has provided the copyright law which defines legal relationships among the parties, and the exact ways in which those relationships are applied are fine-tuned by the courts. That is what CONTU envisioned would happen as the technology developed and the law developed with it.

QUESTION: What do you mean by shrink-wrap, flip-top, and tear-open agreements?

Jon Baumgarten: Those have become shorthand words for a variety of devices that the software publishers have adopted for protection. In one form or another, it relates to a unilateral contract, a contract which the purchase does not sign, which purports to set forth terms—and I use "purport" not in a negative sense, but in an attempt to be neutral—under which the purchaser of software can use it. What you see on the package is a very prominent legend stating that by opening the package, you are deemed to have agreed to the terms set forth in the enclosed agreement.

The terms vary. Some purport to limit the use of the program to use on a single machine. Others purport to govern the circumstances under which archival copies or back-up copies can be made. Others of a more recent vintage deal with whether the program can be reverse engineered—a process by which the protected expression is analyzed to determine the underlying, unprotected idea.

There are two trends in the industry that I have been exposed to. The software houses have been using these licenses for a number of years. They are not only using them, but are strengthening them by dealing expressly with reverse engineering.

Conventional publishers, many of whom are engaged in software publishing, are starting to ask why such licenses are necessary. They say, "We always sold books. Why are we licensing computer software?"

The answer seems to be manifold. One, they are used in the hope that they will maintain a producer/end-user relationship and contractual terms that will be deemed to preserve trade secret protection in mass-distributed programs. Two, they are used to try and avoid rental. If that person is merely a licensee or lessee of the copy, that person does not have the right under the copyright law to rent without the consent of the copyright owner. Three, they are used to trying to avoid the consequences of Section 117 and to restate the circumstances under which archival or back-up copies can be made.

I think there was also a theory that if you marketed computer programs in this way, they were not sales, and therefore you were not subject to considerations under the Uniform Commercial Code dealing with implied warranties of fitness and the like. At the same time they were seeking to remove such warranties they had the traditional Uniform Commercial Code however, warranty disclaimers on the programs.

They are now being used to try to control reverse engineering. However, you will find a more questioning attitude among conventional publishers because of their history, but I do not think that the industry is ready to give them up.

Rick Giardina: I think the key element is the hold-over. Most of the people that started the microcomputer industry were involved with mainframe computers, and many were software developers. They had a tradition of licensing the software through a large corporation or an individual for use. They did not want to sell it because they did not want to lose control of it. So, they would license it for use.

Also, they are a response to what was seen initially in the industry's history as not a clear addressing by the Government as to what rights there really were. There were some concerns of whether software was copyrightable or whether it should be protected as a trade secret. So, the plan was to cover all bases. As the copyright law is increasingly becoming the method of protection, we are backing off of this licensing approach, and I think it will be gone within the next 5 to 10 years.

Thomas Olson: You mentioned that there were discussions about legislation about rental of software. In October 1984, Senator Charles Mathias (R-MD) and Senator Patrick Leahy (D-VT) introduced a bill on that subject, their theory being that it is very much the same situation as the record rental situation that resulted in enactment of the record rental bill in early October 1984.

Jon Baumgarten: Would you care to say something just briefly about the concerns you have expressed about whether the industry can solve the code-breaking device problem that has arisen under Section 117, selling devices on the grounds that enable customers to exercise their privileges? You have raised in formal discussions in the past the possibility that the industry can solve this by making the copies available themselves, and then a correlative amendment can be made to 117. Could you say a word about that?

Thomas Olson: I have suggested a variety of ways of dealing with this problem, but I basically think any solution must address two problems simultaneously. The first is that because software is fragile, people generally do need back-up copies. And it is a problem if software sellers deliver a copy of the software that has copy protection and then abandon their customers by giving them no way of preparing back-up copies. On the other hand, there is a problem if you have unlimited copying of software. We need to find some way of satisfying both of those concerns.

One suggestion that I have made is that allowing customers to make their own back-up copies is only one way of getting them. The companies themselves can provide back-up copies at the time of sale or they can provide users with back-up copies very promptly if the users need them. If the industry had a uniform policy of doing that, then there would be no need for people to prepare their own back-up copies, and the people who promote commercial breaking of copy protection would no longer have any argument for cutting into the legitimacy of their business.

Jon Baumgarten: Deborah, would you like to give us any insights into the chairman's thinking about the next session and computer measures? (Deborah Leavy is staff counsel to Chairman Robert Kastenmeier's (D-WI) Subcommittee on Copyrights in the House).

Deborah Leavy: Mr. Kastenmeier, as you all know, is very interested in new technology questions and how they affect the copyright law, and vice versa. I think that sometimes his thinking is to look at the new questions in somewhat traditional terms, and I think that some of the translations of new technology to older, more traditional questions will give some insight into his thinking.

For instance, in the record rental legislation, it was very important to him to protect the traditional rights of nonprofit educational institutions and libraries to continue their activities.

I think that, similarly, he would look in the software area to determine what are the traditional public interest or public domain uses to which this kind of software, in ways similar to other materials such as books, records, or motion pictures, has been or should be put. He would want to continue to have the copyright law protect those public uses, and at the same time protect proprietors.

Jon Baumgarten: An editorial comment: I think that we are fortunate that we have as chairmen of the respective committees in the House and the Senate two members who, although they do not always agree with each other, have both proven themselves over and over again to be very sensitive to the issues posed by the new technology, to what the law can do and what the law cannot do, and are willing to be both innovative and circumspect in plotting out the answers that can be contributed by legal and nonlegal solutions, which is one of the issues we are addressing today.

QUESTION: A point of clarification with regard to the first sale doctrine as it relates to phono records. Tom [Mr. Olson] and you have suggested that it stops record rental. As I understand it, it just eliminates the first sale defense. That does not, per se, prohibit any record rental.

Jon Baumgarten: Again, we are trying to telescope things here. They do not stop record rentals. They require the authorization of the record company and the music publisher before the rental can be engaged in.

QUESTION: Does it even do that?

Jon Baumgarten: Yes, that it does, not retroactively, but for stock in hand after the effective date of the new law, the phono records cannot be rented except in limited, nonprofit areas that Deborah referred to.

Deborah Leavy: One clarification is that there are no misdemeanor penalties. As a matter of fact, there are no criminal penalties at all.

Jon Baumgarten: I think the gentleman's question was whether it actually stops it. It stops it to the extent that if you are not in one of the nonprofit areas that Deborah mentioned and you are talking about stock acquired by the outlet after the effective date of the new statute, then technically the authorization of both the record company and the music publisher is required.

Michael Tyler: I need a clarification. What is the current status of either the case law or Section 117 interpretation on Lotus or many other companies that give you a back-up copy with the original when you pay your money? And what is one's right as a purchaser to make archival copies if they give it to you now, as opposed to what future legislation might entail?

Jon Baumgarten: I think perhaps the safest answer is that the statute itself does not discriminate between situations and does not require a showing of need as to the condition of the defense. That showing of need is one of the things that Tom Olsen referred to as a possible amendment to the legislation.

I think that a plaintiff's counsel would probably argue that you can read into the statute a need basis and that if the archival copy is already there; the customer does not require it. It is not that far from the argument that was made in *Atari v. JS & A* in which Atari said that you do not have to make archival copies of cartridge-based ROM programs because they are not subject to the kind of electromagnetic failure that Congress was concerned about.

—————————————— four ——————————————
TECHNICAL APPROACHES TO SOFTWARE PROTECTION

Neil Iscoe*

I. INTRODUCTION

The technical protection of software involves the physical techniques vendors use to prevent the unauthorized use of their software. These techniques range from the use of copy-protected disks through external physical devices to specially constructed central processing unit (CPU) chips.

This chapter explains the underlying approaches of the technical methods of software protection. The concept of a program seeking a simple authorization before properly performing is followed by an examination of the more sophisticated methods of protection. Both the physical methods of protection and the software techniques required to implement protection are discussed, along with the policy issues created by current and future methods of technical protection.

---

* Neil Iscoe served as President of Statcom, Inc. of Austin, Texas from 1979–1985. He is now completing requirements for a Ph.D. in Computer Science at the University of Texas in Austin.

Technical protection of software has gained importance as the number of microcomputers has increased. Although protection schemes exist for minicomputer and mainframe computer programs, the method of distribution of this type of software means that license agreements are generally signed before the software is transferred to the user. Furthermore, mainframe software usually requires a large amount of support, updates, and other items that require users to stay in contact with the vendor. Consequently, theft in the minicomputer and mainframe computer marketplace is not considered a problem that requires a technical protection solution. However, the high-volume, mass-market nature of microcomputer software distribution has resulted in a situation in which a substantial amount of theft currently exists (see Chapter 2).

Although there are relatively few facts about the economic consequences of piracy, some insight into the problem can be gained by reviewing the information contained in the computer trade press. Discussions of the issues confronting users and software vendors have been published previously.[1-5] Editorial stands against software theft also can be found. [6,7] Legal protection in the form of trade secrets and copyright laws does exist for software vendors. Jon Baumgarten and Michael Keplinger have addressed the legal issues of software protection in Chapter 3. Additional information on copyright and its rela-

---

[1] J. Wollman, "Software Piracy and Protection—Are You Breaking The Law?," *Popular Computing*, Vol. 1, no. 4 (April 1982): 99–106.

[2] Martin A. Goetz, "At Stake: Competition, Growth, Survival," in "The Hard Fight for Software Protection," *Computerworld*, Vol. 13, no. 37 (September 10, 1979): 15–33.

[3] J. Seymour, "Special Report: The Software Outlaws," *Today's Office*, Vol. 13, no. 37 (August 1984): 20–34.

[4] C. R. Engholm, "No Justifications Allowed: Software Piracy Simply Equals Theft," *Infoworld*, Vol. 4, no. 11 (March 1982): 50–51.

[5] P. Freiberger, "Pirates Bedevil Angry and Frustrated Software Vendors," *Infoworld*, Vol. 4, no. 11 (March 1982): 31.

[6] C. Morgan, "How Can We Stop Software Piracy?," *Byte*, Vol. 6, no. 5 (May 1981): 6–10.

[7] D. Mersich, "Pirates Better Seek a New Line of Work," *Canadian Datasystems*, Vol. 6, no. 5 (December 1983): 21.

tionship to software has been published.[8,9] Reports have also been published for those interested in a lay interpretation of software protection.[10-13]

Although large-scale commercial theft and distribution of software, by and large, are deterred by our current legal system, the relative ease of copying a piece of software, combined with the lack of social sanctions against "borrowing" copies of software, have resulted in a situation in which individuals, clubs, dealers, and corporations routinely steal software. Consequently, reliable methods of physically protecting software are required to deter software theft.

Because the nature of software piracy is such that most casual theft is never detected, perhaps the most important goal of the technical protection of software is to keep honest people honest. A protection scheme should cause as little disruption as possible to the normal use and backup procedures for a program. It should be as inexpensive as possible and have a minimal effect on the authorized use of a program.

The methods required to technically protect software raise a number of new legal questions, including the following: Do certain methods of protection imply that the software vendor is licensing the machine and not the end user? What laws are broken when a software protection device is copied? Is it illegal to distribute information concerning how to patch out an au-

---

[8] J. Baumgarten, "Copyright and Computer Software Including Data Bases and Chip Technology" (Notes), Paskus, Gordon and Hyman, Washington, DC (August 1983).

[9] M. Keplinger, "Computer Software and Copyright: Current Developments," In *"Software Protection: Current Developments in Copyright and Patent and Their Relationship to Trade Secret,* Law and Business, Inc. (Harcourt Brace Jovanovich, Inc.), pp. 15–32.

[10] C. N. Mooers, "Preventing Software Piracy," *Computer,* Vol. 10, no. 3 (March 1977): 29–30.

[11] R. H. Stern, "The Case of the Purloined Object Code: Can It Be Solved? II. Approaches to Software Protection." *Byte,* Vol. 7, no. 10 (October 1982): 210–222.

[12] J. Kamenetz, "Software Protection: A Legal Overview," *Microcomputing,* Vol. 6, no. 7 (July 1982): 76–82.

[13] D. Mersich, "Can You Really Protect Your Program Against Infringement," *Canadian Datasystems,* Vol. 10, no. 3 (March 1980): 76–77.

thorization call in a piece of software or how to emulate a copy protection device?

2. COMMERCIAL SOFTWARE PROTECTION

The first popular program that was protected with something beyond a license agreement was the VisiCalc spreadsheet program. Using a simple disk protection scheme, VisiCorp helped its early sales revenue by discouraging casual copying of its program.

As of summer 1984, most of the major microcomputer software vendors were using at least some type of disk protection scheme. And over 30 companies were in the business of developing and marketing software protection devices and techniques.[14-16]

Although most software companies are already using at least one technical protection system, vendors are actively searching for better systems, individually and through their trade associations.

The Association of Data Processing Service Organizations (ADAPSO) represents most of the major software manufacturers in this country. It is actively pursuing a four-part program to stop the theft of software:

1. Education—Creating the awareness that theft is wrong.

2. Legislation—Monitoring current and proposing future legislative activity in the software protection areas.

3. Technical Protection Methods—Creating a classification and report, as well as beginning the process of eventual software standards.

[14] S. Auditore, "Software Security and the Pinstriped Pirate," *Unix/World* (March/April 1984): 38–44.

[15] Staff Report, "Protecting Proprietary Software," *Mini-Micro Systems* (August 1984): 78–79.

[16] G. Legg, "The Integrator," *Mini-Micro Systems* (April 1984): 109–114.

4. Serial Port Protocol Standard—Public process of creating a communication protocol and physical connection standard for serial port devices.

3. A LOOK AT SOFTWARE—SOME DEFINITIONS

Before beginning the examination of the methods of protecting software, some terms commonly used in describing software products and piracy activities should be reviewed.

Software is the code that runs within a computer. When the protection of software is discussed, the concern is with the code that is distributed on a high-volume basis in microcomputers.

Protection of software indicates an interest in the methods and techniques that will hinder or prevent someone from making unauthorized use of a copy of the object code version of a computer program.

Object code is the form of a computer program that a computer "understands."To create object code, a programmer uses a compiler to translate the source code of a program into something that the computer can directly use.

Source code is the original form of a program before it is compiled into object code. FORTRAN, Pascal, COBOL, C, and Ada are popular computer languages used by computer programmers. A source code version of a program is written by a programmer or programming team. Often exceeding 10,000 lines of information, the source code of a program is the primary method of communicating information between the programmer and the computer.

A compiler converts source code to object code. An object code version of a program is the version generally distributed on a disk. (Because most significant programs are not written in BASIC, the run time interpretation of BASIC programs will not be considered.) The compilers for these languages convert a version of the code that humans can understand into a version that machines can use. For the purposes of this discussion, assembly language will be considered to be source code and assemblers will be considered as compilers (Figure 4–1).

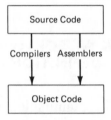

Figure 4–1. Compiling source code

Technical protection of software concerns the physical techniques and devices used to protect against the unauthorized use of the object code version of a program. It is assumed that the source code version of a program is protected through trade secrets practices, including employee agreements.

4. THE PROTECTION ENVIRONMENT

The discussion of software protection begins with an examination of what it means for a program to have authorization to properly execute. In general, if the software fails to find the expected authorization, then it refuses to run (Figure 4–2).

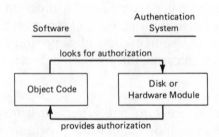

Figure 4–2. Typical authorization scheme

Generally speaking, there are four types of authorization schemes:

- *Identification code:* The software requests and must receive a simple signal or serial number before proceeding.

- *Identification code with active protection:* An identification code system that has additional software that tries to protect itself from being patched.

- *Encrypted software:* The software is encrypted when stored on disks. When used with a special processor, the software sometimes stays encrypted while in the memory.

- *Control logic:* The authorization scheme becomes an integral part of the control logic of the program.

In the case of a standard check for an identification code, the program makes a simple call for authorization before it starts to run (Figure 4–3).

1. Begin execution of the program.
2. Make an authorization call.
   2a. If the authorization is bad, then abort.
   2b. If the authorization is good, continue with 3.
3. Finish execution of the program.

Figure 4–3.   An authorization call

When attempting to break this authorization scheme, a hacker cannot look directly at the source code to find the call for authorization, since a program running within a computer is in object code format.

The pirate begins by executing a standard programming tool called a debugger. A debugger is usually used to help locate programming errors and is easily available from a number of sources.[17] To use a debugger to steal the code, the pirate first loads in the object code that is designated for attack.

The expertise required to use a debugger is a knowledge of a particular microprocessor, an aptitude for programming, and

---

[17] A. R. Grogan, "Decompilation & Disassembly: Undoing Software Protection," *The Computer Lawyer,* Vol. 1, no. 2 (February 1984): 1–11.

a great deal of tenacity. These qualifications can be found in most hackers from age 12 and up.

The debugger allows the pirate to examine the program one step at a time. Depending on the skill and sometimes the luck of the person using the debugger, the hacker will eventually find the section of the code in which the authorization call is made. At this point, the pirate is ready to disable the authorization.

Using a technique called "patching," the pirate replaces (patches) the old code with some special code of his or her own. Depending on the way the authorization call actually appears, the pirate can remove the call, jump around the call, or in some other way disable the call.

These techniques center on Step 2 in Figure 4–3. One form a patch might take would be to replace "make an authorization call" with a statement such as "new 2: Go to 3." This solution instructs the computer to skip past the authorization checks. Another form is to replace Step 2 with a statement such as "new 2: Always return authorized" (without asking for authorization). This solution makes the program think that a correct authorization has been performed. A third alternative is "new 2: Replace 3 with NOP." NOP is a command meaning "no operation" or do nothing. This is, in effect, the same as jumping around the code (Figure 4–4).

1. Begin execution of the program.
2. Go to 3 (or NOP, etc.).
3. Finish execution of the program.

Figure 4–4. Patching out the authorization check

After patching the program, the pirate has a working program in the memory of the computer that will never again try to check for an authorization. However, the pirate is not yet finished because the new version of the program is still in the computer's memory and will disappear when the power is turned off.

The next step after patching the code is to write the modified program onto a disk. In the example given here, this is accomplished with a few simple commands to the debugger. The modified program that now exists on disk will no longer request authorization because the authorization portion of the program no longer exists. Although this example may seem trivial, many of the popular programs sold today can be patched in the described manner. One of the most popular spreadsheet programs requires only a 5-byte patch to disable its protection scheme.

Once a pirate discovers where to put the patch, the information is disseminated via bulletin boards, club newsletters, and other more traditional forms of communication.[18] Publication of the patching information means that nontechnical users who wish to follow relatively simple cookbook-type instructions can disable the protection systems on their own copies of software.

It should be noted that the simple authorization scheme that can be defeated with a patch makes all copies of a particular piece of software vulnerable once the patch is discovered. Apparently, it is not illegal to publish patching information. In fact, some otherwise honest individuals publish the information required to disable an authorization so that licensed copies of software can be used on hard disks.

4.1 The Authorization Signal

An authorization signal originates from some type of device or medium that supplies information to the software on request. Software protection devices can be classified into categories based on the type of device that supplies the authorization, along with the functionality of the software authorization and signal scheme.

The following are the classifications of software protection devices, beginning with devices that create authorization signals:

---

[18] J. Markoff, "Bulletin Boards Respond To The Pirate's Cry, 'Gimme Shelter' (Software Piracy)," *Infoworld,* Vol. 4, no. 11 (March 1982): 45–47.

- *Protected disks:* Disks that have some type of unique signature that the software looks for before running.

- *Hardware devices:* Methods that require some type of hardware, such as

  - *Serial and parallel port boxes:* A box or device that attaches to the computer through a standard serial (RS-232) or parallel port.
  - *Mice, keyboards, and other external hardware:* External devices that attach to the computer through non-standard interfaces.
  - *Devices with no physical connection to the computer:* A code box or other type of device that displays a signal to the user, who then types that signal into the keyboard.
  - *Cryptoprocessors:* A special processor chip that replaces the normal processor inside the computer.
  - *Other boards or special chips that are installed inside the computer:* Includes encryption chips, programs stored in special read-only memories (ROMs), and other devices that require connections inside the computer.

4.1.1. Protected Disks

In the microcomputer marketplace, software currently is distributed on floppy disks. Although electronic distribution may eventually change the distribution system for software, [19,20] the current distribution on a magnetic media source provides a convenient method of authentication.

To understand disk protection schemes, it is useful to look in a general way at how a computer views the information that is stored on a floppy disk. In Figure 4–5 it can be seen that data are stored on a disk in sectors within tracks. Tracks resemble those found on a record; sectors are as familiar as a slice of pie.

---

[19] H. Jones, "Legal and Business Issues in Electronic Distribution and Downloading of Software and Recent Developments in Microcomputer Software Publishing," In *Electronic & Software Publishing, Law, Technology, and Business.*

[20] E. Dyson, *The Computer Lawyer* Vol. 1, no. 3 (March 1984): 1–6.

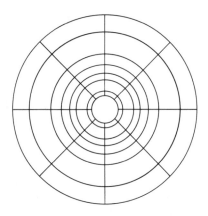

Figure 4–5. Disk layout

For example, the IBM Personal Computer (PC) format has 40 tracks per side and eight (or nine for PC DOS 2.) 512-byte sectors per track.

When a computer reads or writes information, it first selects a particular track and sector. A disk operating system organizes these sectors into convenient units called files. A program is contained within a file that is a collection of sectors on the disk.

An operating system is designed to allow users to copy files from disk to disk. A disk protection system must defeat the ability of the operating system to make normal copies of a file on a disk to protect a program. Disk protection schemes operate by placing a "signature" on the disk. A signature is a unique method of telling the program that it has an authorization to proceed. Returning to the example of an IBM PC, an individual sector within a particular track will be examined in detail.

For the computer to know which sector it is examining, there is an address marker as shown in Figure 4–6. The address marker contains (1) Cylinder (C), which is a number from 0 to 39 indicating the track; (2) Head (H), which is either 0 or 1 indicating the side of the disk; (3) Record (R), which is a number from 1 to N indicating the sector number of that particular track (the value of N is dependent on the version of the operating system); (4) a factor N which determines the size of the sector; the base 2 is raised to the power N and then multiplied by 128 to produce the number of bytes of data in the sector [in this case N is 2, causing a sector to contain (2 EXP 2) * 128 = 512 bytes]; and (5) cyclical redundancy check (CRC), which is an error code to verify that the previous information was written correctly. This information is followed by a gap that contains other types of control codes. That is then followed by the data and finished with a final CRC that acts as an error-correcting code for the data.

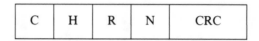

Figure 4–6. A disk sector address marker

Typical "soft" signatures are marks written to the disk that, although they conform to specifications, do not act exactly as the operating system expects them to act. Examples of signature systems commonly in use include extra address marks without data, data with improperly written CRCs, and spurious control codes.

A more recent type of signature is called a hard signature. Hard refers to the fact that these schemes use some type of method to damage the medium. The resulting hole, blemish, or burned area is then used as a signature. By contrast, a soft signature is one that is written electronically onto the disk.

4.1.2 Piracy and Disk Protection

Copying of a soft signature is accomplished by using special copy programs that have the ability to bypass the operating system and use lower level routines to copy each and every byte exactly as it was written onto the disk. These copy routines are commercially available from a variety of sources, and as of the fall of 1984, were available for under $50.

Most disk copying programs are updated regularly to beat whatever protection scheme a company has designed. Some of the copy programs are quite sophisticated and are sold by individuals who have firm beliefs that protecting a program from copying is in itself wrong. Regardless of the personal beliefs of the creators of copy programs, most deliver their software with stern warning labels that explain that their programs are to be used only for making legal archival copies of copyrighted programs. Although many magazines refuse to allow vendors of copy programs to advertise, there does not appear to be any legal barrier to the sale of software that can be used to create legal archival copies of a program.

Although it is presumed that most of these programs are purchased by pirates, law-abiding users purchase this type of software to make legitimate archival copies of their licensed software. The nonlarcenous motivations for copying a piece of software include protecting a disk from coffee, magnetized paper clips, cigarette smoke, hot closed automobiles, and a variety of other hazards that tend to destroy magnetic media.

4.1.3 Summary of Issues Associated with Disk Protection

Vendors of disk protection systems offer a variety of options to software vendors. Some of the considerations involved in the software manufacturer's purchase of a particular disk protection system include the following:

1. Type of signature

   This includes whether the signature is hard (physical) or soft (magnetic); whether the signature is erased by formatting, can be made unique for a particular software vendor, or can be exactly replicated for bulk distribution.

2. Bulk copying equipment

   The software vendor wants to know whether this type of equipment must be used and, if not, then whether it can be used.

3. Availability of disks

   Costs and sources for the type of media that have signatures.

4. Copying speed

If bulk copying equipment is not used, then how long does it take to produce a disk?

5. Skill required to defeat

Disk protection schemes can be defeated by patching out the authorization call or copying the signature. Some disk protection vendors offer sophisticated software that makes patching more difficult. Other vendors offer special signatures that are hard to copy.

Users are affected by the software vendor's choice of a particular protection scheme. The advantage of a disk protection scheme for the user is that it is a simple, inexpensive system that can be moved easily from machine to machine. The disadvantages are that a floppy disk generally needs to be left in the machine, even when a hard disk is used; the system cannot be used in the case of a diskless network; and users must order a replacement disk if they damage the original disk that they purchased.

4.2 Hardware Components that Affect Software Protection

Read-only memory (ROM) is memory that is initialized at the factory. ROMs are named for the fact that, unlike random access memory (RAM), they can only be read and not written. Erasable programmable read-only memory (EPROM or PROM) chips can be erased with an ultraviolet light and programmed with an inexpensive but special machine. In general, clearly copyrighted software that is stored in any type of ROM is considered to be relatively secure against general piracy. The legal restrictions that deter commercial pirates tend to discourage piracy of programs stored in ROMs and also because the equipment required for copying them has been somewhat too expensive for home use.

One device that could make home copying economically feasible was the Prom Blaster marketed by a company called

JS & A. In the case of *Atari v. JS & A,* the court issued an injunction that stopped JS & A from selling the device, since the court believed that its only purpose was to violate the law.

4.2.1 External and Internal Port Devices

A device attached directly to a computer's serial or parallel port is another way to provide an authentication signal (Figure 4-7). This method of authorization works by electronically providing a signal on request of the software.

A serial port is a computer's asynchronous communication port. Typically conforming to the RS-232 communications standard of the Electronic Industries Association, a serial port provides a 25-pin male or female connection between the computer and the outside world. Serial port protection devices come in a variety of sizes and configurations. They all provide an authorization signal to a piece of software. However, methods of accomplishing the transmission of a signal vary considerably.

A signature on a disk and an external port device are both methods of producing authorization signals. For the disk to produce an authorization signal, it must be in a disk drive. Similarly, a serial box must be plugged into a port to produce an authorization signal. It is claimed that most serial boxes are transparent to the computer system. This means that the computer can use its serial port to communicate with a peripheral (such as a printer) without being hampered by the presence of the security device. The dilemma of transparency is that the computer must be able to communicate with the serial box to ask for and receive an authorization signal. If the box is truly transparent, then the computer will be unable to communicate with it. However, if the box is not transparent, then it will

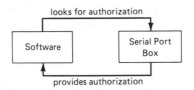

Figure 4-7. Serial Port (RS-232) Authorization

interfere with the peripheral with which the computer is communicating.

Efforts are being made by ADAPSO to come up with a standard method for electronic communication and physical connection of a serial port-type security device to the computer. They hope that proper coordination will prevent a multitude of incompatible serial devices from being thrust on the user community.

4.2.2 The Installation Problem

With the disk protection schemes discussed previously, the software vendor coordinated mating the authorization signal with the software. Because the software is shipped on a floppy disk, it is easy for the manufacturer to put both an authorization signal (the signature) and the program on the same disk. However, the problem becomes more complex when a hardware device is used to supply the authorization signal. One solution is for the software manufacturer to match a hardware device (and its authorization signal) to each piece of software at the time that they are shipped. Unfortunately for the user, this system results in a separate hardware device for each piece of software that the user wishes to run. This means that multiple hardware devices are required if the user wishes to run more than one piece of software on a particular machine.

Daisychaining is the term that describes plugging a series of serial port boxes simultaneously into the same serial port. Although most manufacturers of serial port devices allow daisychaining, the effect on the user is to create a chain of hardware that must be moved from machine to machine. Software protection vendors have come up with a variety of schemes to get around the installation problem. These include the building of boxes that can read cards with magnetic stripes, accept a variety of key-type devices, and allow fusebox-type, plug-in connectors.

4.2.3 Other External Devices

Although serial port-type devices have been described here, there are many other ways to attach external physical devices to a computer. Keyboards, "mice" pointers, game paddles, and many other types of common computer devices can be used as the source of authorization signals. Serial port devices are preferred because many computers have at least one available serial port that can be used for attaching a device.

4.2.4 Devices With No Physical Connection to the Computer

A separate device category exists for a special type of code system that does not require a physical connection to the computer. This system requires the user to complete the authorization sequence produced by the device. One vendor's system makes the software display a special code on the screen. The user reads the computer screen and types the code into the device. The device then produces the authorization code on its own display. The user reads the device display and types the authorization into the computer. A variation on this theme is provided by a software protection vendor that offers a device that decodes a special computer screen image. By this method, the user holds a domino-sized device up to the computer screen. The device reads the screen image and creates the authorization code on its own internal display. As before, the user types the authorization into the computer before the program will continue.

4.3 Encryption

4.3.1 Introduction

Many of the commercial software protection systems and much of the protection literature make reference to various encryption techniques. Although a discussion of encryption and cryptology is beyond the scope of this chapter, the basic concepts and methodologies will be reviewed to enable a more complete discussion of protection methods. More complete introductions to cryptography have been published previously.[21,22] An overview of encryption products also can be found.[23]

The data encryption standard (DES)[24] (Figure 4–8) is the algorithm of the National Bureau of Standards (NBS) for encryption and decryption of data. DES assumes that both the transmitter and receiver of data have secure access to a common 64-bit key. Using a previously agreed-upon key, the person sending a message uses the DES algorithm with his or her key to translate the message into encyphered text. The recipient of the now unintelligible message is able to decode it only by using the same key with the DES algorithm.

NBS notes that their key specification results in an effective yield of "over 70,000,000,000,000,000 (seventy quadrillion) possible keys of 56 bits. . . ." By using a computer capable of

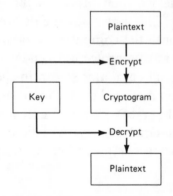

Figure 4–8. Data encryption standard

[21] A. Lempel, "Cryptology in Transition," *Computing Surveys* Vol. 11, no. 4 (1979): 285–305.

[22] W. Diffie and M. E. Hellman, "Privacy and Authentication: An Introduction to Cryptography," *Proceedings of the IEEE* Vol. 67, no. 3 (1979): 397–427.

[23] G. Legg, "Encryption Software Guards Valuable Data," *EDN,* Vol. 28, no. 13 (July 7, 1983): 258–264.

[24] *Data Encryption Standard,* Federal Information Processing Standard Publication 46 (Washington, D.C.: National Bureau of Standards, January 1977).

performing one operation every microsecond, it would take many years to exhaustively test all possible keys. Although a code breaker would not have to test all of the possibilities to break an encyphered message, the DES is considered by most people to be secure for nonmilitary transactions. Dissenting views have also been presented, however.[25]

4.3.2 Public Key

The public key cryptography system (Figure 4–9) requires two keys. Each person who wishes to use the system has both an encryption key and a decryption key. Encryption keys are made public, in a directory or a file, whereas their corresponding decryption key is kept secret.

To use the system, a person sending a message would first look up the public encryption key of the intended recipient. Then, using the recipient's encryption key and a public key algorithm, the person would encode and send the message. Anyone intercepting the message would be unable to decode the text without the unique decryption key held by the intended recipient. The person receiving the now unintelligible message

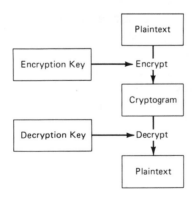

Figure 4–9. Public-key crypto-system

---
[25] Cushman, "Data-encryption Chips Provide Security—But Is It False Security?," *EDN*, Vol. 27, no. 3 (February 1982): 39–45.

would use his or her own secret decryption key and the same public algorithm to decode the message. Note that it is never necessary for users to disclose their decryption keys. Not even the person sending the original message has access to the decryption key held by the receiver.

The public key system has the advantage that key security is not as severe a problem as with the DES. Furthermore, it has the unique feature of being able to be used in reverse to perform a technique of verification known as a signature. To create a signature, a person would use his or her secret key to encrypt a message. The recipient would then use the sender's public key to decrypt the message. If the message were decoded correctly (that is, if an intelligible response appears), then the recipient is assured that the message was encoded by the sender (or by someone with access to the sender's private key).

4.3.3 RSA Public Key Algorithm

By far the most popular public key algorithm was developed by Rivest, Shamir, and Adleman and is generally referred to as the RSA system.[26] Providing both security and computational efficiency, the system is generally regarded as the de facto standard public key algorithm.

It is possible to calculate a decryption key given an encryption key and a high-speed computer. However, RSA points out that the use of a very efficient algorithm with a computer capable of carrying out one million operations per second could break a 50-digit key in less than four hours. It would take 74 years to break a 100-digit key and almost four billion years to break a 200-digit key.

4.3.4 Protection Applications

Encryption techniques are used to hide information from those individuals who do not have authorization to see that information. Consequently, encryption techniques have been

---

[26] R. L. Rivest, A. Shamir, and L. Adleman, "A Method of Obtaining Digital Signatures and Public-Key Cryptosystems," *Communications of ACM* Vol. 26, no. 1 (January 1983): 96–99.

widely investigated as a way of helping to protect software from theft.

The uses of encryption techniques for software protection range from encrypting the object code on a disk and using software to load a decrypted copy to the use of special encryption chips or cryptoprocessors.

4.3.5 Cryptoprocessors

The term "crypto-microprocessor" was coined by Best[27] to describe a microprocessor that is able to execute encrypted instructions. Best has proposed that a modified version of the DES algorithm be used to decrypt instructions in memory. Because the instructions are encrypted while in the memory, there is no authorization signal to patch out. Consequently, the use of a debugger is not sufficient to produce a copy that will run without the processor in place.

The major difficulty with cryptoprocessor-type schemes revolves around the previously discussed installation problem. As with other hardware devices, there must be some type of method for the installation of multiple pieces of software on the same computer. Cryptoprocessors have the additional problem that software installed on a particular machine cannot be transported to another machine without an additional authorization code.

Albert and Morse[28] have described methods of key management that circumvent some of the installation problems introduced by cryptoprocessors. However, even with automated key management schemes, the installation of a piece of software on a particular computer creates a de facto license to a machine rather than a user. This creates problems for users, as well as

[27] R. M. Best, "Preventing Software Piracy with Cryptomicroprocessors," *Proc Compcon* (Los Alamitos, California: IEEE-CS Press, Spring 1980): 466–469.

[28] D. J. Albert and S. P. Morse, "Combatting Software Piracy by Encryption and Key Management," *Computer,* Vol. 17, no. 4 (April 1984): 68–72.

computer service technicians, who often swap computers when carrying out service agreements.

4.4 Toward More Sophisticated Authorization Schemes

There are a variety of ways to make authorization signals more complex. Some software protection vendors use special timing, secret checks, and a variety of other tricks to prevent a pirate from patching out the authorization. However, a determined pirate can not only beat these schemes, but having beaten them the pirate can publish information on how to steal a particular piece of software.

An authorization scheme that cannot be readily broken was proposed in the September 1984 issue of *Communications of the ACM*.[29] Using the concept of control logic and a special processor inside a serial box, the authors show how such a scheme can be used to devise a very good authorization system.

5. SUMMARY

One of the dilemmas introduced by a good protection scheme is that the better the scheme is, the motivation to break it becomes greater. Hundreds of thousands of adventuresome young computer fanatics are available to fight the systems designed by protection companies.

Clearly, there are no technical panaceas. A system is only as strong as its weakest link. However, the industry is working on a number of different methods of refining both the systems that produce authorization codes and the type of authorizations.

Perhaps keeping honest people honest is the most valuable service that the technical protection of software can offer the

---

[29] T. Maude and D. Maude, "Hardware Protection Against Software Piracy," *Communications of the ACM* Vol. 27, no. 9 (September 1984): 950–959.

computer industry. For, it seems likely that software theft will continue as long as other types of theft continue.

DISCUSSION

Stephen P. Morse: Some additional classification of protection schemes should be helpful. One such organization is shown in Table 4–1.

There are several key issues, in addition to those mentioned in the paper, that should be considered when considering any technical protection scheme. For a solution to be acceptable in the marketplace, it must be unobtrusive to the legitimate users. If users find a solution obtrusive, they won't buy the software, and hence the protection scheme would be counterproductive. Users would consider any solution obtrusive that prohibits them from running programs directly from hard disks, running programs over a network, making back-up copies to protect themselves from a failure of the media containing the distributed copy, running programs off a floppy disk of their choice on which they have placed several related application programs, and running programs on any of the computers that are in a lab consisting of a pool of shared computers. They would also consider obtrusive any solution that requires them to take some unusual action (such as plug in a special read-only memory [ROM]) before they can execute a particular package.

With any proposed solution, consideration must be given to who pays the price and who reaps the benefit. An otherwise attractive solution may put the costs on parties who receive no benefits and hence are unwilling to pay. For example, most solutions involving modifications to the hardware place the costs on the hardware manufacturer, whereas the benefits would most likely go to the software vendors. Many solutions require the user to pay a price, namely obtrusiveness as discussed above, with no apparent benefits to the user.

TABLE 4–1.
Classification of Anti-Piracy Solutions

I. Software requests verification
  A. Uncopyable signature on distribution media
    1. Soft signature—nonstandard format of media
    2. Hard signature—physical damage to media
  B. Hardware system parameter
    1. Serial number
    2. Unique ROM bits
    3. Timing parameters
  C. External device
    1. RS–232 serial port devices
II. Processor (or extension thereof) requests verification
  A. Decrypting processor
  B. External device
    1. Decryption and execution
    2. Decryption only
III. Memory provides limited access
  A. Kaufman's non-random-accessing method
  B. Intel's authenticated EPROM
  C. Motorola's security bit EPROM
  D. Seeq's security algorithm

To be cost effective, the level of protection should be geared to the level of threat. For example, there is little threat of piracy in the game market because the tools employed by pirates (debuggers and disassemblers) usually are not available in this market. On the other hand, the threat of piracy of the microcode is great because the financial benefits to such a pirate can be enormous.

Any solution that bases security on an encryption scheme (other than a one-time pad) runs a high risk of being eventually broken as technology advances.

No mention was made of piracy tools other than debuggers to disable the verification code. Other tools worth noting are in-circuit emulators (ICE) and memory-image copiers (Wildcard).

Finally, I have comments on some of the points made in the paper. Iscoe mentions that VisiCorp's disk protection scheme discouraged the casual copying of the VisiCalc program and thereby helped VisiCorp's early revenues. It should also be noted that fear of piracy kept VisiCorp from releasing VisiCalc to the CP/M market, thereby hindering its revenues.

Iscoe mentions that most significant programs are not written in BASIC and hence he does not consider the case of interpreters. This is not so. BASIC, because of its interpretive nature, is extremely popular among microprocessor hobbyists, and many of them eventually produce marketable products. Examples are VisiFile and VisiTrend. Furthermore, my firm distributes a significant accounting package written in BASIC. FORTH, another interpretive language, is used extensively for computer games.

The following disadvantages to the decrypting processor approach are sometimes claimed:

- The decrypting processor is licensed to the machine, not the user. This is not a disadvantage because one copy of the software can be licensed to a stated number of machines.

- The processor is not user-installable. If this refers to the decrypting-processor chip, it would be installed by the system manufacturer at the time the system is built. If this refers to the software, it is indeed user installable.

- If distribution of the decrypting processor refers to key distribution, there are known solutions to the key management problem. If this refers to software distribution, there are no disadvantages.

John Maxfield: Would you agree that all of these schemes can be defeated and that they all have extreme disadvantages to users of software?

Stephen Morse: The one area that is not impossible but very difficult to defeat is encryption. There, the weak spot is the strength of the encryption method itself.

John Maxfield: Isn't microcode a form of encryption, in that if you have encrypted the microcode and if you change the bits and bytes around, you just end up with more microcode?

Stephen Morse: I wouldn't call that encryption. You're just redefining the microcode in that sense.

John Maxfield: I can see that encryption, based on my experiences with the people who are cracking and copying the software, is the only secure method. But encryption costs the user in terms of hardware or additional software or additional time.

Stephen Morse: The thing that I advocated in my paper[30] was an encryptive processor that can operate in both encrypted and unencrypted modes. The big problem there was key distribution. In fact, the bulk of that paper discussed how to solve the key management problem. Once that is done, it will be transparent to the end users. They will see no difference. There will be a slight installation procedure to go through when they get the software, but they won't find that obtrusive in any way.

John Maxfield: There has been talk that perhaps there is no point in trying to protect games. They are going to be cracked, copied, and distributed just as quickly as if there were no protection at all. Perhaps if the manufacturers did not try to stop the cracking, it would reduce the cost of the software. Maybe then the pirates wouldn't be quite so motivated; there is no challenge.

Rick Giardina: We have looked into a lot of protection mechanisms, and one of the things I haven't heard mentioned is that one of the requirements invariably is the addition of one more manufacturing step. That is an element that software vendors and manufacturers are looking at very hard because the addition of another step is a problem. It is not a major one, but it is a problem.

What we have discovered is that technical protection schemes tend to fall into one of two categories: (1) those that are easy

---

[30] D. J. Albert and S. P. Morse, "Combatting Software Piracy by Encryption and Key Management," *Computer,* Vol. 17, no. 4 (April 1984): 68–72.

to implement and easy to defeat and (2) those that are hard to implement and hard to break.

It is possible to end up with some serious problems because if one uses a very expensive system, the effect is the same. Once it is broken, you must get a new system because you end up on the bulletin board.

So we are looking at options of (1) cheap systems, just to try to cut off unsophisticated pirates, which then must be changed when it is compromised, or (2) go the other route and hope that the protection will last a few months or years before having to complete an entirely new retooling process when it is defeated.

five

ELECTRONIC BULLETIN BOARDS: A NEW THREAT TO COMPUTER SYSTEMS

**Donn B. Parker
and John F. Maxfield***

I. INTRODUCTION

Access to computers is increasingly occurring from terminals directly connected by private PBX circuits, circuits leased from telephone companies, and dialed public telephone circuits. This electronic access to computers is facilitating anonymous, unauthorized entry, which is an extension of physical trespassing onto private property. Such trespassing is an outgrowth of the phone phreaking (telephone toll fraud) and computer hacking (pushing and exploring computers to their limits) that have intrigued young people since the late 1950s. Business, governmental, and institutional computers and communication circuits are regularly attacked, often by juvenile delinquents using false names, although discussions with hacker informants have indicated possible participation by career criminals, terrorists, and organized criminal gangs.

* Donn B. Parker is an information security management consultant, researcher on computer abuse and crime. John F. Maxfield is a computer crime consultant and President of a company called BOARDSCAN.

No valid measurements of the size of the problem exist. The nature and extent of the problem are known only from limited reports of loss and interviews with several perpetrators. Such a study is currently being performed at Stanford Research Institute (SRI) International under a grant from the U.S. Department of Justice, Bureau of Justice Statistics. Loss estimates by victims have ranged up to several hundred thousand dollars in a few individual cases, and ongoing attacks against communications companies have resulted in monthly losses of millions of dollars, their security officers estimate.[1] One large corporation reported a total loss, including staff time, of $260,000. Victims mostly have been naive, computer-using organizations with a surprising lack of computer safeguards and telephone companies with large amounts of vulnerable equipment that cannot be easily or quickly changed.

As organizations start to protect themselves, perpetrators and their methods of attack are expected to become much more sophisticated in response. Solutions must be comprehensive yet constrained to avoid unacceptable consequences such as economic loss and civil rights violations. Although the purpose of this chapter is not to suggest possible solutions, four approaches become apparent in studying this problem: (1) changing services to be more resistant; (2) legislating appropriate criminal statutes with vigorous prosecution; (3) changing values, especially among young entrants in the computer field; and (4) establishing safeguards to be built into the hardware and software of computer systems.

2. BACKGROUND

This chapter focuses on unauthorized computer and communication systems access by three classes of intruders. Abuses are committed by (1) malicious hackers and phone phreaks who are mostly juveniles not a part of the victimized organizations

---

[1] Donn B. Parker, *Fighting Computer Crime* (New York: Charles Scribner's Sons, 1983), pp. 23–27.

and (2) trusted employees within these organizations. More recently, a new class has emerged consisting of (3) career criminals who are gaining technical skills, often acquired in training courses taught in many prisons, and who see profitable opportunities in unauthorized access to computers. A spectrum of computer criminals thus emerges: malicious juvenile hackers and phreaks are at one end of the spectrum; the middle of the spectrum is occupied by the trusted, amateur white-collar business criminal; and the other end of the spectrum consists of career criminals, organized criminal gangs that use computers in their businesses, and terrorists such as those who have attacked more than 30 computer centers in Italy and France. A study of 1,500 reported and documented cases of computer crime at SRI International found that these perpetrators were found to have widely different goals and motivations.[2]

Malicious hackers and phreaks in the first class often treat access to computers as an end in itself, focusing on achieving total control of individual computers so that they can play the role of an electronic god. This class usually does not have financial gain in mind. They are striving to prove themselves: to gain recognition from their peers in the hacking and phreaking culture, which could be described as misguided meritocracy.[3,4]

Based on more than 40 interviews of computer criminals conducted by the Computer Security Program at SRI International and on studies by Donald Cressey at the University of California, Santa Barbara,[5] we believe that amateur white-collar criminals see themselves as problem solvers, not as criminals. Their intent is to solve various severe personal problems by violating positions of trust, while causing the least amount of harm to the fewest number of people. Recognition of this

---

[2] U.S. Department of Justice, Criminal Justice Resource Manual on Computer Crime (Washington, D.C.: U.S. Department of Justice, Bureau of Justice Statistics, 1980).

[3] Joseph Weizenbaum, *Computer Power and Human Reason* (San Francisco: W. H. Freeman, 1976), p. 116.

[4] Sherry Turkel, *The Second Self, Computers and The Human Spirit* (New York: Simon and Schuster, 1984).

[5] Donald R. Cressey, *Other People's Money, A Study in the Social Psychology of Embezzlement* (Belmont, California: Wadsworth, 1971).

self-perception is important to develop deterrents to crime. In contrast, the livelihood of career or professional criminals comes from engaging in criminal activities. They view computers as the means to make financial gain and are proud of their criminal status.

Some people move from one part of this spectrum to another, making it difficult to definitively categorize these criminals. Hackers, for example, may progress from engaging in non-financial-seeking activities to criminal activities to make enough money to continue hacking and to pay for the equipment and services they use. Hackers may also develop intense problems and become amateur white-collar criminals. Unfortunately, there are no valid statistics to assess the relative size of these groups.

The methods used by all three types of perpetrators differ only to the extent that amateur white-collar computer criminals tend to gain authorized access to computer systems but subsequently engage in unauthorized activities within that system. Career criminals work both from a position of trust, as do the amateur white-collar criminals, and through the impersonation of authorized computer users.

Hackers can be divided into three subgroups: (1) benign hackers, who are authorized users of computer systems, usually in educational institutions, who engage in pushing computers to their limits, sometimes causing losses to other users; (2) unsavory hackers, who are unauthorized computer and communication systems users, who have impersonated authorized users or who have uninvited access without the need to submit to an authorization process; and (3) malicious computer hackers, who engage in unauthorized breaking and entering of computer systems with intent to do harm.

All three hacker subgroups are outgrowths of the phone phreaking, or telephone toll fraud, of the 1950s and 1960s. Twenty-five years ago, an elite phone phreak had to have extensive technical expertise and knowledge of electronics. Today, the picture has changed with the popularity of home computers and home modems. Phone phreaking (and computer hacking) has taken on a new dimension; readily available underground publications and bulletin board systems (described later in this chapter) contain the necessary information, minimizing the technical skills needed.

Phone phreaking began in the late 1950s with the advent of direct long-distance dialing. Several persons, including John Maxfield, one of the authors of this chapter, independently developed the device that later became known as the Blue Box, so named because the first one captured by police in 1961 in a raid on a betting parlor in Brooklyn, New York, was painted blue. Throughout the 1960s, numerous phreaks were identified and arrested, although little or no publicity was generated in the press. Not until October 1971, with the publication of the *Esquire* magazine article, "Secrets of the Little Blue Box,"[6] and the arrest and conviction of John Draper, alias Cap'n Crunch, did phone phreaking become a nationally known phenomenon.

The introduction of time-sharing in the late 1960s opened another door for illegal electronic activity. Students now could explore mainframe computers. In the beginning, hacking was even encouraged as a learning tool. By the mid-1970s, however, hackers had caused so much harm that many schools began installing countermeasures to limit this kind of abuse.

In 1978, the first computer hobbyist bulletin board systems (BBSs) appeared. These early systems usually ran on borrowed computers. Inexpensive teletypewriter terminals were used because the early home computers lacked sufficient capability to be used as terminals. Finally, in 1980, the first true computer BBSs began to appear in Los Angeles and New York City and were used for many legitimate purposes. From the very beginning, however, some of these BBSs were used for disseminating illicit information. John Maxfield served as a paid informant for the FBI to investigate BBSs during this period. The Starcom BBS, the MOMS BBS in Los Angeles, and the OSUNY BBS in New York City were the forerunners of today's underground network. By the end of 1982, more than 500 BBSs were in operation nationwide, as determined by a count of BBS telephone numbers and names listed in several BBSs. As of Sep-

---

[6] Ron Rosenbaum, "Secrets of the Little Blue Box," *Esquire*, October 1971, reprinted as "The First Computer Freaks," *Esquire*, June 1983, pp. 376–391.

tember 1984, at least 2,000 systems existed, with more coming on line each day. A significant fraction of these BBSs contained illicit information, perhaps unknown to their operators.

When MCI entered into competition with AT&T's long-distance service in 1980, the phone phreaks were ready with their toll fraud methods and BBS communications. Using a technique pioneered by Cap'n Crunch and his blue computer, software was developed for the purpose of scanning by sequentially searching and testing for valid private customer billing codes used by the fledgling communications companies. These new common carriers were forced to use these billing codes because the caller line identification (ANI) used to bill AT&T long-distance calls was denied these new carriers. It appears that this weakness of the billing scheme promoted the growth of phone phreaking and the spread of BBSs; at this point it was extremely easy to place fraudulent toll calls. As the sale of home computers and modems began to boom and judging from the number of BBSs and their frequently busy telephone lines, thousands of people learned about phreaking and hacking from the underground BBSs and the free, oftentimes stolen, computer programs that could be copied from their memories.

After the appearance of computer time-sharing networks, such as ARPANET and TELENET, hackers could explore many connected computers in most major cities by using local-access telephone numbers. By 1982, ARPANET and TELENET had been thoroughly penetrated and used at will by hackers. Clubs such as the inexperienced Milwaukee 414 Gang[7] and the elite experts' Inner Circle hacker gang sprang into being. Considering the hundreds of thousands of juveniles equipped with home computers and modems, it is likely that tens of thousands of them regularly attacked the systems. Some adults found in Maxfield's monitoring of BBSs, motivated by the potential for financial gain, openly aided and abetted some hackers. A new breed of criminal emerged which appears to be here to stay.

---

[7] *Computer and Communications Security and Privacy,* Hearings Before the Subcommittee on Transportation, Aviation, and Materials of the Committee on Science and Technology, U.S. House of Representatives, September 26, 1983, no. 46, pp. 14–53.

Since January 1983, John Maxfield has identified 560 continuously active hackers and phreaks and their practices, including credit card fraud and other crimes. The tabulated results are included in the Appendix at the end of this chapter.

The early computer hackers tended to be of college age, primarily because their first exposure to computers occurred at that educational level. With the advent of home computers and the teaching of computer basics in the lower grades, the average age of the hacker has probably dropped. Today, the overwhelming majority of known BBS owners and users are teenagers. Teenagers tend to form cliques and peer groups, so the formation of phone phreak and hacker gangs seems inevitable. The parents of these bright teenagers usually do not understand the power of the computer, which means that the teenagers are not subject to the same parental restrictions that would govern their other activities. Many parents view the home computer as an excellent babysitting device. If their sons or daughters spend the evening quietly in their rooms with the computer instead of visiting the local pool hall or video game parlor, the parents feel reassured that their offspring are not getting into trouble. In reality, these teenagers may be engaging in electronic gang activities, including the illicit copying of proprietary computer programs. The implications of this are serious. The copying losses to the software industry alone are millions of dollars annually, according to trade media quotes of spokesmen for software companies and the Association of Data Processing Service Organizations (ADAPSO).

Some gang leaders tend to be older, more experienced teenagers, perhaps college students, who are interested in hacking not for the intellectual challenge, but for the financial rewards. Some gang leaders are adults who are financially motivated. Several of the major figures behind the cracking and distribution of pirated software for resale to the public are adults. One adult gang leader openly solicited credit card numbers from juvenile members in exchange for hard disk drives and other equipment that the adult would order fraudulently. Some teenaged leaders bask in the tremendous notoriety and acclaim that they receive from their peers and strive to be the biggest hacker by breaking into the greatest number of computer systems.

The gangs may be local, such as the Milwaukee 414 Gang, national, such as the Inner Circle Gang, or even international, such as CHAOS, a Commodore C-64 malicious hacking and illicit copying club, with headquarters in the Federal Republic of Germany. In all cases, a BBS was the gang's main base of operations and served as a secure communications center. The 414 Gang had a private BBS that was so secret it had no name. The Inner Circle had the Securityland BBS, as well as illegitimate accounts on GTE's TELEMAIL network. CHAOS operates on a variety of BBSs in both the United States and Germany.

Another international aspect of the problem comes from overseas intrusions that start as pranks but have the potential of becoming a serious international incident. One BBS listed the phone number of Queen Elizabeth's private secretary. Windsor Castle then received a number of prank calls from juveniles in the United States. More serious is the stated intention of some hackers to try to penetrate Russian computers via their phone system. One incident reported recently involved the recruitment of French teenagers by their tax authorities to penetrate Swiss computers to find data on French citizens' accounts.

3. BULLETIN BOARD SYSTEMS

A bulletin board system (BBS) exists to enable microcomputer users to communicate and exchange information. This communication may consist of private messages, public messages, such as requests for help or equipment for sale, computer programs, or just about any information that can be transferred by telephone lines and modems. Many computer clubs have set up BBSs for the benefit of their members. A club member can ask for and receive help with a computer-related problem and can make copies of public-domain programs stored in them.

Unsavory BBSs found in Maxfield's monitoring include those that cater exclusively to people looking for sexual partners.[8]

---

[8] "Computers: X-Rated, The Joys of Compusex," *Time*, 14 May 1984, p. E5.

One national service was discovered in New Orleans that traded children for sexual purposes, resulting in several criminal convictions. Some of these on-line dating services cater to homosexuals. Many of the monitored BBSs fall into the category of pirate systems that stock the latest copyrighted game and business software and allow them to be freely exchanged and traded. A partially organized network of BBSs exists across the United States for the sole purpose of distributing stolen computer programs. Still other BBSs cater to those who desire to break the law in other ways. On one of these BBSs, instructions are given on how to avoid payment of long-distance call charges, how to steal services from time-sharing companies, how to make nitroglycerine and lock picks, and how to engage in a wide range of other criminal activities.

A BBS consists of a microcomputer such as a TRS-80, an Apple II, or a Commodore C-64. Connected to the computer may be several floppy diskette disk drives, a modem, and perhaps a printer. A high-volume nonremovable disk drive may be used as a substitute for floppy disk drives. Because information storage and retrieval is the main purpose of the system, the more disk drives and the larger their capacity, the more information (e.g., messages and programs) that can be stored for retrieval by on-line callers.

A typical minimum system would consist of an Apple II+ with two disk drives and a modem. Such a system would cost about $2,000. At the other end of the spectrum would be a system with multiple phone modems and lines to permit multiple users. One such system in the Midwest has eight phone lines and two 40-megabyte (40 million characters) hard disk drives and runs on an Altos 68000 UNIX computer. The value of this hobbyist BBS is about $25,000.

It is easy to become captivated by BBSs and the exotic electronic underground associated with them. Although a BBS is not inherently evil, it does tend to contribute to electronic crime. People who use BBSs extensively have very high telephone bills. It is very easy to use a billing code belonging to a customer of one of the alternative long-distance services such as Sprint or MCI. Calls placed in this manner, in which equal-access protection is not in effect, cannot be billed properly, nor can the originator be identified. If the telephone company staff try to call the recipient of the fraudulent call, they will be answered by a modem and microcomputer. Even if the BBS operator is cooperative, learning the identity of the BBS caller is difficult because most fraudulent callers use handles instead of their real names.

Any successful BBS almost always has inadequate disk storage space. Given the widespread use of credit cards and the availability of telephone-order vendors that carry computer equipment, there is a strong temptation to use BBSs for credit card fraud. Credit card numbers are widely traded and posted in underground BBSs. Prime targets are the credit cards with high credit limits that allow the fraudulent purchase of a hard disk drive costing $3,000 to $5,000. System operators of underground BBSs have openly bragged about the new hard disk drives acquired for their systems in this manner. Most young hackers cannot afford a $10,000 microcomputer system, yet BBSs with this much equipment owned by juveniles are quite commonplace among the 100 BBSs monitored by Maxfield.

A BBS can use a variety of BBS software, either commercially produced or homemade. Some of the popular BBS programs are Networks and T-Net (and their pirated equivalents) for the Apple computer. Typical BBS software has most or all of the following features: public bulletin section, public text and data files, privately addressed message section, program section, and user lists.

The message sections divide the messages into various categories such as general, for sale, help, and meeting announcements. After accessing these sections from a menu of choices, the user may view the message titles, read any or all of the messages, post a new message, or delete a previously posted message. To limit objectionable messages, most systems will not allow messages to be posted until the submitter has been validated by the operator or has called the BBS several times.

In addition to the messages, the user may view special files that can only be placed there by the system operator. Examples of such files would be lists of other BBS systems, instructions for use of the system, and news items. Sometimes these files are combined with the program section and may contain documentation for the available programs.

The privately addressed message section allows communications between individually specified users. Messages can only be read by the intended recipient or the system operator. In underground boards, it is this type of section in which much of the illegal information, such as credit card numbers, is exchanged and accounts for about half of the storage space on a typical system. Most BBSs list other users to facilitate the use of the private message section. Obviously, mail cannot be sent to someone who does not use that particular BBS. Sometimes the user list gives the user's telephone number and address, but most often it lists only the user's name or handle.

Interestingly, BBSs monitored by Maxfield were often the victims of the very hacker community they supported. The crashing of a well-established BBS or even a rival gang's BBS is common. Because of the hacker problem and the user's anonymity, most BBSs assign a private password to each user and only allow access to post messages if the new user gives his or her real name and telephone number to the system operator in a private message. Validation of the user typically takes 24 to 48 hours, depending on the responsiveness of the system operator. Validation may also involve raising a user's security level so as to access parts of the BBS that otherwise would be inaccessible.

The operator of a pirate BBS acquires a large collection of free software from the users. Many of the early pirate boards would allow users to obtain copies of four or five programs only if they first supplied one new program. This strategy ensured that the system operator would always acquire the newest programs as they became available on the underground market. Software collections consisting of more than 1,000 programs are not uncommon. Most juveniles who set up BBSs do so for this reason alone. Some unscrupulous adults obtain commercial software in this manner so that they can be resold to unsuspecting clients.

Most underground BBSs require new users to prove that they too are members of the underground by providing the BBS operator with some sort of illegal information, perhaps an

MCI customer code or a credit card number, before granting full access to the BBS. The BBS operator (or sysop) is the person most likely to benefit by permitting underground activity on the BBS.

All BBSs must advertise their presence to attract users and new information. Information about BBSs can usually be obtained at local computer club meetings through casual conversations. Once validated on one system, a user can obtain a list of other systems from which lists of more systems can be obtained.

Identifying whether a BBS is part of the underground is relatively easy. Most underground systems have obvious names such as Applecrackers, Twilight Phone, Forbidden Zone, and Securityland. A few masquerade as normal, legitimate systems with nondescript names. If a BBS has many selections listing special message categories such as underground, special access, phone phreak, hacking, technical, and restricted, it is probably an underground system. Some BBS operators try to hide these illicit sections by making them invisible to a user who does not have the necessary security clearance. Most users tend to be careless, however. If a hidden section exists, reference to it may be found in a message posted in another section. Another excellent way to tell whether a BBS caters to illegal uses is to note whether the BBS operator has posted a disclaimer claiming freedom of speech and absolving the operator from any liability because of message content. The tougher the wording of this disclaimer, the greater the illegality of the information stored in the BBS is likely to be.

> The sysops take no responsibility for any messages, files, or other incriminating information on the boards, or in the General section, because those files were all uploaded by anonymous users.
>
> "Do you work for or are you affiliated with any Government, detective, or police agency, public or private, or would you ever reveal any information gained from this BBS to any of the above, or do you work for any type of long-distance company, public or private, and/or would you release any information gained from this BBS to any long-distance service or its affiliates? Please

answer yes or no." (Answering yes causes the computer to abruptly disconnect.)

These underground systems often publish illicit information, including the following:

- Lists of customer billing codes and common carrier access numbers

- Plans and instructions for blue, red, black, and silver toll fraud boxes

- Access numbers, passwords, and log-on procedures for computer systems

- Procedures for wiretapping and phone bugging

- Instructions on how to pass oneself off as a computer or telephone repairman or other trusted person to gain information or access to be used for fraud

- Plans and instructions in the art of picking locks

- Do-it-yourself instructions for the home manufacture of explosives, poisons, and incendiary devices

- Lists of phone numbers of famous people, Government installations, computer systems, and telephone operator call-routing codes

- Lists of credit card numbers to be used to order merchandise over the telephone for resale or trade

- Ways to invade the privacy of individuals through access to their computerized credit and financial records

- Ways to harass or harm individuals either over the phone or by other means

- Programs to convert one's microcomputer into a blue box or to use it for scanning for modem numbers or customer billing codes

As time passes and the BBS operators experience little or no control of their activities by law enforcement officials, they become more and more egregious. Some BBSs contain information of great use to both organized crime and foreign powers.

4. SOURCES OF ILLICIT INFORMATION

Some hacker gangs set up group excursions to industrial parks or office complexes to scavenge information and equipment from the trash dumpsters behind buildings, according to hackers who have been interviewed. Dumpster diving is a major source of passwords, system documentation, and other information. Credit card numbers are also obtained in this manner by salvaging the carbons from charge slips. Computer and electronic store garbage cans are a favorite hunting ground. Other major targets are telephone company switching centers and vehicle garages. This is known from cases resulting in criminal convictions reported in the news media followed by investigation by the SRI International Computer Security Program.[9,10]

All too often, unscrupulous or careless employees of major corporations pass on details of computer operations to friendly hackers. In some cases, the hacker has legal access to the computer center as an equipment repairman or delivery person. Hackers often pose as customers, vendors, or employees and try to obtain information over the telephone about system access and passwords.[11] Many times, this method succeeds when other methods have failed, but there are no statistics on its frequency of occurrence.

As a last resort, physical theft is often attempted. A common ploy is the interception of mail containing customer account codes or passwords, according to messages monitored in BBSs. Occasionally, break-ins and theft of documentation, terminals,

---

[9] Donn B. Parker, *Crime by Computer*, (New York: Charles Scribner's Sons, 1978) pp. 12–40.

[10] Parker, *Fighting Computer Crime*, pp. 130–188.

[11] Parker, *Fighting Computer Crime*, pp. 130–188.

or other equipment are preliminary actions to prepare for a major hacker attack on a computer system. In 1981, the Roscoe Gang in Los Angeles attempted this in its attacks on the Pacific Telephone Cosmos System. Most of the participants were convicted.[12]

Programmable, smart modems that allow computer-controlled phone number dialing and special software are used to find computer access numbers or customer billing codes. Numerous programs exist for almost any combination of microcomputer and modem which can perform sequential or random dialing of trial numbers until a modem is detected by its high-pitched tone response or a billing code is compromised. Some of these programs test upwards of 1,000 numbers an hour. The recent movie *Wargames* showed in great detail the operation of one of these scanner programs. Some hackers specialize in scanning and publish long lists of codes and telephone numbers.

Most of this information eventually appears in underground BBSs. Once posted there, the information is picked up and reposted widely. Some juveniles, in an effort to impress their peers, gather up every little tidbit and repost it on all the boards that they call. Much of the information that is posted in this manner is old or useless because it has passed through so many hands. Any sensitive or extremely useful information is not publicly posted right away. Most hacker gangs will not post new information unless it is on their own BBS.

Maxfield posted a test message in 1983 on a California BBS. Only 1 hour and 20 minutes later the same message was posted on a New York BBS. Within 1 week, the message had been reposted on dozens of BBSs nationwide. It can be useful to plant false or erroneous information in this manner to confuse inexperienced hackers.

Organized crime gangs could use the underground BBSs in much the same manner as the teenaged hacker gangs for gambling, drugs, and prostitution intelligence communication. There is a limited amount of evidence that has been obtained by monitoring BBS messages that organized crime elements control a number of BBS systems in the Midwest, the New York City

---

[12] Parker, *Fighting Computer Crime,* pp. 130–188.

area, and Florida. One informant knows of a BBS that is located in an off-track betting parlor. Teenagers are easily recruited to act as information gatherers; they work for little or nothing and sometimes do not know how they are being used. Maxfield and other adult hackers have been approached and offered large sums of money to tamper with banking and credit data computers.

5. CONTROLS

Various legal remedies, both civil and criminal, are available, but no nationally uniform code of law exists. The Federal justice system lacks a central clearinghouse for computer and telecommunications crime control and cannot deal well with juveniles. The U.S. Small Business Administration has recently started such a clearinghouse to assist small businesses. Computer hacker attacks tend to be multijurisdictional nightmares that traditional law enforcement agencies do not handle very well. When the 414 Gang was breaking into computers in New York, California, and New Mexico from their homes in Milwaukee, they were only caught through an intensive call-tracing effort that took many hours and only after they had penetrated some computer systems for months.

Users are not the only individuals at fault. The BBS operator controls access to the system through the user validation process, determines the format of the system, and decides what the various message topics are to be. It is the operator of an underground board, not the user, who makes a BBS available for illegal information. If the operator has to validate a user for special access to an underground section, it appears that the operator is a party to any wrongdoing, regardless of posted disclaimers.

The issue of freedom of speech is a sensitive one, however. Perhaps a licensing arrangement such as the one used for ham radio operators and those who use Citizens Band radios is in order. Possession of an unlicensed BBS could be handled similarly to possession of an unlicensed radio transmitter.

For a time, the State of Oklahoma had telephone tariff restrictions that specified that an extra $50 be paid for connecting a modem to a telephone. This charge was subsequently dropped under protest by home computer owners. If this sort of charge were applied to lines used by a BBS, it could eliminate all but the few who were willing to pay extra for the privilege of owning a BBS. The telephone line connected to a successful BBS is always busy. Thus, an extra tariff could be justified on the grounds that more than the normal amount of circuit time would be used.

Finally, public awareness of the problem, the changing of values among young technologists, and the elimination of teen-ager-run systems by concerned parents would go a long way toward controlling the problem. Several BBSs were shut down last year when the leader of the 414 Gang bragged about them on a network television show. Only then did the father of one of the BBS operators find out what his son was really doing with the home computer.

APPENDIX

Since January 1983, John Maxfield has systematically recorded the identity and practices of hackers and phreaks during his monitoring of BBSs, newsletters, meetings, and telephone calls as a full-time occupation. He has concentrated on the most visible and flagrant participants throughout the United States. However, contacts have tended to concentrate in the greater Detroit metropolitan area (within area code 313). Approximately 100 BBSs were routinely monitored, with each having an average of 200 to 300 names on their user lists, but only the continuously active individuals were identified and counted. When individuals became inactive, their names were dropped from the file. Ten of the more virulent BBSs were studied in detail. New ones appear daily, and others sometimes disappear and possibly reappear again.

The tabulation of 560 individuals is provided (Table 5–1), with subtotals for each type of activity they engage in as indicated. Note that many individuals engage in more than one activity; for example, most hackers are also phone phreaks and are counted in two or more types of activities; therefore, the subtotals add up to much more than the total. These data should not be taken as representative of the problem and should not be used to extrapolate estimates for other areas or the United States as a whole. They are an indication that there are at least this number of individuals in one major metropolitan area and in each activity type. In addition, percentages for subtotals should not be calculated because the total of all individuals found is biased in unknown ways, making the subtotals in relation to the total meaningless. For example, because the most active individuals tend to be recorded, the proportion of adults is probably artificially high. Individuals are identified by a combination of real name or fictitious name (handle) and telephone number.

TABLE 5–1.
Number of Hackers and Phone Phreaks and Activities Engaged in From January 1983 to October 1984

Activity	*Number*
Total Known To Be Continuously Active Since Discovery From January 1983 to October 1984	560
Known To Be Over 17 Years Old	135
Area Code 313 Residents (Southeast Michigan, Detroit Area)	202
Engaged in Copyrighted Program Theft as:	
Copiers	308
Protection Crackers	85
Sellers	18
Subtotal	411
Phone Phreakers	
Toll Thieves	246
Theft of Services Experts	172
Sellers	15
Blue Box Manufacturers	8
Subtotal	441

TABLE 5–1. *Continued*

Number of Hackers and Phone Phreaks and Activities Engaged in From January 1983 to October 1984

Activity	Number
Computer Hackers	
Beginners	111
Experts	92
Sellers or Traders of Information	9
Subtotal	212
Stolen Credit Card Number	
Users	42
Suppliers	30
Sellers or Traders	9
Subtotal	81
Stolen Merchandise Fencers	13
BBS Operators	86
Newsletter Publishers and Authors	17
Illegal Computer Program Authors	12
Criminal Convictions	
Phreaking	13
Computer Access and Fraud	8
Other Crimes	4
Subtotal	25

DISCUSSION

Joseph Tompkins: As a reader, I was hoping that they had been a little more specific, using the combination of the Stanford Research Institute study of 1,400 actual computer crime cases and John Maxfield's hands-on personal experience, and provided more specific, more analytical information about the extent of computer intrusion.

How strong is the evidence of organized crime involvement in bulletin board systems? What is the link there? How has it been used so far? Concerning the Appendix, which I think is useful, it would be helpful, particularly for more nontechnical people, if some of the words had been defined, and the basis for some of the categorizations would have been helpful.

For example, how do the authors know how many people are copiers, how many people are engaged in copying? How do the authors define protection crackers, and how do they know how many there were? How do they know how many computer hackers are beginners as opposed to experts, which are categories that are used in the Appendix?

In conclusion, I think the paper is a very useful discussion of bulletin board systems. It's an area that we ought to be more concerned about, and I think the paper is a very useful and relevant starting point.

Daniel Burk: We heard, on the one hand, that there is no real worry about the pranks. On the other hand, we heard about the pranks we really are worried about: when somebody calls the Queen of England, it is not a problem, but when somebody calls a Russian computer, it becomes a problem. It seems to me that you cannot really eliminate calling the Queen of England as a problem because of what it leads to.

John Maxfield: There is no way to say which people go in which category, because there is a spectrum of such activities. Someone who starts out by calling the Queen of England may end up by cracking a Russian computer. There is no way of knowing in advance how to categorize them.

As you notice from the numbers [of phone phreakers and pirates], there's an overlap. In other words, most pirates pirate the software by phone phreaking to get it. [They] call a bulletin board across the country and don't pay for the phone call to download the stolen software. Many of the phone phreaks are pirates.

Marvin Schaefer: In the attacks you have seen described on computers and computer systems, how technical have they been? Are they mostly identifications of passwords and things such as this?

John Maxfield: Most of the attacks are unsophisticated. However, there appears to be an escalation of the sophisticated jobs. These teenagers are growing up and going to college, and they are learning how to hack a computer at that point. Then they get out or drop out of school, and they are looking for a means to support themselves so they fall back on their hacking skills.

Donn Parker: Most of the really sophisticated attacks are done because the achievement of the attack is an end in itself. If you were a crook trying to determine how to get into a computer system, it doesn't take long to figure out that these Trojan horse attacks are ridiculous when all you have to do is dive in a dumpster or bribe someone.

I spend a great deal of my consulting time just spoof-proofing my clients' people to make them resistant to giving out information. The most dangerous kids in the world are your sons and daughters, the sons and daughters of trusted computer users.

COMMENT: Crime statistics in this area are impossible, but one relevant statistic is the tremendous increase in computers. There were 5,000 personal computers in 1978. There are about 5 million now, and by the end of the decade there are going to be about 80 million personal computers. So you're talking about an exponential increase in the technology, and you're going to get a lot more good and bad people.

QUESTION: I have a question about the small number of people that you said had criminal convictions besides their hacking activity. Were these people criminals first and then get into computers later? Did they learn it in prison, or were they people who were involved in computers and as a result of that occasionally collected convictions?

John Maxfield: Well, it's a little of both. As I said, there's no way to really put them into separate categories. I've got one gentleman in Oregon who regularly taps into satellite telephone traffic. He has a felony firearms conviction from 12 years ago. Now, what he did in between and what led up to the felony firearms conviction, I don't know, but this man started out as a career criminal and decided that he should get into hacking because there's money in it. I know some other people who were busted as phone phreaks in their college days, and now they are out there selling blue boxes to the mob, or whomever. I do not think that you learn these skills in prison. It does concern some people that there's data processing training being given in prisons. Then, on the other hand, a lot of people say that we should hire these hackers because they're the ones who know. Here I am, essentially a hacker myself. I have never really been on the dark side of it, but I'm a hacker and I'm involved on the dark side.

Is it a good idea to have these people around? SRI has a couple of them working for them. One gentleman, 10 years ago, broke into SRI's computer, was hired, and became one of their best people. I don't think you can do this with all of them.

What we are seeing here is that the technology is filtering down the social strata. I have been involved with a computer users group in the Detroit area since its beginnings 9 years ago, and I take care of the membership roster. Initially, the club members consisted of the people out in the high-income suburbs, and now close to half of our applications are coming from the city of Detroit, and these people own expensive IBM personal computers.

So, again, the increase in the number of home computers is introducing this technology to larger groups of people, not just the intellectual elite and the financially secure, but also the middle and lower classes.

A computer is not inherently an evil thing like a gun. We have all kinds of legislation on gun safety and gun regulation. A computer is not inherently evil, but it's a powerful tool, and you can use it to destroy as well as to build. This is where there is a vacuum in regulation. Everybody has the tools, but there is no control on the use of those tools.

QUESTION: What kind of targeting was seen against Federal systems by the hackers? Anything unusual?

Donn Parker: No. The targeting mostly is ARPANET. There have also been cases of NASA facilities and Los Alamos being targeted, wherever there are Digital Equipment Corporation computer systems. Those are the favorite targets because that's what the kids have learned on. They know those systems very thoroughly, so they search out those kinds of systems. So, if it is against Federal agencies, it is mostly against the engineering and scientific laboratories rather than any type of business application.

John Maxfield: In my travels through the underground bulletin boards, I have seen phone numbers that are purported to be the NORAD computers in Colorado and various Government agencies—CIA, FBI—in the Washington, D.C., area. In some cases there were passwords also listed for these computers. I have no knowledge myself as to whether any of this information was accurate, because in a case like that I just turn it over to the Department of Defense and let them worry about it. However, the attacks on systems of that level of sophistication probably are not going to be very successful because the security measures are already in place. Most of the penetrations into Government computers that I have seen evidence of in my bulletin board explorations are usually into a small laboratory machine which is unclassified.

six

LEGAL AND MANAGERIAL APPROACHES TO INTRUSION PROTECTION

Susan H. Nycum
and Daniel L. Appelman*

I. INTRODUCTION

Intrusion, or the unauthorized access to computer systems and computerized data bases, has been of increasing concern to the Federal Government and the private sector as they become ever more dependent on computer services. Estimates of the extent of the intrusion problem cannot be given with any degree of confidence because the unauthorized access may long go undetected. Even when agencies or businesses become aware of an unauthorized access, they may never report it. In many jurisdictions, intrusion itself does not constitute a crime.

This chapter surveys the present status of state computer crime legislation in addressing the problem of unauthorized access to computer systems and data bases. It highlights major areas of difficulty encountered in interpreting, applying, and enforcing these state laws. Greater uniformity in state legislation

---

* Susan Nycum and Daniel Appelman are with the law firm of Gaston, Snow, and Ely Bartlett, of Palo Alto, California, specializing in computer security issues.

and a more concerted, coordinated effort on the state and Federal levels would be likely to enhance the deterrence and prosecution of those involved in computer crimes. The particular need for legislation to deter those acts of unauthorized access which constitute trespassing, without resulting in any significant alteration, destruction, or disruption of computer services, will be discussed. There follows an analysis of existing and proposed Federal legislation and the advantages of enacting Federal statutes which deal explicitly with computer crimes. Several managerial procedures which would help to discourage intrusion are summarized. A summary of the roles that business and agency management, the states, and the Federal Government may play in attempting to contain and control the incidence of computer crime concludes the paper.

2. STATUS OF STATE LEGISLATION

2.1 Present Status

As of September 1984, 33 states had enacted legislation making certain instances of unauthorized access to computer systems and data bases a crime. The appendix to this chapter lists those states which have computer crime statutes, all of which have been enacted during the last 6 years. This rapid proliferation of computer crime legislation reflects an increasing social awareness that traditional criminal laws may not effectively deal with computer crimes. Although the passage of such legislation on the state level is viewed by many as a positive step in the deterrence and prosecution of those involved in computer crimes, several areas of difficulty have emerged which merit discussion.

2.1.1 Unclear Definitions

A fundamental weakness of many state computer crime statutes is their inability to define simply and clearly the elements of the crimes so that those charged with their enforcement can easily apply the definitions to suspected activities. It is theoretically possible in Colorado, for example, to commit computer fraud by using a television, a radio, or a videotape recorder without authorization, because the definition of "computer" in that state's computer crime law includes "any electronic device performing memory functions in the manipulation of electronic or magnetic impulses."[1]

Nevada has adopted much the same language but has made the foregoing definition more clear by explicitly excluding devices "such as a radio or television transmitter or receiver, television camera, videotape recorder, sound recorder, phonograph, or similar device. . . ." In so doing, however, Nevada also adds complexity to its statute by requiring that law enforcers determine that such noncomputing devices are "used for reproducing information in oral or visual form without changing the nature or content of the information unless such a device is connected to and used by a computer."[2] This qualification appears to be not only circular, but too broad as well. For example, those who edit commercials out of a television broadcast by means of an employer's videocassette recorder might be deemed to be committing computer fraud.

Another example of unclear definitions is Arizona's inclusion of the term "approach" as being one kind of access to a computer system which, if unauthorized, would be a crime under the law. If construed literally, any unauthorized physical proximity by an individual to a computer would constitute a felony.[3] This language can be traced to the earliest Federal bill (S. 1766), which was criticized by Susan H. Nycum and Donn B. Parker at the time of its introduction. Unhappily, a number of state legislatures adopted parts of that early bill. When terms are unclear, they are difficult to apply. Individuals who enforce the statutes are most often not computer experts, nor are the judges and juries who hear the evidence. It is therefore essential that

---

[1] Colo. Rev. Stat. Computer Crime 18–5.5–101 (1979).

[2] Nev. Rev. Stat. Title 52, Ch. 501, 3 (1984).

[3] Ariz. Rev. Stat. Ann., Ch. 23 13–2301 (1978). " 'Access' means to approach, instruct, communicate with, store data in, retrieve data from, or otherwise make use of any resources of a computer, computer system, or computer network."

the terms used to define the crimes be easily understood and applied, or the statutes cannot be effectively utilized.

2.1.2 Lack of Impetus for Reporting Computer Crimes

Many computer criminals go unpunished because the victims do not report the crimes. Victims of computer crimes often see the crime as a sign of the vulnerability of their business operations. The publicity connected with computer crimes can also threaten to estrange future business opportunities. A more immediate effect is that if the crime is reported but prosecution is subsequently declined, the likelihood exists that the alleged perpetrator will sue the victim for defamation or wrongful termination. The result is that some intruders may not be brought to justice and the lack of prosecution may weaken the deterrent effect of the legislation.

The Georgia legislature attempted to provide a controversial solution to this problem. The Criminal Code of Georgia makes it:

> . . . the duty of every business; partnership; college; university; person; state, country, or local governmental agency or department or branch thereof; corporation; or other business entity which has reasonable grounds to believe that a violation of this article has been committed to report promptly the suspected violation to law enforcement authorities.[4]

This statute provides immunity from liability for making such reports and makes the failure to report a computer crime a crime in itself.

The instances in which failure to report a crime is made a crime are very rare and whether this part of the Georgia legislation could withstand a challenge of its constitutionality is questionable. Additionally, the state could have enacted civil liabilities as an alternative to criminal penalties for failing to report a computer crime. For these and other reasons, Georgia has not actively enforced the statute, and no other state has

---

[4] Ga. Code 26–9954(a) (1981).

passed similar legislation. We do not advocate it as an acceptable solution to the problem of unreported computer crime.

2.1.3 Lack of Simple Trespass Violation

It has been suggested that truly effective computer crime legislation would include criminal penalties for the full range of acts incident to gaining unauthorized access to computer systems and data bases. Most state computer crime laws address the need for sanctions against those who cause injury or the disruption of computer systems and services in the course of their intrusions. However, the security and integrity of computer programs and data can also be compromised by the unauthorized access itself, apart from any damage that might otherwise result. It is therefore arguable that society should discourage "browsing" and "joyriding" through computer systems, even if no monetary damage results from these activities.

Intrusion on computer systems and data bases has been likened to criminal trespassing, an offense which has traditionally not required either the element of injury or an intent by the trespasser to cause injury to the property of another.[5] However, many states which have enacted computer crime laws require some damage, or at least an intent to cause some loss, before the activity in question becomes criminal.[6] Although the Virginia statute, for example, does not require an actual injury to the property or person of another, it does specify that the perpetrator must have at least an intent to cause a malfunction or to temporarily remove data, programs, or software from a computer to be convicted of computer trespassing.[7] The crimes of computer invasion of privacy and personal trespassing by computer also require similar intent.[8] In Colorado, however, one can be

---

[5] 87 Corpus Juris Secundum *Trespass* (1954).

[6] As of this writing, actual injury or at least an intent to cause injury was a required element of computer crime legislation in the states of Alaska, Arizona, California, Connecticut, Massachusetts, Minnesota, Nevada, Ohio, Utah, Virginia, Washington, and Wyoming.

[7] Code of Virginia Crimes and Offenses, 18.2–152.4 (1984).

[8] Id. 18.2–152.5, 152.7.

convicted of a computer crime merely for using a computer without authorization.[9]

If computer crime legislation is adopted in part to deter acts of which society strenuously disapproves, the definition of a crime should not hinge merely on whether injury results or is intended, but rather on whether unauthorized access itself is the kind of behavior society should penalize. It is possible that the criminalization of mere intrusion, without monetary loss or invasion of privacy, might deter far more serious acts of computer crime. The failure of many state statutes to make intrusion without injury or intent to injure a crime may well be a serious deficiency in state legislation.

2.1.4 Lack of Consistency from State to State

As in most criminal statutes, computer crime legislation usually includes a recitation of specific offenses, a definition of terms which themselves define the elements of the offenses, and a list of penalties to which commission of the enumerated crimes subjects the perpetrator. Although it is not unusual for any of these items to vary from state to state, computer crime statutes are particularly inconsistent. Perhaps this has something to do with the exceedingly technological nature of the acts and the comparatively recent acceptance of intrusion as a crime.

Computer crime, however, has another characteristic which makes the lack of consistency among jurisdictions particularly unfortunate. It is frequently an interstate crime. Apart from the complex jurisdictional issues which computer crime engenders when facilitated by telecommunications media, significant variations from statute to statute discourage unified and consistent law enforcement and provide mixed messages to perpetrators. In 1983, for example, the 414 Gang in Milwaukee accessed computers in Wisconsin, New Mexico, and New York. New York had no computer crime law; Wisconsin and New Mexico

---

[9] Colo. Rev. Stat. Computer Crime 18–5.5–102 (1979). Both states, of course, require the traditional mens rea of knowing that the use or access is unauthorized. The issue here is whether something more is required, i.e., the presence of an intent to cause loss and not merely the intent to accomplish the access without authorization.

did, but their provisions were different, even though the acts committed were identical.

A few examples of inconsistencies in the definitions of important terms and penalties included in state computer laws follow.

Terms. Common terms found throughout the computer crime laws of the 33 states that have such laws include "access," "computer," "property," "data," and "loss" or "injury." The definitions of each of these terms, their simplicity, and the ease of application help to determine how successfully and effectively these new statutes will be used to deter and prosecute computer crimes.

"Access" to a computer system or data base is often one element of a criminal offense under the statutes. The most common definition found in state legislation for the word "access" is "to approach, instruct, communicate with, store data in, retrieve data from, or otherwise make use of any resources of a computer, computer system, or computer network."[10] The Montana definition substitutes the words "obtain the use of" for "access," deletes the word "approaches," and adds the concept that access includes causing another to do all of the things for which doing it oneself would be a crime.[11] In New Mexico, "access" is defined as making "use of any resources of a computer, computer system, or computer network."[12]

Of these three statutes, New Mexico's appears to be the easiest to apply. The inclusion of the word "approach" in the Arizona statute may cause complications, because "approach" can mean merely gaining physical proximity, as well as whatever else was intended by the drafters. The discrepancy between the statutes of Montana and the other two states with respect to vicarious acts could result in the imposition of a felony in one case and the complete absence of culpability in the others.

The term "computer" is also given a variety of meanings in the state statutes. Perhaps the most common definition of the word "computer" is Colorado's, which reads:

---

[10] Ariz. Rev. Stat. Ann., Ch. 23 13–2301 (1978).
[11] Mont. Code Ann. Crimes 45–2–101 (1981).
[12] N.M. Stat. Ann. Article 16A 30–16A–2 (1979).

. . . an electronic device which performs logic, arithmetic, or memory functions by the manipulations of electronic or magnetic impulses and includes all input, output, processing, storage, software, or communication facilities which are connected or related to such a device in a system or network.[13]

Among the simplest of the definitions of "computer" is Connecticut's: "a programmable electronic device capable of accepting and processing data."[14] In Virginia, the term "computer" means:

. . . an electronic, magnetic, optical, hydraulic, or organic device or group of devices which, pursuant to a computer program, to human instruction, or to permanent instructions contained in the device or group of devices, can automatically perform computer operations with or on computer data and can communicate the results to another computer or to a person. The term 'computer' includes any connected or directly related device, equipment, or facility which enables the computer to store, retrieve, or communicate computer programs, computer data, or the results of computer operations to or from a person, another computer, or another device.[15]

Definitions such as these may be more successful if they were less dependent on technology. In the years since the first computer crime bill was passed, computer technology has advanced rapidly and will continue to do so. The efforts of states such as Virginia to anticipate every possible mode of data processing must inevitably be frustrated by innovation and change. Moreover, it is becoming clear that the focus of computer crime statutes should shift toward the deterrence and sanctioning of acts which cause damage or disruption to the data and programs stored in computers or computerized data bases rather than to the equipment or media on which that information resides.

The term that appears to give drafters of various state laws particular difficulty is "property." Florida, Missouri, and Ten-

---

[13] Colo. Rev. Stat. Computer Crime 18–5.5–101 (1979).
[14] Conn. Public Act 84–2–6 (1984).
[15] Va. Code, Crimes and Offenses 18.2–152.2 (1984).

nessee define "intellectual property" as being distinct from "property." In Connecticut, property means "anything of value including data."[16] In Arizona, the statute defines property as "financial instruments, information, including electronically produced data, computer software, and programs in either machine- or human-readable form, and anything of value, tangible or intangible."[17] In Illinois, property is defined as "anything of value." The statute then provides a recitation of examples of property, but it seems to be irrelevant, because by definition it is not exhaustive.[18]

The variations in the definition of property again illustrate the lack of agreement among the states on how to define elements of computer crime. Some states undertake what is hoped to be a comprehensive listing of the categories and kinds of property. Other states adopt some general and all-inclusive phrases.[19]

Intent. One of the important requisites of criminal culpability is the criminal intent of the perpetrator. Different crimes require different levels of intent. These are most commonly specified in the statute itself; if not, they must at least be established by judicial interpretation. Criminal intent can range from "reckless" (which may be akin to "gross negligence") to "malicious" and "wanton." In general, the more serious the crime and the more onerous the penalty, the higher is the threshold definition of criminal intent.

The computer crime statutes of most states follow Florida's example by creating a threshold which is defined as "willfully, knowingly, and without authorization."[20] In New Mexico, how-

---

[16] Conn. Public Act 84–206.

[17] Ariz. Rev. Stat. Ann., Ch. 23 13–2301 (1978).

[18] Ill. Rev. Stat., Criminal Law and Procedure, Art. 15, Ch. 38 15–1 (1979).

[19] Although it is beyond the purpose of this paper, the definition of property within most state jurisdictions is in need of overhaul. Many states still rely on definitions from the sixteenth century English common law, focusing on tangible personal property, and as such are inapplicable to modern concepts of intellectual property such as trade secrets and newer representations of assets such as electronic impulses, computer cycles, and computer time.

[20] Fla. Stat. Crimes, 815.01–815.07 (1978).

ever, the defendant would not be guilty of committing any computer crime whatsoever unless his or her intent was proved to be "intentional, malicious, and without authorization."[21] This statute was ineffective in the prosecution of the 414 Gang perpetrators, as their acts were not provably malicious.

New state statutes lower the threshold of intent. Idaho, Wyoming, Missouri, and Iowa include computer crimes undertaken "knowingly and without authorization." Delaware's statute may be one of the most liberal with regard to the degree of intent required. Under that law, any alteration or destruction done "intentionally and without authorization" would qualify as a crime.[22] Connecticut, too, makes alteration, deletion, or tampering a crime if done "intentionally or recklessly and without authorization."[23] The statute in Virginia, as well as the proposed statute for the District of Columbia, are among the best examples of this trend.[24]

Authorities have suggested that the many degrees of computer crime have not yet been widely accepted. Computer crime statutes must deter those who would trespass or invade the privacy of others just as they deter those who would cause damage or injury to computers and data. The schemes of deterrence and prosecution of computer crimes are not complete as long as people may, without fear of legal sanctions, browse without permission among private records and use computer services without authorization. Law enforcers face severe obstacles in coordinating their efforts to prosecute computer crime when the definitions of intent vary so radically from state to state.

Penalties. The penalties prescribed by the computer crime statutes of the 33 states that have such statutes vary widely. To some extent, these variations are due to differences in defining

---

[21] N.M. Stat. Ann., Article 16A 30 (1979).

[22] Del. Code Ann., Title 11, 858 (1982).

[23] Conn. Public Act 84-2-6 (1984).

[24] Virginia is one of the few states to statutorily link computer crime with the invasion of privacy. Code of Virginia Crimes and Offenses, 18.2-1.52.5. The proposed statute for the District of Columbia would also include invasion of privacy by computer as a crime.

threshold levels of criminal activity. However, even in those instances in which the activities are similar, penalties can vary greatly from state to state. In California, for example, the maximum penalty for damaging a computer is 3 years in prison and $5,000.[25] Minnesota can penalize its computer criminals much more harshly. Anyone who damages a computer may be imprisoned for up to 10 years and may be fined up to $50,000. It also provides a much greater range of penalties for the different degrees of damage caused by the perpetrator.[26]

The disparity in the penalties for computer crimes among the states is not so unusual. Differences can also be observed from state to state in the penalties for a great number of other crimes. These simply reflect social attitudes and priorities about particular kinds of criminal activity. To the extent that these differences make law enforcement more difficult in some places than in others or result in less uniform deterrence and prosecution of computer crimes throughout the country, we may have to live with them rather than attempt to change them. However, social attitudes often change with time. The dependence of society on computer services and the increasing incidence of serious acts of intrusion into computer systems and data bases may prompt reexamination of the schemes of penalties attached to these acts. It may also strengthen the impetus to enact comprehensive Federal legislation.

2.1.5 Jurisdiction

State courts must establish jurisdiction both over the subject matter of a crime and over the accused in order to maintain criminal proceedings successfully and constitutionally. A computer crime committed completely within one state's jurisdiction may, of course, be prosecuted in that state. The defendant's due process needs are satisfied, because he or she committed the crime within the state and is subject to its laws. In addition to the person, the state has jurisdiction over the offense itself because the crime was committed entirely within the state.

---

[25] Cal. Penal Code 502(e) (West 1981).
[26] Minn. Stat. Criminal Code, 609.87–609.89 (1982).

One of the most important weaknesses of the efforts to deter and prosecute computer criminals through the enactment of state legislation has to do with the numerous instances of interstate intrusion. In recent years, the natural joining of data processing services with the telecommunications media has meant that individuals using the telephone can dial and obtain access to computers and data in other states as easily as in their own. When that occurs, questions often arise with regard to which state has jurisdiction over the crime.

Jurisdiction Over the Offense. Jurisdiction over the offense resides solely in the courts of the state in which the crime is committed, and its laws govern.[27] A crime is deemed "committed" in any state in which an essential part of the crime occurs. The California legislature, for example, has recognized that an obscene telephone call is deemed committed either at the place the call was made or at the place it was received.[28] The law also recognizes that the victim state may have jurisdiction over an offense in which a person, although in another state, sets in motion a force which operates to affect another state.[29] In addition, the state the accused was located at the time of the crime's commission may also have jurisdiction over the offense, but only if the statute either expressly provides for this or if the acts committed in the state the accused was located constituted part of a continuing crime according to an applicable statute of that state.[30]

This possible dual jurisdiction of the courts over the subject matter of the offense is particularly troublesome in the context of computer crimes. It is conceivable that someone accused of an interstate computer offense may be charged under the law of the state in which the intrusion took place, under the law of the state in which the telephone call was placed, or both.

---

[27] *Huntington v. Attrill* 146 U.S. 657 (189); 21 Am. Jur. 2d, *Criminal Law,* 383; *People v. MacDonald* 24 Cal. App. 2d 702, 709 (1938); *State v. Volpe* 113 Conn. 288 (1931), 155 Atl. 223; *Idaho v. Cochran* 98 Idaho 862, 538 P.2d 791 (1975).

[28] Cal. Penal Code 653(m), Subd. c. (West 1983).

[29] 21 Am. Jur. 2d 346, p. 599.

[30] Id.

Does it really make sense for a state to have subject matter jurisdiction over a computer crime just because a telephone call was placed there?

The penalties of the states and even the types of offenses charged under computer crime statutes differ substantially. Seventeen states have not yet enacted computer crime statutes and therefore could prosecute only under traditional theft or malicious mischief laws, which may not be appropriate for the offenses committed. The uneven results of such varied ways in which an interstate computer offense could be handled are evident. For instance, an individual located in Connecticut who recklessly disrupts computer services valued at more than $10,000 in Minnesota would be guilty of no computer crime under Minnesota law, because there the act must be intentional, but would be guilty of a felony under Connecticut law with a maximum jail sentence of 20 years.

Jurisdiction Over the Person. The competency of a court to hear an interstate computer crime case is further complicated by the need for jurisdiction over the person. If the accused resides outside of the state in which the intrusion takes place and that state wants to prosecute the case, it must gain jurisdiction over the accused by one of four alternative methods: extradition proceedings, voluntary submission of the accused to the jurisdiction of the victim state, sufficient contacts with the state for the accused to be subject to service of process, or voluntary surrender of the accused by the Governor of his or her state to the state seeking to prosecute.

The state in which the accused is located automatically has jurisdiction over that person.[31] However, that state may not have jurisdiction over the offense if not expressly provided for by statute or if the offense is not a continuing crime.[32] For instance, if a person were to trespass a computer located in another state, the accused's state would not be permitted to prosecute unless it is provided for by the legislature, because trespassing is not necessarily a continuing crime. The victim's

---

[31] 22 Corpus Juris Secundum Criminal Procedure 144 (1954).
[32] Id.

state would have jurisdiction over the offense but may have difficulty obtaining jurisdiction over the person.

Because of the complex jurisdictional issues which accompany those instances of unauthorized intrusion into computer systems and data bases located across state boundaries, state officials may be unable to prosecute computer criminals when they would otherwise wish to do so. Intruders can use the jurisdictional complications to shield themselves from criminal prosecution. When state officials do decide to attempt prosecution, their efforts may be frustrated because of the complexities in gaining jurisdiction over both the offense and the person. These difficulties also act as a deterrent to the vigorous prosecution of interstate computer crime. The uncertainty officials face may cause many state law enforcers, even those with strong state legislation, to decide to direct their resources and energies elsewhere.

2.2 Trends in State Legislation

As states become increasingly aware of the need for strong, easily applied legislation, better statutes are being drafted and old ones are being amended. Three issues will be addressed: the need for reduced thresholds of criminal intent, legislation making simple trespassing by computer (without damage) a crime, and legislation focusing specifically on the jurisdictional issues.

2.2.1 Reduced Threshold of Criminal Intent

Under the laws of many states, unauthorized access to a computer system is a crime, but only if the intrusion was accompanied by malicious intent. California's computer crime statute has recently been amended to make any intentional and knowingly unauthorized, but nonmalicious, computer access also punishable. The amendment also provides that a computer owner may recover his or her attorney's fees in any civil action for damages caused by unlawful computer access.[33] The Cali-

---

[33] Cal. Penal Code.

fornia amendment is typical of current efforts to deter and prosecute acts of intrusion which may be committed without the degree of intent formerly required in many jurisdictions.

2.2.2 Simple Trespass

Many commentators have argued that simple, intentional access that does not cause injury should not be subject to penal justice. Others, however, have noted the inconvenience and encouragement which results if intruders become aware that the states have no recourse to discourage their forays into computer systems. The California amendment described above expands the range of penalties, depending on the extent of damage suffered. Even if no direct injury had been suffered and no damage had been caused, the first-time perpetrator of the unauthorized access would have committed an infraction simply by entering a computer system, network, or program knowing that access to it is prohibited by the owner. Subsequent offenses would be misdemeanors and would be subject to a fine. This amendment makes it much easier to prosecute and hopefully deter those who would obtain access to computer systems in those instances in which no substantial injury or disruption occurs.

Currently under consideration in the District of Columbia is a bill that would also make criminal any use of a computer without authority, whether or not such use resulted in damages. Such unauthorized use, if committed maliciously, would be punishable by a fine not exceeding $1,000 or a maximum term of 15 years in jail or both; if done without malice, the maximum term would be 3 years, but, curiously, no fine is specified. Thus, under the proposed statute, maliciously committed unauthorized access might result in a fine only, but conviction on a charge of nonmalicious access would necessitate a jail term.

2.2.3 Jurisdiction

The proposed legislation in the District of Columbia (the District) also includes a section on jurisdiction which could become a model for other states. Briefly, the crimes covered would be considered to have occurred in the District if (1) any act in furtherance of the crime was performed therein, (2) the victim had his or her principal place of business in the District, (3) the criminal (any criminal) had control or possession in the District of any proceeds of the violation or any material objects or instrumentalities that were used in the furtherance of the crime, or (4) any access to a computer was made by wire or by any other means of communication from, to, or through the District of Columbia. This section, if constitutional, ensures jurisdiction if any aspect of the crime were to touch the District. One must question whether or to what extent the District would be prepared to assert jurisdiction to extradite a nonresident who intruded on a computer system also located elsewhere merely because the telephone lines employed by the perpetrator went through a switching system located in the District. In any event, more states have begun to include language regarding jurisdiction to their computer crime laws, presumably because of some of the complexities mentioned earlier in this paper.

2.3 Proposed Direction for the Future

The disastrous implications of a rapid proliferation of criminal activities involving computers, the demonstrated lack of uniformity among the states with respect to much computer crime legislation, and the interstate nature of computer crime itself, argue strongly for a need to formulate and pursue a coordinated effort to deter and vigorously prosecute those involved in computer crimes. This effort might include the development of model computer crime legislation which states could adopt much as they have adopted other uniform laws.[34]

---

[34] The development of model laws and the adoption of uniform codes is not a new idea. The National Conference of Commissioners on Uniform State Laws has provided guidance on increasing uniformity in such areas as commercial law and probate for years. The American Law Institute has provided restatements of many areas of the law in an effort to promote uniformity throughout the states. The adoption of uniform laws can be viewed as an alternative to the increasing federalization and centralization of civil and criminal jurisprudence and so should be attractive to those who do not favor a more comprehensive role for the Federal Government in the prosecution and deterrence of computer crime.

There should also be a more concerted attempt to report and gather useful information about computer crimes and computer crime legislation. States should institute procedures whereby much of this information can be shared.

3. FEDERAL LEGISLATION

Although no Federal legislation has yet been enacted to deal comprehensively with computer crime and the problems associated with unauthorized access to computer systems and data bases, certain existing statutes have applicability to the issues at hand. Although a thorough discussion of these laws is beyond the scope of this paper,[35] the Federal wire fraud statute is particularly important and will be discussed in ensuing sections, along with existing and proposed Federal legislation will be summarized.

3.1 Wire Fraud Statute

Chapter 1343 of Title 18 of the United States Code makes it a crime to use the interstate telephone system for the purpose of executing or attempting to execute a fraud or a scheme to obtain money or property under false pretenses.[36] The courts have been very liberal in defining the term "fraud." Intrusion is usually, if not always, undertaken for the purpose of obtaining information, and the term "property" may or may not be sufficiently broad to include it.

The purpose of the wire fraud statute is to give Federal jurisdiction to many types of crimes otherwise prosecutable only by the states. The statute has the advantage of making prose-

---

[35] Readers who are interested in a more extensive discussion of existing Federal statutes which have some bearing on the prosecution of computer crime are referred to S. H. Nycum, "The Criminal Law Aspects of Computer Abuse Part II: Federal Criminal Codes," 5 Rutgers Journal of Computers and the Law: 297 (1976).

[36] 18. U.S.C. 1343 (1983).

cutions of computer crimes more feasible in instances in which state laws are inadequate or in which state officials decline to prosecute for any of the reasons addressed above. The maximum penalty for a violation of this section of the Code is $1,000 or 5 years in prison or both. In those cases in which imprisonment is not appropriate but a substantial fine is, the statute may not be adequate, and the application of the wire fraud statute to intrusion without injury is not always perfectly clear.

3.2 Existing and Proposed Federal Legislation

Although as of September 1984 no comprehensive Federal computer crime legislation had yet been enacted into law, Congress passed the Small Business Computer Crime Prevention Act. The principal thrust of that statute was to encourage the formation of a task force to study the impact of computer crime on small businesses and to disseminate to small businesses information about managerial approaches to deter computer crime.

In 1977, a bill was introduced which would make virtually all unauthorized use of Federal computers and computers used in interstate commerce a Federal crime. The Federal Computer System Protection Act, the principal sponsors of which have been Sen. Abraham Ribicoff and Rep. Bill Nelson, has been reintroduced in each session of Congress since that time, but without success.

Congress has just passed and sent to the President a bill which would amend the United States Code to provide penalties for fraud and related activities in connection with access devices and computers. The bill would classify as a felony any act to devise a scheme or artifice to gain unauthorized access to privately owned computers or to enter a computer illegally and obtain classified information. It would be a misdemeanor to enter a computer system operated by or on behalf of a government or private entity and get $5,000 worth of use or cause $5,000 worth of damage while tampering. Penalties range from a maximum of $5,000 or twice the value obtained or both for

a first offense, to $10,000 or twice the value of the loss and up
to 10 years in prison.

It is unclear as of this writing how and to what extent this
most recent bill resembles the comprehensive legislation introduced year after year by Sen. Ribicoff and Rep. Nelson. It does,
however, represent an important first step toward addressing
the problem of unauthorized access to computer systems on a
Federal level. Computer crime will not be sufficiently controlled
by the states alone. As one of the most prominent victims of
computer crimes, the Federal Government has a substantial
interest in the deterrence and prosecution of those involved.
With proper legislative guidance, the Department of Justice and
other Federal law enforcement agencies could become partners
with the states in the formulation of coherent, consistent policies
with regard to computer crimes.

4. MANAGEMENT ALTERNATIVES

There is general agreement that legislative initiatives are not
by themselves sufficient to completely deter those seeking unauthorized access to computer systems and data bases. It is also
well recognized that among the victims of computer crimes are
many who could, but have not, taken steps within their own
organizations to discourage computer intruders. These steps may
be technological, managerial, or a combination of the two. The
technological steps will be addressed in Chapter 7. However, a
few words may be appropriate concerning the steps management
may take to make intrusion more difficult.[37] These steps are
among those that have been available for some time and are
relatively easy to implement.

---

[37] There are a number of books on this topic which could be useful to
the reader; among these are the following: W. E. Perry, *Computer Control
and Security* (John Wiley & Sons, 1981); James Martin, *Security Accuracy
and Privacy in Computer Systems* (Prentice Hall, 1973); August Bequai,
How to Prevent Computer Crime (John Wiley & Sons, 1981); Donn Parker,
Computer Security Management (Reston, 1981); and T. A. Rullo, *Advances
in Computer Security Management* (Hayden, 1980).

Management can institute a system of passwords, so that those who are not authorized to access the computer system will have a more difficult time doing so. It can also install an access procedure such that those who attempt unsuccessfully to gain entrance would be disconnected or isolated from the system after a few unsuccessful attempts to gain access.

Many computer system vendors provide a password mechanism preset to a standard number or sequence for maintenance purposes. At a minimum, management should select and change new sequences irregularly but reasonably often. Much of the success of the 414 Gang intrusions was due to the failure of the management of the victim organizations to reset the original password. That password, in fact, was the same as the one used by the perpetrators' own school system. A multipassword control, in which the computer system would not be operational unless the different passwords of at least two individuals were required for system activation, could similarly deter the isolated computer thief from gaining access with obvious disadvantages for legitimate users. Management should sufficiently plan for instituting safeguards at the time of purchase or installation of the computer system when it is least expensive. The addition of safeguards that were not anticipated at the time the computer system was initially procured can be costly and may not be entirely satisfactory.

Many of the instances of intrusion occur after business hours. It may be possible for some businesses to shut down telephone access to their computer systems at those times. Because intrusion is often a matter of repeated attempts to crack codes and procedures, management should also limit the prompting information available on display screens until the user has been properly identified.

Computer displays should give ample notice of the proprietary nature of the system's information and the lack of permission which is implied by the unauthorized user's presence. This gives the user fair warning that the activity is illegal and makes later prosecution easier because it facilitates the showing of intent.

Users should be required to sign agreements containing nondisclosure promises regarding the system. Because many instances of unauthorized use occur because authorized users gave access information to hackers, the binding of authorized users to the nondisclosure obligations will act both as a deterrent and a reminder. It would also facilitate civil action against those who disclose to others the procedures by which they may gain access without authority to computer systems.

Management should perform background investigations on those to whom they wish to give key computer system responsibilities. Collection of this information can be relatively inexpensive if it is limited to checks of previous employers. These activities should be guided by legal counsel to avoid intrusions on the privacy of others and to allay the concerns of sources.

Management can establish systems of incentives to reinforce positive attitudes on the part of its own employees with regard to the need for privacy, security, and integrity of computer systems. Guides can also be formulated that set forth company procedures which employees must follow to preserve computer and data base security.

Over time it has become clear that a base line of security techniques is important. Locking a screen door in a house will never keep out a dedicated trespasser but it can be an effective deterrent against the casual intruder. Similarly, the precautions set forth above are the first steps in a security program on which more sophisticated efforts can be built.

5. CONCLUSIONS

This paper has demonstrated some of the weaknesses inherent in state efforts to deter and prosecute unauthorized access to computer systems. These include the inability to coordinate the definitions of computer crimes and penalties among the states and the particularly complex questions of jurisdiction which computer crimes often present. The joining of computer crimes and the telecommunications media gives rise to the need for consistency among the states' computer crime statutes, a wide range of sanctions which will address with appropriate penalties the many varieties and degrees of unauthorized access, a jurisdictional mandate which will enhance rather than hinder the prosecution of interstate acts of computer crime, and a level of recognition of the seriousness of computer crime which the states cannot provide on their own. Whether one or another of the pieces of proposed Federal legislation should be enacted is beyond the scope of this paper. However, the need for Federal activity in the area of computer crime is undeniable.

Federal legislation could become a model for the states and could serve to reduce the disparities in the treatment of acts of unauthorized access from jurisdiction to jurisdiction. Federal legislation could serve as an alternative to state jurisdiction, rather than preempting it, and could play an important role in the uniform treatment of interstate criminal activity. In appropriate cases, Federal legislation could serve to establish exclusive Federal jurisdiction over particular acts of computer crime and could otherwise fill the void left by states which, for lack of mandate, fail to aggressively prosecute in those instances in which unauthorized access is evident.

Federal legislation, however, offers no panacea. The states must also take the initiative to provide as wide a range of sanctions against computer crimes as is necessary and to define the crimes themselves in such a manner that simple trespassing, as well as more extensive injury, are officially discouraged. Finally, management, too, must and can do more to deter unauthorized access to private computer systems. We urge that a deliberate program of activity on the state, Federal, and private levels is essential for containing and reducing the instances of computer crime in the years ahead.

APPENDIX

Computer Crime Laws Summary

| | *Statutes* | |
State	Effective Date of Statute	Statute
Alaska	Jan. 1, 1980	Criminal Law Article 611.46.985

Computer Crime Laws Summary

State	Effective Date of Statute	Statute
Arizona	Oct. 1, 1978	Chapter 23 Organized Crime and Fraud 13–2301, 13–2302, 13–2316
California	1981	Penal Code 502
	1983	Evidence Code 1500.5, Penal Code 499c
Colorado	July 1, 1979	Computer Crime 18–5.5–101, –102
Connecticut	1984	Public Act 84–206
Delaware	July 21, 1982	Title 11 858 Computer Fraud
Florida	Aug. 1, 1978	Crimes 815.01–815.07
Georgia	July 1, 1981	Criminal Code of Georgia 16–9–90–16–9–95
Hawaii	July 1, 1984	Hawaii Revised Statute 708
Idaho	July 1, 1984	Chapter 22, Title 18, 18–2201, 18–2202
Illinois	Sept. 11, 1979	Criminal Law and Procedure, p. 1, 2, 50, Division I. Criminal Code of 1961, Title III Specific Offenses, Part C: Offenses Directed Against Property Article 15, 15–1, 16–9
Iowa	1984	Crimes 716A.1–716A.16
Maryland	1984	Crimes and Punishment Article 27 45A, 146
Massachusetts	1983	General Laws Chapter 266, 30
Michigan	Mar. 27, 1980	Computers 752.791 through 752.797
Minnesota	Aug. 1, 1982	Criminal Code 609.87–609.89
Missouri	1982	Crimes and Punishment 569.093 through 569.099
Montana	April 21, 1981	Crimes 45–2–101, 45–6–310 through 45–6–311

Computer Crime Laws Summary

State	*Effective Date of Statute*	Statute
Nevada	1984	NRS Title 52 Chapter 501 and NRS Chapter 205
New Mexico	1979	Article 16A Computer Crimes 30–16A–1 through 30–16A–4
North Carolina	Jan. 1, 1980	Criminal Law, Article 60 14–453 through 14–456
North Dakota	July 1, 1984	Volume 2, North Dakota Criminal Code 12.1–06.1
Ohio	July 1, 1983	Crimes Title 29, Chapters 2901, 2913.01
Oklahoma	1984	Title 21, 1951 through 1956
Pennsylvania	1984	Title 18, Crimes and Offenses 3933
Rhode Island	1979	Criminal Offenses Chapter 52 11–52–1 through 11–52–4
South Dakota	1982	South Dakota Codified Laws Chapter 43–43B, South Dakota Wiretap Law 23A–35A–2
Tennessee	April 20, 1983	Criminal Offenses Part 14, 39–3–1401 through 1406
Utah	1979	Offenses Against Property, Part 7, 76–6–701 through 76–6–704
Virginia	1984	Code of Virginia, Crimes and Offenses, 18.2–152.1 through 18.2–152.14
Washington	1984	Revised Code of Washington Annotated, 9A.48.100
Wisconsin	May 1, 1982	Crimes Against Property 943.70
Wyoming	1984	Wyoming Statutes 6–3–501 through 6–3–505

The table is titled *Statutes*.

DISCUSSION

Daniel Burk*: As articulated thoroughly by Nycum's and Appelman's paper, state legislative responses to data base intrusion has resulted in an unmanageable, and indeed amorphous, structure in which variation is the rule. Some of the statutes are overly simplistic; others ignore immediate, discernible problems. Because of the variation, computer owners and users have been left with a hopeless myriad of variations which must lead to similar variations in policies and practices between states. In the meantime, respective state courts have no hope of looking forward to a consolidated body of case law because interpretations by one state court will largely be inapplicable in any other state, even as guidance.

One of the difficulties I had when drafting the legislation for Virginia and the District of Columbia was trying to summarize different pieces of legislation and putting them into one package, with the hope of pulling out the best of all of it.

Unfortunately, one of the difficulties that I had with the paper was that the different portions of the paper address the different problems with the different legislation, but the paper does not suggest the ultimate answer.

As I have been speaking on this topic and have heard criticisms, particularly of the definition of "computer," one of the offers that I very quickly put out is that if you give me your best shot at it, I would be happy to see how we can match it and make Virginia's or any other legislation improve because of it. Uniformly, I have not gotten an answer that has been satisfactory either to myself or to the person who initially leveled the criticism.

One of the points that struck me in reading the paper is that there is a strong interdependence among technical, legal, and management approaches that may not have been amplified

* Daniel Burk is with the law firm of Thomas & Fiske in Alexandria, Virginia. He drafted the computer crime statutes for Virginia and for the District of Columbia.

enough in the paper. I am referring to things as simple as passwords and lock-out devices, and perhaps even encryption devices, to keep data transmission from being intercepted.

The paper alludes to many management solutions, some of which I had thought of, some I had not. Again, the easiest ones are the incorporation of passwords once the mechanism is in the computer, the auditing of unauthorized attempts to use a computer, or simply the notification of appropriate users of appropriate uses of the computer.

There is a great deal of difficulty in separating those different categories. The technical devices are necessary before any kind of audit of unauthorized access can be made. It cannot be determined who was on the computer unless there was a technical device to keep track of it.

One can go through a management process of routinely and irregularly changing the passwords. Similarly, if it is decided that after three attempts anybody who has put in a password improperly will be blocked, the technical device is again needed.

The technical and management devices interplay very extensively with the legal solutions. The technical devices are needed to be able to detect a crime and to present proof that the crime actually existed if any of the legislative solutions are to be pursued.

It may be necessary for management to send out notices describing to the employees or the users of a computer system that x, y, and z are appropriate uses, but a, b, and c are not, because most of the legislation talks about someone being without authorization. The opposite side of that is the easy defense that there was reasonable justification. Written notice may be necessary to negate that reasonable justification.

Needless to say, the technical devices or the management schemes will do very little if there is no fear of any ultimate prosecution. The management devices may do nothing more than have someone be afraid of the possibility of being fired, which works fine for the innocent or slightly curious employee. However, those who have decided that their money is not going to be made as employees, but instead will be made by temporarily being the employee long enough to reap illicit benefits, are not going to be concerned about the firing threat. The legal prohibitions may be needed to deter these people.

One of the problems is that we know that Federal legislation might be uniform, but it is not an either/or proposition. It is absolutely necessary that we have both. The first source of uniformity should come from the Federal level and should give Federal law enforcement agencies concurrent jurisdiction over crimes that, for any of a number of reasons, cross state geographical borders, and exclusive jurisdiction should be taken over those crimes peculiarly of a Federal nature. The recent passage of Federal legislation (H.R. 5616, codified as 18 U.S.C. 1029) has, perhaps, been more detrimental than successful because of its limited scope. Indeed, it is possible that the passage of H.R. 5616 in the 98th Congress may exacerbate the absence of a strong Federal role if Congress focuses its attention on modifying H.R. 5616 rather than on formulating and passing comprehensive legislation. This result should be strenuously avoided.

The second type of uniformity on a nationwide basis should come from a uniform state legislation proposal which might be drafted by a body like the National Conference of Commissioners on Uniform State Laws. This type of drafting body has neither the pressures of political support, sponsorship, or authorship nor the time constraints of a legislative session and can therefore consider thoroughly the various legislations throughout the country, as well as any issues which may be uniformly lacking in all legislation. If enough states accepted the uniform legislation, a body of case law would arise on a nationwide basis that could then be used as guidance for other states' courts and for computer users and owners throughout the country. At this time, enough separate experiences have been gained in the 33 states with this type of legislation to prepare an effective model act that could avoid many of the weaknesses of the separate states' efforts. Delay in such an initiative would only serve to perpetuate the difficulties and inconsistencies described by Nycum and Appelman.

One area in which all of the legislation seems to fall short is in consideration of the prosectorial difficulties involved in which important confidential information, perhaps rising to the level of trade secrets, must be disclosed to prove the method by which a perpetrator accessed a data base. Such disclosure, if made public even in a criminal setting, may spur more repetition of the intrusion than fear. Consideration should be given both at the Federal and state levels to codifying the principles set forth in cases such as *United States v. Ruiz-Estrella,* 481 F. 2d 723 (2nd Cir. 1973), and *Perez v. Metz,* 459 F. Supp. 131 (S.D.N.Y. 1977), in which the courts recognized that a criminal's right to a public trial should be balanced against the Government's or the complainant's need to isolate certain portions of the proceedings to be kept by the clerk of the court under seal.

Any legislation should also take into account the interdependence of the legal solutions on both technical and managerial solutions. For example, technical devices that monitor unauthorized access are critical in detecting criminal activity for purposes of prosecution. Furthermore, technical restraints may require the sanction of law both to act as an additional deterrent and as a method of "blessing" technical restraints in general.

Equally, legal solutions that are based on the presence or absence of authorization for the would-be offender are dependent on steps taken by the management of the computer installation to ensure that the scope of authorization of a particular employee or user is unquestionable. Yet, the best and most thorough managerial solutions, even combined with the most sophisticated technical solutions, may not prevent dedicated criminals from using the power of a computer as an instrument in their criminal activities. Accordingly, legislation as a partner in the solution can never be ignored.

In short, uniform legislation resulting from both a Federal initiative and from an initiative taken to create a uniform computer crimes act would help solve some of the weaknesses present in the legal structure proscribing computer intrusion. In addition, consideration of methods to protect the complainant's confidential data and trade secrets, thereby making prosecution more attractive, should be considered at all levels. Finally, all legislation should encourage the concurrent use of technical and managerial solutions.

Marvin Schaefer: I'm curious about contributory negligence on the part of the victim. If places choose to disregard the warnings and advice given by the manufacturers and vendors and are subsequently victimized by people who use a standard attack that has been published on the bulletin boards for years, has there been any chance of contributory negligence as a defense?

Daniel Appelman: If you're talking about civil liability, contributory negligence may well be a factor. Management should and must do all it can to deter computer crime without state or Federal legislation.

QUESTION: Still another reason for not getting a conviction would be the lack of being able to prove criminal intent. I would be interested in hearing comments on the inclusion of some kind of an electronic "no-trespassing" sign at log-on time that would state something to the effect that any attempt to access this computer beyond this point would be a criminal act subject to prosecution.

Daniel Appelman: It will go a long way toward forestalling a criminal case from being thrown out of court for lack of criminal intent if you do insert proprietary notices that there may be a criminal violation involved.

Daniel Burk: There are still two problems. Suppose I don't lock my front door and an intruder has been walking in every day for two years without my knowledge of it and I suddenly discover it. I don't believe that I have any less of a right to have the state press charges simply because my door has been unlocked and that is the way I choose to live. Now, it may be careless of me and I may have more difficulty in a civil suit, but the intruder has not trespassed any less simply because I don't have a sign out. You also have a problem with making it an obligation to put up a sign in that you're creating a burden on the computer user to try and keep up with all of the improper means of access.

I think a sign, as a practical solution, is a good step. It will take care of the more benign cases of somebody entering the front door and claiming, "I thought I had all rights to it." However, I do not believe that it should be an obligation of the computer owners to have to do it.

John Maxfield: I put in a warning only after an illegal access has been detected—in other words, a password has failed. Then, a notice is given stating that this appears to be an illegal access and proceeding further could subject the user to prosecution. However, to put something up there and make it a requirement, I think, is asking for problems. Most intruders do know what they're doing. They may say "I didn't know what I was doing," but that's not really true.

Donn Parker: I strongly believe in these due notices. However, most of the clients that I work with strongly disagree because they are trying to make these systems as friendly as they possibly can. They are always balancing the friendliness versus the stridency.

COMMENT: Another method is to have employees sign for passwords, thereby agreeing to the rules if they are to take part in the data processing system of that company as an employee. If they don't choose to play by the rules, stay off the system.

Daniel Burk: That is exactly one of the management solutions that I propose to our clients.

Donn Parker: Schools are doing that almost uniformly now when they provide computing [courses] for students. In fact, we are trying to get them to resign those statements at least once a year.

John Maxfield: Most of the commercial data base systems have a contract that when you accept user service, you agree to these terms: "You abuse our system and we'll take action; here is what we consider to be proper use of the system."

What happens in many of these computer intrusion cases, especially those in which juveniles get in, is that management says, "we want this system to be so easy to use a child could use it," and that is exactly what happens.

seven
TECHNICAL SOLUTIONS TO THE COMPUTER SECURITY INTRUSION PROBLEM

Eugene F. Troy,
Stuart W. Katzke,
and Dennis D. Steinauer*

I. BACKGROUND AND SCOPE

Computer security involves the protection of information resources and services against threats such as environmental and natural hazards, accidents and against errors, omissions, and intentional acts of people. Computer security is needed because such threats can result in the loss of confidentiality, integrity, and availability of information resources. Although the direct impact on an organization can be significant (for example, loss of a client data base), it is often the indirect impacts (such as disruption of customer services) that have more serious consequences.

To maintain the confidentiality, integrity, and availability of information resources, threats must be counterbalanced with cost-effective controls that will reduce the risks to acceptable

* The authors are at the Institute for Computer Sciences and Technology at the National Bureau of Standards in Gaithersburg, Maryland. They work in the Computer Security Management and Evaluation Group on the issues discussed in this chapter.

levels. Typically, a risk assessment process is used to select a combination of management and technical controls that provides protection from those risks which are of most concern.

This paper focuses on a specific area within the broad scope of computer security risk management, namely the intrusion problem. In the following sections, the intrusion problem will be defined, classes of threats identified, and some technical approaches to reduce risk described.

2. DEFINITION OF THE PROBLEM

2.1 Basic Definition of Intrusion

"Intrusion" is the willful use of information resources (equipment, documentation, software, services, or data) by an unauthorized person. It does not include violations of trust, which are the intentional misuse of information resources by persons who are authorized to use such resources for their normal job functions. Nor does this definition include the use of unauthorized information resources by some accidental means (for example, accidentally finding another person's file in the residue of a memory dump).

Technically, this definition of intrusion includes the unauthorized (and often illegal) copying or use of licensed or proprietary software. However, this software "piracy" problem has been covered earlier.

2.2 Classes of Intrusion

A wide range of potential threats could result from intrusion. For the purposes of discussion, several general classes of intrusion will be defined.

Physical Access and Theft. Physical access and theft include the theft of equipment, software, documentation, and data by individuals who obtain physical access to areas in which such resources are kept.

Unauthorized User Access. Unauthorized user access is the access to (reading, copying, modifying, or destroying) or the use of information resources (such as data files, proprietary software, and computers) by individuals who are not authorized to do so as part of their normal job function. Organizations are vulnerable to this threat when they fail to establish administrative and technical safeguards for controlling access to information resources. Individuals may obtain these resources in two ways. The primary distinction between the two methods is the degree to which the access point and information path to the target system can be physically protected.

Direct Use. User terminals or other points of access (for example, remote job entry stations) may be directly connected to the host computer by cable. In this case, the host is usually in the same or a nearby building. Included here is the use of a personal computer (PC) where the user and host PC are in the same room.

Remote Use. A user may be at a site that is remotely connected to a host computer by telephone or a more elaborate computer network.

Communications Intrusion. Communication intrusion involves the interception of information as it flows through a communications network. Vulnerable components of a network include the physical links that carry the information (such as dedicated lines, telephone dial-up lines, and microwave, satellite, and local area networks) and the points or nodes through which the information is switched from one communication path to another. It is not unusual for a communication network to include combinations of several transmission media (for example, dedicated lines and microwave transmission).

Interception of information is considered to be passive when transmitted data are only monitored or copied. Wiretapping and radio reception of the data are the most common methods of passive intrusion. With active intrusion, a receiver-transmitter is installed in the communication line, and intercepted data are retransmitted. The data will be unchanged until a special "looked for" event causes the monitoring mechanism to modify the data. Alternatively, the intruder may capture the data for re-transmission at a later time (for example, replay of a funds transfer request). Spoofing and misrouting are specific examples of threats resulting from the modification of transmitted messages. Spoofing involves techniques that induce users to take incorrect actions. Misrouting causes a message to be sent to the wrong location.

Compromising Emanations. All electronic equipment emanates electromagnetic signals. For some equipment, such as computers, communication lines, and data terminals, these emanations may carry information that can be detected by appropriately placed monitoring devices.

3. APPLICABLE TECHNICAL CONTROL MECHANISMS

There are several classes of controls that can be used to reduce the risks arising from the threats of intrusion discussed above. Some of these controls are well known, although they may not be widely applied. However, there is another group of useful controls that tend to be more technical in nature and include new approaches or more traditional methods which have been significantly improved. They are the principal subject of this paper.

3.1 Basic Requirements of Control Mechanisms

To prevent the unauthorized use of systems and data, effective control mechanisms must have the following qualities: (1) process integrity, which is a basic trustworthiness that provides assurance that the mechanism works as it should; (2) auditability, which is the ability to record information that may be significant in detecting and recovering from intrusion attempts and other security-related events; and (3) recoverability and robustness, which is the ability to maintain the integrity of the access control despite intrusion attempts, other untoward events, or system failures.

3.2 Control Mechanism Types

There are several basic categories of controls that can provide protection against the intrusion problem. (1) Physical protection involves the protection of the physical equipment and its operating environment. (2) Emanations control is the suppression or shielding of compromising electronic emanations. (3) Threat monitoring is carried out by monitoring security-related events in the system and its environment. (4) System and data access control is controlling which users have access to the individual system resources. (5) Port protection involves the prevention of unauthorized access to system communication ports. (6) Cryptography is the transformation of data into an unintelligible form for transmission or storage. These control mechanisms are illustrated in Figure 7-1. Each type of control mechanism will be discussed briefly.

3.3 Physical Protection

Although physical protection measures normally do not qualify as technical controls, they provide the bare minimum level of protection against intruders. Unless physical security can be provided, none of the other control types can be effective. Physical protection mainly refers to the creation of barriers, such as walls, doors, and guards, between the computer hardware and people who do not require access to it. A second, and equally important, strategy involves the protection of hardware and storage media from disasters, such as fire, water damage, and other natural causes, by the use of vaults, fire suppression mechanisms, proper construction, and alarm devices. These strategies work together because good protection from natural disasters often helps provide a measure of protection from intruders.

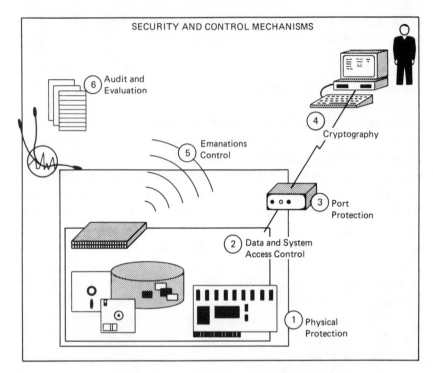

Figure 7-1. Control mechanism types

3.4 Emanations Control

All electronic equipment emanates electromagnetic signals, and these emanations may carry information which can be detected by appropriately placed monitoring devices. Specific technical details regarding the nature and extent of the problem of compromising emanations are classified by the National Security Agency. For this reason, the ease with which such signals can be intercepted is not well documented in the public literature. For most nonmilitary applications, emanation risks, at present, can be considered small in comparison with the many other types of security exposures that are often present.

Security measures intended to combat this problem are known as TEMPEST controls. Such controls usually involve equipment that has been specially shielded or modified to minimize emanations. TEMPEST-certified devices include a variety of printers, terminals, word processors, and personal computers. Large devices (for example, mainframe processors) and systems consisting of interconnected certified devices are not individually TEMPEST certified. Rather, the entire area in which such equipment resides must be specially shielded and certified.

Applications involving classified (national security) data generally must be processed on TEMPEST-certified systems. For unclassified applications, classified, it is the user's responsibility to determine whether the risk justifies the extra cost. The National Security Agency maintains a public list of equipment that has been certified to meet minimum criteria for the suppression of compromising emanations.

3.5 Threat Monitoring

The threat monitoring class of controls is concerned with the detection of events, activities, or situations which may represent a successful or attempted system intrusion. It consists of two parts: logging of information about all security-related system events of interest (also called audit recording) and variance detection, which uses the information to identify whether a security threat exists. It is especially important to protect these logs from unauthorized access and modification. System-level access control mechanisms can be used for this purpose. If a computer system routinely enforces highly effective access control mechanisms, it is less important to perform stringent threat monitoring.

The operating systems of most large- and medium-sized computers have some ability to collect information about unusual events that occur in the system. To use this capability, the operating system must be given directions about the types of events to record in the journal file. Security-related events logged should include, as a minimum, all failed attempts to gain access to any sensitive resources, such as programs or files. As the sensitivity of the resources in the system increases, the information about their use should increase proportionally.

Variance detection is a method of examining the security information collected in the journal to identify events or patterns that are suspicious. Normally, programs must be written to do this in a batch mode. Dynamic threat monitoring is a form of variance detection that identifies intrusion attacks as they occur and generates alarms so that the security force can respond immediately. In the more common batch form of threat monitoring, the journal contents are processed once a day, or less frequently, to produce reports that are scanned by management. These reports help identify whether the system is being attacked, from what source, and to what end. Responses that shore up system security can then be tailored to the threats.

3.6 System and Data Access Controls

System and data access controls are facilities built into the hardware and software components of the host system to be protected. They are intended to ensure that only authorized individuals may gain access to systems and the data contained in them. A more extensive form of the same mechanism also ensures that specific conditions of access, such as time of day or terminal type, are met. These controls are described in depth in Section 4.

3.7 Port Protection

A new class of hardware devices, port protection devices, has been developed that directly protects the computer's communications ports, to which the terminals or dial-up telephone lines are connected. These devices are enclosed in boxes physically separate from the computer and its software. They operate as external-access controls, independent of any controls that exist in the computer hardware, operating system, or applications. Port protection devices are particularly useful for providing a minimal level of security when dial-up telephone access is required for systems with weak internal controls. This set of devices is more thoroughly discussed in Section 5.

3.8 Cryptography

Cryptography is primarily intended to provide protection for information which must travel through some sort of insecure channel—a path in which the information cannot be protected from interception or modification. Cryptography is the transformation of information into a form that cannot be understood by an intruder who does not have the proper codes to reverse the transformation. Cryptography helps to ensure that intercepted information is unintelligible to interceptors or that any modifications made by them are detectable by authorized recipients. Cryptography is also useful for the secure storage of information on magnetic media and as an indirect method of user authentication. The subject of cryptography will be treated in depth in Section 6.

4. SYSTEM AND DATA ACCESS CONTROLS

Data processing resources are often sufficiently valuable, sensitive, or private that it is imprudent and often illegal to allow indiscriminate access to them. System and data access controls are designed to prevent unauthorized access to information resources. Their origins date back to early computer systems in which it was necessary to protect system software (the operating system) from being destroyed or overwritten ("clobbered") by the system's single user. As systems matured, to permit multiple users to share a computer (called multiprogramming), protection mechanisms were needed to (1) maintain isolation between the operating system's and user's processes and (2) provide for controlled sharing of system resources among users. Continuing changes in computer system architectures have resulted in today's time-shared minicomputers and mainframe computers. Both require sophisticated hardware and software mechanisms for restricting a user's access to only authorized system and information resources.

4.1 Description of System and Data Access Controls

The subject of access control encompasses the definition of the rules governing the allocation of access privileges to system resources to the user community, implementation of automated mechanisms to enforce these rules, and establishment of administrative practices and procedures necessary for effective and secure operations. Access controls provide the means whereby management can control interactions among people and system resources (including devices, software, communication lines, and data objects) because the privilege to access a resource can be selectively granted to, or withheld from, individual users. This means that access requests—for example, to read a data file or to execute a specific program—are mediated by system security components to verify the privilege or authorization of the requestor before granting access.

An access control mechanism should, to the degree specified by management, enable only authorized users (or computer processors acting on their behalf) to perform only those authorized functions only on those data to which they are authorized access, using only those hardware and software resources they are authorized to use.

In general, the principle of least privilege is usually recommended. The less a person using the system is allowed to do (consistent with the work the person is required to do), the safer will be the system's other users and the individual's own processes and resources.

4.2 Problems Addressed

Access controls provide a particularly effective solution to a significant portion of the intrusion problem. If used and administered properly, they are effective in ensuring that directly or remotely connected users of a computer system cannot read, copy, modify, destroy, or use information resources unless they are authorized to do so.

An important point to remember is that access control enforcement is based on the identity of the requesting user and on the user's privileges. Consequently, the process of user identification and authentication is critical. An individual masquerading as a legitimate user will be permitted the same access privileges as the legitimate user if the identification and authentication process can be fooled or subverted. Many reported break-ins have resulted from inadequacies in the user identification and authentication process (see below), the access control mechanisms, or both.

Although the primary objectives of access controls are to prevent the unauthorized disclosure and to maintain the integrity of information resources, access controls can also be used to provide the following: (1) allocation of limited resources among a user community competing for their use, by enforcing the conditions under which the resources may be used; (2) collection of information about resource usage for billing and accounting purposes (who, what, and for how long etc.); (3) separation of distinct organizational entities by restricting the access of groups of users to only certain groups of data based on their organization and job functions (the principles of least privilege and need to know should apply); (4) control and monitoring of patterns of computer usage for the purpose of efficient and effective resource utilization; and (5) specific implementations of local or organization-wide computer security policies.

4.3 Basic Access Control Techniques

This section discusses the importance of user identity verification as a precondition for effective access controls, defines a functional model for the access control process, and discusses the implementation of the access control mechanism by several system components.

4.3.1 User Identity Verification

Verification of user identity is essential if access to information resources is to be controlled on the basis of user privileges. Furthermore, users cannot be held accountable for their actions unless they (or processes acting on their behalf) are positively identified. Identity verification usually involves a two-step process. Identification occurs when the user provides an identifier (the name by which the user is known) to the system. The user's identifier is unique, is unlikely to change, and need not be kept secret. It is used for access control, security recording in a journal file, and other purposes such as accounting and billing. Authentication occurs when the individual passes some further test which proves that the user is actually the person associated with the identifier.

There are three basic techniques by which individuals can "prove" their identities. Individuals can present the following for verification: (1) known information such as a password, numerical combinations, or other information known only to the user; (2) objects possessed by the user, such as a magnetically encoded card or a key for a lock; and (3) physiological, behavioral, or morphological attributes of the user such as signatures, fingerprints, voiceprints, or palm prints.

Of all three basic techniques, passwords are the most commonly used automated method of identity verification. If password generation and distribution are effectively administered and if passwords are adequately protected by users and the system, then passwords can be used with a degree of reliability that is adequate for most systems. When necessary, passwords can be used in conjunction with other methods to obtain a higher degree of reliability. Of all the methods, passwords are the least expensive. The National Bureau of Standards is currently working on a Federal standard for using passwords which specifies management and technical requirements for password systems. The Department of Defense (DOD) Computer Security Center is also developing a password standard for use within the Defense Department community.

For systems with very stringent security requirements, the principle of "mutual distrust" should be used. In other words, not only should a system user authenticate himself or herself to the host computer, but the computer should be able to verify its own identity to the user.

4.3.2 Functional Model for Access Controls

The following model elements are the seven major components that are necessary to perform the access control process.

Subject. The subject is an entity that initiates access requests and possesses access privileges. Examples include individual users and the programs they cause to be executed on their behalf.

Object. The object is a resource resident in the computer system, to which access is restricted for purposes of protection or controlled sharing. Common examples include data files, the records or fields they contain, programs, and hardware devices.

Mode of Access. The mode of access is the operation to be performed on the requested object by the requesting subject. Examples include the "read", "write", and "execute" functions.

Decision Criteria. Decision criteria are the data and algorithm used to describe whether an access request should be permitted or denied. The three primary components—subject, object, and mode of access—must enter into the decision. Other useful criteria include time of day, the content of requested data, passwords, and the context in which a program is invoked.

System Response. System response is the action taken by the system when an unauthorized access attempt is detected. Examples include termination of the session, notification of the offending program or terminal, and notification of security personnel.

Security Log. The security log is a journal that includes events of relevance to access authorization. Of interest are events that could trigger a log entry and the information that an entry should contain. Examples of loggable events are all requests and denials for access to sensitive objects.

Control of Authorization Data. Control of authorization data is a policy or procedure for managing the authorization data, particularly those data governing the assignment and revocation of access privileges. Information about subjects, objects, and the privileges that hold between them must be stored within the system, and facilities must be provided for entering, reviewing, updating, and protecting this information. These facilities may be centralized (that is, utilized by a few designated individuals) or may be distributed throughout the user community.

4.3.3 Implementation of Access Controls

Elements of the model can be successfully implemented by a variety of strategies or architectures. Consider the relationships presented in Figure 7–2. Four major system components—the hardware, operating system, data base management system (DBMS), and application software—are presented. The arrows show potential dependencies of one component on another. Although each of these components can implement access controls within its domain of protection, the access control mechanisms of higher level components usually depend on the mechanisms of lower level components.

Hardware. Hardware protection mechanisms are necessary in time-shared, multiuser computers to physically isolate or partition user processes and to support rapid switching in the execution of user processes. Privileged instructions, process state switching, memory mapping, and bounds registers are a few of the hardware capabilities that are used to maintain physical separation between users. Machines that lack hardware protection mechanisms (personal computers for example) do not pro-

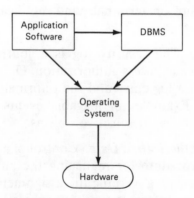

Figure 7–2. Basic access control components and dependencies

vide a firm base on which to build protection mechanisms at higher levels of the system.

Operating System. Because of its position as the principal interface between applications software and the underlying machine, the operating system (OS) is ideally placed to provide logical separation between users. Users (and the processes that are executed on their behalf) are considered logical entities because they are represented by a number of cooperating software components. By utilizing the physical protection mechanisms of the hardware, the OS is able to control the scheduling, initiation, and execution of user processes in such a way as to ensure the efficient sharing of system resources (for example, main memory, input and output devices, mass storage, and communication lines), as well as to provide logical access controls that enforce controlled sharing. At this level, subjects may be individual users or processes (executing programs), objects may be data files or software programs, and modes of access to objects include read, write, and execute.

Because there is a considerable amount of variability in the level of access control protection provided by vendors in their operating systems, numerous add-on products have appeared in the marketplace to enhance the security of vendor-supplied systems. Although the result of using these products does improve the ability of a system to enforce controlled access, adding-on security is not comparable with designing and implementing a secure system, as discussed below.

The application software and the data base management system (DBMS) are dependent on fundamental access controls provided by the OS (Figure 7–2). Consequently, the integrity and trust of the OS are of prime importance when implementing controls in these upper level software components. Significant developments in the theory and the construction of high-security, "trusted" systems have occurred over the past few years, culminating in the establishment of the DOD Computer Security Center and the publication of the Center's Trusted Computer System Evaluation Criteria.[1] With regard to access controls, the

---

[1] U.S. Department of Defense, *Department of Defense Trusted Computer*

criteria are based on a basic objective stating that trusted systems will control access to information such that only properly authorized individuals will be permitted to use specific system resources or to read, write, create, or delete information managed by the system's security controls.

The approach advocates the following basic requirements: (1) a well-defined security policy and model; (2) a method for formal specification and verification of the system (from high-level system specifications through its implementation in code) to ensure correct implementation of the security policy; and (3) a security kernel (which is a small, centralized, and highly protected portion of the code in the OS), the main function of which is to perform authorization checking. Because the kernel implements critical portions of the security policy, its formal specification and verification is essential.

If the goal of the DOD Computer Security Center is achieved, one can expect to see commercially available trusted operating systems that could form a secure base on which to build computer applications. These will reduce the degree of trust that must be placed in application systems.

Data Base Management Systems. DBMSs provide individual users and user applications with the ability to store, manipulate, and retrieve data that are entrusted to the DBMS. When access to information maintained by DBMS software must be controlled, the DBMS can provide powerful and effective enforcement capabilities. Examples of such capabilities include the following:

(1) Restriction of user access to only a user-view or subschema of the data base—some DBMSs allow the data base manager to define only those portions of the data base that users need for their job functions and to control access to that subset of data. From the user's point of view, the data base appears to contain only the data related to the job that must be done.

System Evaluation Criteria (Fort George G. Meade, Maryland: Department of Defense Computer Security Center, August 15, 1983).

(2) Password protection of specific files, records, or fields within records—many DBMSs (such as those following the CODASYL model) permit the attachment of passwords to individual data items (such as files) and permit access to those items only if the correct password is known by the user when an access request is made. The passwords discussed here are in addition to those required for user identification and verification at the time of log in.

(3) Query modification—used in some relational DBMSs, query modification involves the appending of additional conditions onto a user's query against the data base. Query modification is an example of how decision criteria can be implemented at the DBMS level in the access control functional model. Before a response to a user's question is provided (for example, "Which employees have had psychiatric care?"), the additional conditions are evaluated to determine whether the user has a need to know the information (such as, "Is the user an employee in the health unit and is the user a medical doctor?").

In most cases, the DBMS is viewed by the operating system as an executing process which must be scheduled, isolated from other processes, and protected. Thus, ensuring the integrity of the code, directories, dictionaries, and other working files of the DBMS is primarily the responsibility of the OS. Other processes that are executed on the same machine must not be permitted to access data being managed by the DBMS. The ability of the DBMS to maintain access controls over its user community cannot be ensured if the integrity of the OS cannot be guaranteed.

Application Software. Application programs, like DBMSs, depend on the OS to protect their data from other processes that are executed on the same machine. Also, like DBMSs, application programs can control access of their users to application data. There are several reasons why access controls might need to be implemented in application software. The first reason is that there are inadequate OS controls. When operating systems provide little or no access control facilities, supplementary access control mechanisms can be placed in the application software. However, if the OS cannot be trusted (if it contains flaws that can be exploited to obtain system and user data), then application software controls will not provide a high degree of protection. This is typically the case with personal computer OSs. Use of other technical anti-intrusion methods, such as cryptography or port protection, may have to be used in this case.

The second reason for implementation of access controls is to allow for restricted user interface. As an analog to the concept of user-views and subschema found in DBMSs, application software can limit the type of actions a user may request of the application system. For example, based on the user's identity, the application may allow the user to invoke only the specific subset of the available transactions that is needed for performance of the job function. This technique is particularly effective when the user is constrained to interface only with the application software during the log-in sequence, is terminated from all system activity at the time of logging off, and is not permitted to escape from the application software while executing authorized transactions (for example, escaping to the OS command mode).

The third reason for access controls is to allow for known subjects and objects. When the entities that comprise the subjects and objects are only known at the application level and not by the OS or DBMS, then responsibility for access control rests with the application program. For example, clerks in a regional office (subjects) may be executing data entry transactions (objects) of a payroll application. From the application perspective, clerks and transactions are known entities. However, from the OS view, the application software process is a subject and the application data files are objects. The level of granularity of clerks and transactions is inappropriate for OS control, requiring access controls to be placed at the application program level.

Application software can utilize the capabilities of a DBMS for storage, manipulation, and retrieval of application data. When this occurs, access controls at the application level may supplement, complement, and depend on those implemented in the DBMS.

5. PORT PROTECTION DEVICES

Port protection devices (PPDs) are a relatively new class of components that provide control over the initial entry into a system by terminal-based users and help create a secure dial-up communications environment. In general, these devices were developed to address the problem of unidentifiable users attempting to access a system remotely, over dial-up telephone lines. PPDs provide a level of user authentication. In addition, the devices operate independently from the host system, thereby offering improved prospects for integrity control, because they are located between the host and the communications line. Figure 7–3 illustrates a typical configuration.

5.1 General Description

PPDs are connected to the computer's dial-up port and are used to interrogate all callers for proper identification before they may be connected to the computer. These devices are

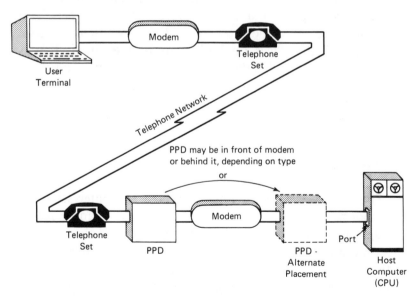

Figure 7–3. Port protection devices—typical configuration

physically external to the host computer system and operate independently of the host operating system. Devices of this type are designed to reinforce the protective measures that already exist in a computer's operating system, or they can add a measure of security to systems which have no inherent access controls.

Conceptually, the PPD functions as a black box placed in series on the communications line to mediate all initial accesses between dial-up terminal users and the host. Its purpose is to augment the host's user identification and authentication security capabilities. No call to the host can be completed unless the PPD permits the connection. Most PPDs are unable to communicate directly with the host and in operation are invisible to the host. The PPD may be embedded in a modem or other communications equipment, as long as it is physically and logically separate from the host and is not under host program control.

The PPD is a one-end security solution, because it is placed only on the host computer end of the communications circuit. Any user with the proper PPD identification access code, analogous to a password, may access the system.

There are a number of newer devices, much more restrictive in access control, that are not covered in this paper. These devices may be called the two-end solution, because they involve special matched devices on both ends of the circuit that are able to recognize each other in some secure way. The user is not necessarily required to enter any access code, because the keyed pair of devices automatically enter into a dialog and establish the legitimacy of the user's connection with the host.

5.2 Problems Addressed

The PPD is designed to help the host computer screen out unauthorized callers. Any computer system that can be reached through the public telephone system or through other common telecommunications carriers is potentially vulnerable to penetration. Hackers as well as more serious computer criminals can exploit a number of common computer security weaknesses by using inexpensive personal computer equipment. They can write simple programs to operate inexpensive modems that will automatically make systematic searches of telephone exchanges and discover telephone numbers connected to computer systems. Once connected, these intruders can readily identify many computers by their methods of interaction with callers and then use a series of well-known techniques to attempt penetration.

5.3 Techniques and Functions Performed

5.3.1 Minimum Expected Functions

All PPDs consist principally of two components. First, they have an internal microprocessor that makes user authentication and access control decisions. The second major component is a small amount of electrically alterable read-only memory (EAROM) to store information about the legitimate system users. The EAROM usually contains a table of acceptable user codes, any one of which will permit access to the host computer port. It may also include other identifying and call-back information. In a functional sense, this information and the decisions the PPD makes about it can be viewed as a special layer of password-based access control that is independent of any other authentication process.

As a first step to permitting connection with the host, a PPD typically will prompt a dial-up user to enter an access code. The PPD then compares the code with the EAROM table. If a match exists in the table, the PPD connects the user to the host communications port. From that point on, the user goes through the normal host computer log-on sequences to establish the session connection. If the code that was entered by the caller cannot be found in the table, the PPD may permit a small number of additional attempts and then will hang up if no valid code has been entered. This feature helps the devices resist the brute force attack, in which the caller attempts numerous passwords, usually by programming a personal computer to make a random search.

Once a potential user has been able to satisfy the access code requirements of the PPD, then he or she will be required to comply separately with any access controls used by the host computer (see Section 4).

PPDs are not encryption devices. They do not have the capability of protecting any data passing between the terminal and host from monitoring by unauthorized parties (wiretapping). The access codes for the PPD, any sign-on information for the computer system, and any transmitted data are still vulnerable to tapping. When this additional type of protection is required, encryption devices that use the digital encryption standard developed by the National Bureau of Standards should be used on all external communications lines.

5.3.2 Additional Security Functions

In addition to the required special password, most PPDs have one or more extra security features.

Camouflage. Some PPDs camouflage the existence of a computer port on the line. Hiding the carrier tone of the modem significantly deters the common hacker ploy of using an auto-dial modem and hobby computer to search telephone exchanges for the steady whistle indicating a computer-access telephone number. For example, one device on the market answers with a synthesized human voice, and another type is completely silent once it picks up the line.

The camouflage approach may have drawbacks in practical applications. Many portable terminals and personal computers designed for use as terminals will be unable to communicate with PPDs which use voice response. These machines, including the new group of "knee-top" or "notebook" computers, typically are equipped with internal modems and plugs which connect directly to the telephone line without using a standard voice handset. For these, the user would have to place a separate call using a voice telephone for the sole purpose of interacting with a voice-oriented PPD. Then, some means must be available for switching over the direct-connect modem after clearance to the host is given.

Call-back. Call-back is one of the original PPD features and has tended incorrectly to become synonymous with the entire class of PPDs. Call-back is available on many but not all PPDs. Each legitimate user of a computer system is expected to have a routine terminal work location and associated telephone number. A PPD equipped with the call-back capability can keep a person who has stolen a legal access code from gaining entry to the system being protected. The PPD does this by storing the access code and a telephone number for each valid system user. Once the PPD verifies the access code entered by the user, it hangs up and independently places a return call to the expected user location. This second call is required to make the connection to the host computer system.

Call-back procedures do provide additional security, because the potential system user not only must have the right access code, but also must be using a telephone that matches it. However, this feature may not be useful for many organizations. There are three immediate problems that arise. The first is that each connection is delayed up to a minute while the second call is placed, which may annoy and inconvenience the users. The second problem is that many regular users are very mobile, such as traveling auditors and salespeople, and do not have fixed telephone numbers to which the system can call back. Most units can disable the call-back feature for selected users, but that also reduces the intended security. A third practical problem may come up if the management of the central computer facility is unwilling to be billed for all telephone connection time, which results when the PPD initiates the second call for hookup to the computer.

Logging. The ability to log users when they enter and exit the system, as well as when access violations occur, is an important security characteristic. Some PPDs provide extensive logging capabilities, including the ability to collect and print out a variety of communications usage statistics, in addition to security-related information such as failed access attempts. It is desirable if the PPD unit is at least able to indicate whether invalid access attempts have been made, so that other security actions may be taken to identify the problem. Some units meet this need by storing a number of the most recent invalid codes used or by making light-emitting diode (LED) displays to indicate the number of invalid attempts. Several of the low-end PPDs have no logging capability at all.

5.3.3 Other Security Characteristics of PPDs

Separation of Function. PPDs are physically and logically distinct from the host computer and its internal security functions. In effect, they are part of the system's communications network equipment. For additional security, the responsibility for maintaining these units and their access code structures may be separated from normal system user authorization and password management. The latter is normally a function of the computer operations or technical support staff. The separation of functions induced by having two separate organizational elements control different parts of the total external dial-up access process is a very powerful security mechanism because it requires collusion between persons doing different job functions before violations can occur.

Access Code Security Versus Entry Methods. PPDs vary significantly in the ways in which they implement various functions. There are three basic methods used for entry of the access code. These methods have important security implications, because there are differences in code sizes and complexities among them. Two methods use the telephone set for code entry and the third method uses the terminal's keyboard.

The first method of entry is via the user's voice in responding to a synthesized voice from the PPD which counts through a series of numbers. There are normally only three digits in the code for this method, and each number can be from zero to nine. The possible number of access codes for this method is 1,000, which is well within the range of brute force intruder cracking attempts.

The second method of access code entry takes advantage of the touch-tone keypad on the telephone set. The user is normally prompted by a synthesized voice from the PPD to key in the access code, which is usually a series of five numbers. It is possible to use the two special characters on the keypad (* and

#), in addition to the 10 numbers, for a total set of less than one-quarter of a million possible codes. This is also within cracking range of the hobby computer, which can program an auto-dial modem to enter a random series of codes as long as the PPD will permit the connection to continue.

In several of the newer PPDs, a third method is used, by which the user enters the access code directly via a terminal keyboard. These PPDs operate on the digital side of the modem rather than the analog (voice) side, so they can communicate directly with terminals. When the user dials a computer telephone which has one of these PPDs installed, the PPD automatically makes a connection to the terminal through the modem. The user must then key the password on the terminal keyboard.

Use of the terminal keyboard rather than the telephone touch-tone keypad to enter the access code permits a much larger selection of characters for the code. PPDs of this type can commonly use most or all of the 128 ASCII characters that can be generated on standard terminal keyboards. These characters consist of upper and lower case letters, numbers, special and graphics symbols, and even nonprinting "control characters." A short, five-character ASCII access code can have over 34 billion combinations and is relatively resistant to all telephone-based brute force intrusion attempts.

PPDs should stay abreast of the present technology that system users desire and expect. Many terminals now contain or are coupled to auto-dial modems that are directly connected to telephone lines. These configurations do not require telephone handsets for voice traffic to establish communication with the host. Most installations of this type do not even have provisions for attachment of the telephone handset. The preferred method for user convenience is to permit all connection dialog to take place via the terminal screen and keyboard. Consequently, to reintroduce the requirement for touch-tone or voice communication with a PPD for security purposes is a step backward and must be justified by legitimate security concerns.

5.4 Selection and Size Considerations

The primary considerations for selecting PPDs are the number of ports or lines to protect, the degree of security control desired, and the convenience of system users. Other important concerns are cost per unit, ease of administration and maintenance, and number of users to be supported per line.

5.4.1 Number of Ports Protected

Most PPDs available today are small units designed to protect a single port. They are about the same size as a standard asynchronous modem, and a few of the newer models are even integrated with the modem in the same enclosure. These would be appropriate for a personal computer or a larger computer with a small number of dial-up lines to protect. Larger multiline units are available in various sizes, from 2 to 64 lines in standard configurations, and one unit has the ability to expand to as many as 384 lines. Costs range from $369 to $1,495 for single-line units and can go to as low as $204 per line for multiline units. Large PPDs can cost significantly less per line because a single set of chassis and power supply components is used, and circuit boards are added as required for more telephone lines and user access code tables.

5.4.2 Security Control Criteria

The important features to examine in terms of security controls are the maximum number of user access codes stored, the access code type and size, any camouflage of the port, the presence of a call-back capability, event logging capability, and action taken on invalid access attempts.

Number of Access Codes. The PPD should be able to store one access code for each expected user of the dial-up line to ensure proper separation and control. The sharing of access codes and system passwords is not a good security practice, because it does not permit adequate individual accountability.

Code Type and Size. The access code type may be a standard numerical code or the ASCII code set used by a terminal keyboard. As discussed above, the use of ASCII permits a much greater range of possible access codes, which increases the resistance to intrusion attempts. The number of possible elements in the access code is normally at least six for most units. Smaller numbers would reduce the resistance to intrusion.

Camouflaging. Port camouflaging by the use of verbal response or blank screens can be a desirable feature for reducing identification and possible harassment. However, if other security features are strong enough, camouflaging does not significantly add to the security of the system.

Call-back. A call-back capability in effect creates a double access code hurdle for system users to surmount. They must have both pieces of the combination, the access code itself, and the proper terminal telephone number to connect to the host computer. This increases the security level, but it must be carefully balanced against user convenience and other factors such as telephone billing procedures.

Event logging. As described above, PPDs vary significantly in event logging capabilities from none to extensive. As a minimum, it would be useful if the unit were able to indicate whether a number of invalid access attempts had been made. In systems which have high-level security requirements, it would be appropriate for the unit to keep a record, via printer or disk file, of information on all valid and invalid access attempts, including the identification of users and time stamping. One unit which uses call-back is able to store and display telephone numbers that are used in invalid attempts.

Invalid Attempts. All PPDs that are now available are designed to terminate the telephone connection when invalid access codes are entered, which is a very desirable security feature. As noted above, some have the logging capability to record this type of event. Some units permit only a single attempt and then hang up, and other units either permit a small, fixed number of attempts or permit the administrator to set the allowable number of attempts. The smaller the number of attempts that are permitted, the higher the security of the system will be. This must be balanced by convenience factors, because legitimate system users should not be unduly penalized for making simple entry mistakes.

5.4.3 Product Comparison Table

In Table 7–1 are described 17 PPDs that are known to be available as of the summer of 1984. Additional units of this type are being announced frequently because of the growing public interest in preventing computer intrusion. A number of other new communications security devices, which fall outside the strict one-end port protection definition used in this paper, are available but are not included in this table. The PPDs are compared in terms of 11 significant characteristics discussed in this paper. It should be noted that, because security needs vary greatly, not all of these characteristics are important in every application. This table is provided for purposes of demonstration only, with the understanding that it is not the policy of the National Bureau of Standards to endorse any product.

5.4.4 User Convenience Factors Versus Enhanced Security

In the final analysis, computer systems are designed to be used by people to conduct their legitimate business. User convenience, also called user-friendliness, is an important issue and should be paramount within security requirements. It is necessary to determine the nature and extent of the threats facing a computer system and to evaluate the inherent sensitivity of data to manipulation or disclosure to determine a valid level of security for the system. PPDs are effective security tools, but first it must be determined that they are necessary to protect the system. On the negative side, they can make the process of legitimate user connection to the computer significantly more difficult. PPD features that can affect system user convenience are access code entry methods, code type and size, call-back capability, and the number of invalid tries that are permitted. The most important of these are code entry methods and call-back, both of which, if not thoughtfully implemented, have the potential of reversing the automation trend by increasing the difficulty of user access procedures and requiring manual intervention.

6. CRYPTOGRAPHY

Much has been said about the value of cryptographic protection in computer systems. Many commercially available system security products, particularly those intended for personal computers, are based entirely or in part on cryptographic protection. However, before acquiring such products, the user first must understand the purpose and proper application of cryptography to the security situation. Improper application of cryptography may result in minimal protection while leaving users with an unjustified sense of confidence, thereby actually increasing exposure. This section discusses the role of cryptography in information security and presents some implementation considerations.

6.1 Use of Cryptography

The purpose of cryptography is to protect information while it resides in or passes through an insecure environment which cannot be physically protected from access by unauthorized parties. This might include such media as a public telecommunications line, the airwaves, magnetic tapes in transit or unprotected storage, or even an unprotected personal computer system. In general, cryptography can provide two types of protection: privacy and integrity. It can do this in two types of environment: communications channels and data storage media.

6.1.1 Privacy Protection

Cryptographic techniques normally are used to prevent the unauthorized disclosure (reading) of information. This is usually accomplished by having the sender transform (by encryption) clear-text information into cipher text and having the receiver subsequently reverse the process (by decryption). The encryption

TABLE 7-1. Product Comparison Table
Port Protection Devices—Product Characteristics

Product	Vendor	No. Ports/Lines Protected	No. User Access Codes	Access Code Type/Size
Gateway	Adalogic 1522 Wistaria Lane Los Altos, CA 94022 (408) 996-8559	1	20	ASCII (Any Length)
Dialsafe 3 and 3 Plus	Backus Data Systems Inc. 1440 Koll Circle, #110 San Jose, CA 95112 (408) 279-8711	3	65 (Optional to 150)	ASCII ID: 1 to 6 PW: 1 to 6
Sleuth (Formerly Sherlock, Esq)	C. H. Systems 8533 W. Sunset Blvd., #106 Los Angeles, CA 90069 (213) 854-3536	1	74	ASCII ID: 1 to 6 PW: 1 to 6
Defender IIS	Digital Pathways Inc. 1060 E. Meadow Circle Palo Alto, CA 94303 (415) 493-5544	16	1000	Numeric 1 to 7 Char.
Defender II		48 Std. (Optional to 384)	1000 (Optional to 4000)	Numeric 1 to 7 Char.
Entercept	Integrated Applic. Inc. 8600 Harvard Avenue Cleveland, OH 44105 (216) 341-6700	1	1 (Shared by all)	ASCII 1 to 6 Char.
Barrier	International Anasazi Inc. 2914 E. Katella Avenue Orange, CA 92667 (714) 771-7250	1	1 (Shared by all)	ASCII (Any Length)

Product	Company			
Micro Sentry		1	16	Numeric 3 Char.
Computer Sentry	TACT Technology (formerly IMM Corp.) 100 N. 20th St., Philadelphia, PA 19103 (215) 569-1300	1	8	Numeric 6 Char.
Multi Sentry		16 Std. (Optional to 128)	1000	Numeric 1 to 10 Char.
SAU (Secure Access Unit)	Lee MAH Inc. 729 Filbert St. San Francisco, CA 94133 (415) 434-3780	1	99	Numeric 6 Char.
SAM (Secure Access Multiport)		2 to 64 (22 Std.)	256 (Optional to 2304)	Numeric 2 to 15 Char.
Data Sentry	Lockheed-GETEX Co. 1100 Circle, 75 Parkway Atlanta, GA 30339 (404) 951-0878	1	16	ASCII 1 to 20 Char.
Oz Guardian	Tri-Data Inc. 505 E. Middlefield Rd. Mountain View, CA 94039 (415) 969-3700	1	160	ASCII 1 to 250 Char.
Lineguard 2001		1	64	ASCII 1 to 8 Char.
Lineguard 3000	Western Datacom 5083 Market St. Youngstown, OH 44512 (216) 788-6583	2	100	ASCII 1 to 8 Char.
Lineguard 3060		15 Std. (Optional to 60)	100	ASCII 1 to 8 Char.

TABLE 7-1. Product Comparison Table (Continued)
Port Protection Devices—Product Characteristics

Product	Access Code Entry Method	Camouflage of Port	Call-Back Capability	Event Logging Capability	No. of Invalid Tries Permitted
Gateway	Terminal	Partly (Blank Screen)	No	Yes (List on Command)	Set 1 to 10
Dialsafe 3 and 3 Plus	Terminal	No	Yes	Yes Printer (Optional)	3
Sleuth (Formerly Sherlock, Esq)	Terminal	Optional (Originate-Only Modem)	Yes	No	1
Defender IIS	Touch-Tone (Terminal Option)	Yes	Yes	Yes Printer or Disk	3
Defender II	Touch-Tone (Terminal Option)	Yes	Yes	Yes Printer or Disk	3
Entercept	Terminal	Partly (Blank Screen)	No	No (Audible Alarm)	1
Barrier	Terminal	Partly (Blank Screen Optional)	No	No (Visible Alarm)	3

Micro Sentry	Touch-Tone or Voice	Yes	No	No (Visible Alarm and Shutdown)	3
Computer Sentry	Touch-Tone or Voice	Yes	No	No (3 Alarm Modes With Shutdown Optional)	Set 1 to 9
Multi Sentry	Touch-Tone or Voice	Yes	Yes	Yes Printer (Opt.) 3 Alarm Modes, Shutdown (Opt.)	Set 1 to 999
SAU (Secure Access Unit)	Touch-Tone	Yes (Silent on Answer)	Yes	No	1
SAM (Secure Access Multiport)	Touch-Tone	Yes (Silent on Answer)	Yes	Yes Printer (Opt.)	1
Data Sentry	Terminal	No	Yes	Yes (Bad ID's and Phone No.'s Saved)	Set 1 to 9
Oz Guardian	Terminal	No	Yes (May Include 2nd Password)	Yes (No. Invalid Attempts)	1
Lineguard 2001	Terminal	No	Yes	Yes (No. Invalid Attempts)	2
Lineguard 3000	Terminal	No	Yes	Yes (No. Invalid Attempts)	2
Lineguard 3060	Terminal	No	Yes	Yes (Optional Monitor)	2

TABLE 7-1. Product Comparison Table (Continued)
Port Protection Devices—Product Characteristics

Product	Access Code Changing Method	Contains Integral Modem	Standard Config. Cost Per Port/Line
Gateway	Terminal and Password	No	$395
Dialsafe 3 and 3 Plus	Host or Terminal and Password	No	(Gross $1295 for 3 Ports) $432/Port
Sleuth (Formerly Sherlock, Esq)	Terminal, Switch, and Password	No (Needs Hayes Smartmodem)	$465
Defender IIS	Terminal and Password	No	(Gross $6000 for 16 Ports) $375/Port
Defender II	Terminal and Password	(Gross $9800) No	for 48 Ports $204/Port
Entercept	Key and Dip Switches	No	$595
Barrier	CPU or Terminal and Switch	No	$369

Product	Access Method	Dial-Back	Price
Micro Sentry	Phone Pad and Switch	No	$695
Computer Sentry	Phone Pad and Key Switch	No	$1495
Multi Sentry	Terminal, Key, and Password	No	(Gross $21,500 for 16 Ports) $1343/Port
SAU (Secure Access Unit)	Phone Pad and Password	No	$1195
SAM (Secure Access Multiport)	Terminal and Password	No	(Gross $13,750 For 22 Ports) $625/Port
Data Sentry	CPU or Terminal and Password	Yes	$995 Includes Modem
Uz Guardian	Terminal and Password	Yes	$750 Includes Modem
Lineguard 2001	Terminal, Switch, and Password	No	$695
Lineguard 3000	CPU or Terminal and Password	No (Requires Racal-Vadic Chassis)	(Gross $1120 for 2 Ports) $560/Port
Lineguard 3060	CPU or Terminal and Password	No (Requires Racal-Vadic Chassis)	(Gross $3730 for 15 Ports) $249/Port

and decryption processes are controlled by a key or pair of keys established by the sender and receiver. A key is simply a data string (characters or bits) of some specified length. Without the proper key, an intruder who is able to intercept the cipher-text information should not be able to decipher it.

6.1.2 Integrity Protection

In addition to privacy protection, cryptographic techniques can be used to detect the unauthorized modification of data. This is done by using a cryptographic transformation of the contents of a message to produce an authentication code which can be attached to the original message. The recipient performs the same transformation on the received message to generate a code that can be compared with the received code. Any difference between the two codes indicates that the original message was modified while in transit. The transformation is controlled by a secret key, so an intruder able to modify the data will not be able to generate a corresponding valid authentication code.

Such message authentication codes have application in situations in which the integrity of data is important. An example is the protection of funds transfer messages. An American National Standards Institute standard "Financial Institution Message Authentication"[2] provides guidance in this area. This technique can also be used to help ensure that important files or programs have not been modified. It should be noted, however, that this process does nothing to prevent actual data modification—it only enables the detection of such acts.

6.1.3 Communication Protection

The traditional use of cryptography has been to protect messages which must be sent over insecure routes. Modern data communications systems usually include segments that are insecure, including switched telephone lines, microwave links, and satellite links. Local area networks are particularly vulnerable,

---

[2] American National Standards Institute, *Financial Institutions Message Authentication Standard X9.9* (Washington, D.C.: American National Standards Institute, 1982).

because each device on such a network can read all messages being exchanged among other devices and can insert counterfeit messages. Cryptography is a natural (and often the only) method of protecting data in such environments.

6.1.4 Storage Protection

Data can be encrypted before being recorded on storage media, if such media might be exposed to unauthorized users. All types of media can be protected in this manner, including tapes, floppy disks, and hard disks resident on both personal and large computer systems. This is typically accomplished with simple file encryption programs. Cryptography can also be built into computer systems at the basic input/output service level. This enables cryptographic protection of all data stored on disks while relieving applications programs from any concern for the process (because they still deal with unencrypted data at all times). It is even possible to embed cryptographic protection in hardware to protect data in random access memory. However, this requires special modifications to the central processor system and, therefore, is often an unacceptable approach.

6.2 Specific Types of Cryptographic Mechanisms

There is a wide range of cryptographic mechanisms appropriate for use in the protection of computer systems and data. The number of products on the market is growing rapidly. They differ in the type of environment in which they are designed to operate and in the basic methods of cryptography employed. The following is a discussion of several general types of cryptographic mechanisms. Several technical and implementation considerations are discussed below as well.

6.2.1 Communications Cryptography

The first large-scale application of cryptography for computer systems was for data communications lines. A typical application includes a device at each end of a communications link. Between the two devices, all communications are encrypted; outboard of the devices, data are in unencrypted (clear-text) form. The establishment of keys for a given communication session may be determined in several ways. The simplest method is for each user to insert the necessary key manually (for example, with a thumbwheel switch). Some products provide for the automatic insertion of keys with a special hand-carried electronic key insertion device. In addition, some systems provide a key establishment protocol over the common communication link. In this case, a master key is first used for the encryption and secure transmission of keys used in each session.

Most communication cryptographic devices do not interface directly to the communications hardware. The cryptographic device is usually inserted in the digital portion of the communication line between the computer or terminal input/output port and the modem. Several commercial cryptographic devices of this type are available. Some are stand-alone boxes that are connected between the modem and terminal device; others for personal computer systems may consist of printed circuit boards that include both cryptographic and communications interface functions. For large-scale host systems which must handle several incoming communication lines, rack-mounted devices are available. Some devices include key generation and distribution facilities; others leave those activities to the user.

This type of cryptographic device can help ensure the security of data while in communication channels, but provides no protection for information once it has been decrypted and is in the computer system.

6.2.2 Bulk File Cryptography

The easiest manner in which cryptography can be used to protect stored data is to encrypt and decrypt entire files. Typically, a user prepares a file (presumably containing sensitive information) and then runs an encryption utility program to produce a cipher-text version of the file. The original file should then be overwritten (to prevent residue "scavenging"). Before the file is used again, the utility program must be used to decrypt it and produce a clear-text version of the file. In general, the user is responsible for selecting, entering, and remembering the key used for the encryption and decryption process. Commercial cryptographic products usually provide utility programs for bulk file encryption and decryption, as well as a utility to overwrite old files. The majority of these products are implemented entirely in software, but some are built around a cryptographic hardware device.

6.2.3 Integral File Encryption

There are a number of problems with the bulk encryption and decryption of data files. These include general inconvenience, the need to erase clear-text files, and the need for user training. An alternative to file encryption is a cryptographic facility which is integral to the file input/output subsystem. Basically, each block of data to be written to the disk is first encrypted, and each block read from the disk is decrypted before it is passed to the requesting program. This makes the entire cryptographic process almost transparent to the user and eliminates the inconvenience and dangers associated with bulk file procedures. Such facilities may be implemented at the level of the operating system input/output service routines, at the disk controller level, or even within the central processor. Users with sufficient technical expertise can implement such a capability themselves. In addition, there are commercial hardware and software products that may be considered.

6.2.4 General Purpose Cryptographic Facilities

A more flexible approach to cryptography is to provide a general-purpose cryptographic facility that can be used for a variety of applications. Such a facility needs to provide at least three basic functions: key entry, encryption, and decryption. It should be available through standard system interfaces, for example, through a subroutine call or a basic input/output operation. There are a number of board-level cryptographic devices available for personal computer systems (and some large-scale systems) which communicate with the central processor over standard internal bus channels. There are also products which operate as stand-alone devices which communicate with the processor through a standard (usually serial) communications port. Also in the category of general purpose cryptographic facilities are subroutines which can be called by other programs to perform encryption or decryption operations on selected data records.

6.2.5 Application Level Cryptography

In many situations, it may not be possible to provide cryptographic protection at the communications link, file, or disk levels. In such situations, it may be necessary to embed cryptographic protection in the specific application in which it is needed. Some commercial application programs may use cryptography for both data and software protection. Because general purpose hardware or software cryptographic facilities often are not available, such application-level cryptography usually must be implemented in software. This may make it somewhat more vulnerable to modification. However, embedding cryptography at this level has the advantage of not causing system degradation for other applications for which such protection may not be needed.

The above discussion has outlined the basic types of cryptographic facilities that are generally available for data protection. There are, however, several different operational and technical approaches for implementing such mechanisms.

6.3 Technical Considerations

The technical characteristics of various cryptographic mechanisms differ widely. In selecting cryptographic mechanisms or products, several technical considerations are important. These include the following:

• Private versus public key systems

• Cryptographic algorithms

• Hardware versus software implementation

• Key generation and management

- Process integrity

- Cryptographic strength

6.3.1 Private Versus Public Key Systems

There are two basic types of cryptographic systems in common use. A private key cryptosystem requires that the sending and receiving parties share a common cryptographic key. This key must be kept secret (private) to ensure the security of the encrypted information. This requires special precautions and protocols for the distribution of keys. Indeed, the key distribution problem has long been one of the difficulties in the widespread application of cryptography to large communications networks. However, in situations involving small numbers of users, this is generally not a significant problem.

A public key cryptosystem involves pairs of keys: one for encrypting messages and another for decrypting messages. The encrypting key is public, so that anyone who wants to send a message to a given user can use that person's key. Only the recipient, however, has the (secret) decryption key. This type of cryptosystem may possibly reduce certain key management problems and can be attractive for large networks of interconnected users. In both systems, the selection and protection of keys (even public keys) is critical to the overall security of the system. It is possible to combine the use of each type of system to provide very effective security with relatively little administrative overhead.

6.3.2 Cryptographic Algorithms

All cryptosystems require a well-defined process (algorithm) by which information is transformed from clear text to cipher text and back to clear text. It is an accepted principle of cryptology that the strength of a cryptosystem must not be dependent on the secrecy of the algorithm itself. This enables the exchange of information necessary for the design and manufacture of systems incorporating the algorithm. Public availability of the algorithm also permits critical analysis of the algorithm's resistance to cryptanalytic attack.

The Data Encryption Standard (DES) is the cryptographic standard for nonclassified Federal Government applications. The DES is a private key cryptosystem and is described in Federal Information Processing Standards.[3] DES has undergone extensive critical analysis, thus providing a high level of understanding of the level of protection it provides. Federal Government agencies are required to use DES whenever encryption of nonclassified information is needed.

Although there is no standard public key cryptosystem, there are algorithms that have been published in the open literature. Like the DES, they also have received considerable critical review, and the level of protection provided by them is relatively well understood. Several commercially available cryptographic products incorporate either DES or the openly available public key algorithms.

A number of commercial cryptographic products use proprietary (secret) cryptographic algorithms. Such algorithms may operate at higher speeds than such algorithms as the data encryption standard. However, because the algorithms are not made public, it is difficult to obtain an objective evaluation of their cryptographic strength. It is therefore the responsibility of the user to make the necessary determination.

6.3.3 Hardware Versus Software

Cryptographic algorithms can be implemented in either hardware or software. The former approach usually results in much faster operation (one to two orders of magnitude), because the extensive bit-level operations involved in most cryptographic processes are very inefficient in software. Hardware implementations also provide better integrity protection, because hardware is not easily subject to undetected modification as is software. Software implementations, however, are often less expensive and more flexible. Hardware implementations of DES on a single integrated circuit chip are available from at least two manufacturers and are used in a number of cryptographic products.

---

[3] National Bureau of Standards, *Data Encryption Standard* (Washington, D.C.: National Bureau of Standards, January 1977).

It is also worth noting that full compliance with DES requires hardware implementation, although software versions of the DES algorithm are available.

6.3.4 Key Generation and Management

The strength of cryptosystems is largely dependent on the quality, integrity, and secrecy of the keys used to encrypt and decrypt information. Therefore, care must be taken that the keys are randomly or pseudo-randomly selected, and they must be protected from unauthorized disclosure or modification. With many commercial cryptographic products, it is the user's responsibility to generate and distribute cryptographic keys. This often can result in short or trivial (weak) keys.

In addition to this problem, many commercial products do not provide adequate mechanisms for transmitting and storing keys. In all cryptographic systems, keys must be exchanged in a secure manner. For one-key systems (such as the DES), this requires protection of the keys from both substitution and disclosure. This may involve distribution of keys through separate (often manual) channels or through encrypted key exchange protocols. The use of two-key (asymmetric or public key) cryptosystems may possibly reduce the key disclosure problem. However, even for two-key systems the one publicly available key must still be protected from substitution. It is beyond the scope of this chapter, however, to discuss these issues in detail.

6.3.5 Process Integrity

Most cryptographic products are implemented in part in software. If this software is modified (for example, to cause the substitution of trivial keys), the basic integrity of the cryptographic process itself can be undermined. Even hardware-based products may have some exposure if they use the system bus to pass information.

6.3.6 Cryptographic Strength

To date, only one algorithm, the Federal Data Encryption Standard, has undergone detailed examination and has been established as a standard for use by the U.S. Government (except for national security information) and for many private sector applications. Although other cryptosystems and algorithms are available, evaluation of their cryptographic strength is beyond the ability of most users. Therefore, care should be taken before selecting such systems.

6.4 Summary

Cryptography is an important and growing resource for information security. As information is increasingly exposed to potential access by unauthorized parties, particularly with the rapid growth of personal computers and data communications, cryptography offers the only truly effective method of protection. Figure 7–4 provides a summary of the various operational and technical characteristics of cryptographic protection systems.

In the past, cryptography has not been used widely because of inadequate algorithms, lack of necessary hardware, and key management problems. However, most of these problems have been reduced or eliminated. The primary blocks to the widespread implementation of cryptographic protection now seem to be the lack of recognition of the exposures, possible compatibility issues in rapidly developing networks and systems, and the failure to consider implementation of such controls before system design and installation.

7. SUMMARY

Information security technology in practice seems to lag behind what we know can be done about the intrusion problem. Many of the protective mechanisms discussed in this chapter have received renewed interest only after the potential risks of system intrusion began to be recognized by large numbers of users. There is considerable research currently underway to improve on this technology, some of which can be expected to be available relatively soon. The following discussion is intended as a look to the future of information security technology.

Intended Use
Communications Cryptography
Bulk File Cryptography
Integral File Cryptography
General Purpose Cryptographic Facilities
Application-Level Cryptography

Basic Type of Cryptosystem
Single-Key, Symmetric, Private Key
Dual-Key, Asymmetric, Public Key

Type of Algorithm
Proprietary
Nonproprietary
Data Encryption Standard
Other

Type of Implementation
Hardware
Stand-Alone Device
Standard Bus Expansion Board
Integral Device or Chip
Software
Operating System Modificaiton
Subroutine
Stand-Alone Program

Figure 7–4. Characteristics of Cryptographic Facilities

7.1 What is Needed

With the rapid introduction of microprocessor-based systems, including personal computers, the nature of the intrusion problem is changing. Large numbers of new users, the physical accessibility of equipment, the increasing use of data communications, and the decentralization of control combine to make the problems of intrusion protection very complex and difficult to manage. In particular, improvements are needed in mechanisms for user identification, system integrity, and communications security. In addition, standards are necessary to ensure that the mechanisms work together effectively.

7.2 User Identification

Several technologies are available for personal identification and authentication. These are based on physical characteristics of users, such as fingerprints, hand geometry, retinal patterns, and handwriting dynamics. The primary problems in using such mechanisms have been the cost and the lack of secure and reliable methods of transmitting authentication data to the system component which must use it. This has made such technology generally unacceptable for large networks of remote users. These technologies are now being applied, however, to special-purpose systems and personal computers.

The use of "smart card" technology offers considerable promise in the area of user authentication. Smart cards are devices the size of a credit card which contain a microprocessor and memory embedded in plastic. Systems based on such technology can incorporate user identification data, authentication passwords, and even audit trail information. They also have the twin advantages of requiring physical possession of an authentication "token" (the card itself) and being a familiar device for most people.

7.3 Trusted Computer Systems

The topic of trusted computer systems was discussed in Section 3, in connection with the DOD Trusted Systems Criteria. Because the criteria are quite rigorous, no previously existing computer system could qualify beyond the lowest levels. Systems that the manufacturers claim meet the criteria at the higher levels are beginning to appear in the marketplace. These are not yet in widespread use, and to date, only one system has been approved to operate at the highest security level. There is evidence that vendors are starting to use the criteria as design objectives in building both large and small systems. A number of equipment manufacturers are working with the DOD Computer Security Center to see that the criteria are met.

7.4 Communications Security

Cryptographic protection depends on effective transformation algorithms and key management. The former are generally available, although research continues on improved algorithms which can remain secure in the face of future computer technology. One of the main blocks to the widespread use of cryptographic protection has been the lack of acceptable key generation and distribution methods. Recent developments in key management standards and the judicious use of public key cryptosystems can be expected to help lessen this difficulty. Standard methods in this area will enable hardware and software developers to implement cryptographic protection that minimizes user involvement while ensuring general interoperability, both of which have been missing.

In situations in which the primary communications security problem is determined to be initial user authentication, port protection devices and the newer two-end authentication schemes may provide an answer. In the latter, devices placed at each end of a communications link undertake a mutual authentication protocol. Such systems can make use of new smart card technology. They can also be combined with cryptographic mechanisms to provide both authentication and cryptographic protection.

7.5 Standards and Guidance

In addition to improved technical mechanisms, there is a requirement for a level of standardization, or such mechanisms will become inoperable in increasingly integrated environments. Efforts are under way among several voluntary standards organizations, the National Bureau of Standards, and professional organizations to develop standards for additional aspects of system security. In addition to the Data Encryption Standard[4] and the Financial Institution Message Authentication Standard,[5]

---

[4] *Data Encryption Standard.*
[5] *Financial Institutions Message Authentication Standard X9.9.*

additional efforts are under way in the areas of cryptographic key management, network cryptographic implementation, and password management. Other areas of potential standards development include user access control and personal identification.

8. CONCLUSION

This chapter has described the general nature of the computer system intrusion problem and some of the existing technical methods for addressing the problem. It can be expected that technical innovations will continue to improve our ability to provide protection for critical information systems and data. However, technical solutions, although they tend to be automatic and reliable, are not always the most cost effective when all cost factors, such as personal productivity, are considered and balanced against a hard-to-quantify reduction in risk.

Technical controls are one element in an effective overall data security effort. Many of these powerful controls are now generally available, but they have not yet been used to the full measure of their potential.

────────── **DISCUSSION** ──────────

Marvin Schaefer*: We found a long time ago, when trying to do penetration studies for clients in private industry, that three things are true. First, we could not find systems that we were unable to penetrate, with penetrate meaning to take over completely. Second, when we told our clients what we could do, often they would not believe it, and on receiving a convincing demonstration, they would have a shock reaction. They had suddenly recognized that their defenses did not exist and that they were completely compromisable. Third, there was not

---

* Marvin Schaefer is the Chief Scientist of the National Computer Security Center.

anything that they could do to better the situation by patching or correcting the errors that they had discovered in their systems. In our past experience, when someone has tried to patch a system that we had penetrated, they would ask us to do it again. Generally, we would be able to penetrate the system much more quickly because it was only necessary for us to look at the logic of the patch and find an inconsistency between that and what we remembered about the system and exploit that inconsistency. Therefore, patching systems proved to be unsuccessful against skilled interlopers. In the criteria we used to study the systems, we discarded the idea of penetration testing, for the most part, as not being very significant because that kind of testing, like all testing, is a game of wits. On the one hand, the people who are building the system must be able to demonstrate that the system has no weaknesses. Interlopers must find only one weakness, and then they are able to penetrate the system. So, because repeated patching and testing do not work, we believe that strong design principles that are rigidly adhered to, walked through, and studied are the only means by which one can protect any system against penetration by a dedicated adversary. In the Defense Department we are concerned about dedicated adversaries, but we are finding increasingly that the banking community, the Treasury Department, and the Social Security Administration are quite concerned about intruders as well.

My major reaction to the paper by Troy, Katzke, and Steinauer is as follows. In their characterization of intrusion, they do not include the intentional misuse of information resources by persons who are authorized to use such resources in performing their normal job functions. I think that is a narrow definition because one must ask what it means to use one's official job function. If it means the transfer of $100,000 from an account when a client asked for $10,000 to be transferred, it is difficult to answer. I do not think that any of us can derive malicious intent by algorithmic means.

If, on the other hand, doctors are reviewing the financial records of patients in the hospital, other than their own, that might be an abuse of privilege. I would think that controls should be instituted to limit the scope of browsing by such people. If the people who work at Sprint, GTE, or MCI were to dump all of the access numbers and put them onto a bulletin board system, that would certainly be an abuse of privilege. Yet, if they can access any one of the systems, they can probably access all of them, and we must be concerned about that kind of activity.

This is a form of browsing that I call password browsing, which brings me to my first example of why most systems are not well protected with passwords. Various systems use a combination of passwords and encryption to try to separate users from intruders. UNIX is one of the more typical systems. The technique is that the user thinks of a password and types it in. The system runs some kind of a polynomial against it for which no known inverse is available. That produces an encrypted version of the password. The encrypted version is stored in a file that anyone can read. The reasons that it is stored there are twofold. First, system users were afraid that the people who knew the password might die or otherwise become unavailable, and they wanted to be able to get to it. Second, by encrypting passwords with a unique key or algorithm, there would be no reason to apply protection that the system does not control well anyway. The access control in UNIX is rather uncertain.

It turns out that there is a known attack against that; this is not the cryptographic attack that everyone thinks of, but a much simpler one. Most versions of the UNIX have a spelling correction dictionary. The dictionary consists of many English words and proper nouns. If one does an encryption of the entire spelling word dictionary and then tries to match that against the words in the password file, one finds an astounding number of matches, thereby discovering many user passwords.

Is that form of browsing within the purview of users doing their normal job functions? They are allowed access to the spelling correction dictionary. The algorithm used for encryption is public knowledge. The name of the password file is public knowledge. They are acting within their purview. It is not a good way of imposing security.

The use of passwords to protect files in general *seems* to be advocated in the paper. When people must store many passwords in a system, passwords must be redistributed periodically if files are to be protected in that manner. Therefore, password and crypto key redistribution are essentially the same problem. You must have a means of controlling access to passwords and encryption keys or the entire protection scheme is without value. However, one could contend that if you have the controls to restrict access to the encryption keys and to all of the file passwords, you might just as well not use the passwords and keys because the access control mechanism is good enough to prevent people from getting at the data in the first place.

The authors rule out the accidental finding of another person's file in the residue of a memory dump. However, one could deliberately cause a system to crash so that memory dumps would be produced which could then be perused for the contents of user files. That was one of the techniques that I first stumbled onto in the late 1960s. I found the payroll file and found out how underpaid I was compared with my peers.

In the paper it is stated, and I agree, that users should not be granted more authority and more power on the system than they absolutely need to perform their normal job functions. The notion that a process acting on the user's behalf must be as constrained as is the user was properly stated in the chapter, but it was not given enough emphasis.

Throughout the chapters, all of those technological mechanisms that are done to prevent software piracy were discussed: how a program will go in, start executing, and begin signaling, storing things here and there and looking for them later. All of these things are invisible to the users, and all of the information being read by that program, except for information that the user explicitly asks it to read, is invisible as well.

A number of us who participated in the workshop have been involved in riding the so-called Trojan horses. A Trojan horse is something that lives in a new program like WordStar or some such program that does everything, including two-column output and footnotes. If I were on a multi-user system, I would be delighted to be using it from any of the ports at which I could get on, but I would be displeased if every file I was writing was also being sent over to my friend in another building for his perusal. Yet, such a system could certainly do that without my ever knowing it. After all, whatever the SAVE command does is completely unknown to those of us who do not know how DOS works. Therefore, protection against Trojan horses is necessary.

Time bombs have been advocated as a means of protecting software. This means that if the software runs on an unauthorized machine, it zeroes itself out. Or if it finds that the signaling device is not functioning correctly, it destroys what was output as well as itself. For example, the public library system in Montgomery County, Maryland, was held for ransom this year by the people who built their catalog control system. The time came for a renewal of the contract, and the library was told that if they did not renew before a certain date, all of the check-out data in the system would be destroyed.

A few other items were mentioned in the paper that allowed me to make a few observations. The first observation in the mutual authentication protocol was that before I give my password to that system, whatever that system is, I would like to know that I am talking to the operating system and not to an application. If I am entering the system over a telecommunications network, any of the switches along that network might be listening to everything I am typing, whether or not I am using encryption, thanks to other properties of encryption. So I do not know where my password is going.

Another observation is that it is necessary to know the amount of time it takes intruders to determine the passwords. Passwords should be changed very frequently. An eight-character password against a dedicated interloper is good for a few months, at the very most. Therefore, people who pick a password that is their mother's maiden name or whatever are doing themselves a disservice. Those who keep a password for a number of years have probably been compromised, if they have any data worth stealing.

The third observation deals with the notion that an embedded subsystem provides security in some sense. I want to hit on a hard problem, not a fallacy in the paper, but a hard problem. The question is, where are the data? Suppose there is a data base management application in which some people are supposed to see some parts of the common data base and other people are supposed to see other parts of the same data base. Generally, the data reside on a disk, and access to the disk is generally controlled by the operating system. The user can talk either to the operating system or to the data base management system. The point is, if users are not willing to live by the consequences of a decision made by the DBMS, they may choose to try to get to their data directly through the operating system.

Jon Baumgarten: I would like to get the scientific people to focus on what they are trying to do. Are they aiming for a foolproof system, for the most inconvenient system for intruders, or just for something that will hold until Congress can act?

Dennis Steinauer: Before working for the Government, I was responsible for data security for a time-sharing firm. I found that what the industry wants is something that costs nothing and is foolproof. If it costs anything at all, then they want data on its cost-effectiveness. They said they are not going to put anything in unless there is solid data to prove that it is worth it. What is on the other side of that balance sheet? Well, if it is only losses that you did not incur, you are never going to get those data.

From a Government point of view, I am very hesitant to suggest regulation. However, because of the demand on the part of those who must spend the money for controls for some measure of their value, there is probably some minimum standards that need to be established. There will be a user identifier whenever you use a system. Perhaps even for your personal computer, you might have to put a key in it to turn it on. That is obviously very controversial, and it would be difficult to put definitions or specifications onto some of those controls. But, perhaps that is necessary so the user and operating community can stop looking for the quantitative excuse to provide some security. Their excuse will be that they are required to do it.

Stuart Katzke: We would like to see those mechanisms built into the systems in such a way that they are transparent to the user so that they do not provide any obstacle to the user. If I am going through a network and want to communicate with someone, all I would have to do is indicate perhaps whether I wanted a protected line. I identify myself and I am authenticated. I tell the system who I want to talk to and all the other mechanisms take place automatically.

John Maxfield: From the hackers' point of view, if you make that transparent, then you have defeated the hacker. The hackers are looking for holes; they're looking for ways around the doors. If they can't get in the door, they'll try the window. System managers see their systems differently. If system managers implement a particular front-end security program, they must pay to install and maintain it. They will probably have to hire somebody just to assign passwords, to take care of problems when users forget their passwords, and all of the routine maintenance that goes along with it.

So they view it strictly as an expense, and it is an expense that cannot be recovered. If you require them to have a minimum level, then they can't say that they should not spend the money.

Marvin Schaefer: On the no-log-on message issue, there are two things that bother me. One is that the system is not going to identify itself; it is not really any different from the voice-actuated modems or other front-end port protection devices. I think they are good for two weeks against the hacker community before that information will be on the computer bulletin boards. The other thing is that if I am going to identify myself to a computer and give it my password, I would like the computer to identify itself to me.

I also do not like the idea of a card that has all the data. I do like the idea of a person keying in a personal password after the card has gone through and authenticated itself to the system, which has authenticated itself back to the card, so that a lost or stolen card cannot be used without its owner.

There are secure systems, or at least products that can be used securely, but there is not yet enough demand so that they can be profitably sold, even in the United States. Only until the commercial sector demands security is it going to be profitable to offer it. So I think that within the Government we can start putting out regulations. We can do many things, but the add-on security packages did not appear until the people in the SHARE user's group started demanding security for IBM mainframes.

Jon Baumgarten: What are some of the reasons for the lack of user demand in the United States for secure systems? Is it cost? Is it the lack of user-friendliness?

Marvin Schaefer: Certainly, part of it is a lack of user-friendliness. The other problem is that because people are currently using unsecure computers, they are trapped in their existing system. The ability to move to something better is fairly limited, and conversion is very expensive.

Donn Parker: I think that we have to look at the spectrum of people that we are trying to protect against. There are safeguards that will work in one range, and there are much more sophisticated safeguards that must work in the other ranges. We should not condemn a low level of protection because it does not stop the most expert cracker. We need a spectrum of levels of protection because we have a spectrum of levels of enemies.

Jon Baumgarten: Are you suggesting that the only solution is a technical one? Let the company choose the degree of security that it requires to stop the kind of penetration that it wants to stop and everything else goes by the boards.

Donn Parker: No. I am saying exactly the opposite. Technical solutions do not work well at all, unless you put them into a framework in which people will be willing to cooperate and let them work.

John Maxfield: There's a spectrum of abusers. On one end of the spectrum there is a 14-year-old boy with a $250 home computer and all of his friends. Using a brute-force approach, they get into a system and vandalize it, causing untold headaches for months for the staff maintaining the system.

On the other end of the spectrum there are the few highly skilled hackers or intruders who can break just about any operating system known. One of these people can do as much damage as the juveniles.

It is probably easier to stop the low end of the spectrum, but what is happening in industry is that there is not even this level of protection. There needs to be a minimum level which drops somewhere into the center of this spectrum and at least wipes out the bottom half. This would be the minimum standard . . . The experts would have to be dealt with on a completely different level in a completely different way.

Neil Iscoe: One reason there is little user demand for security is that people do not want to put their jobs on the line, for example by saying that their bank has theft. The responsible people do not want to do that for obvious reasons, and bank management does not want them to do it for their own reasons.

From a bank standpoint, banks do have theft. Banks also have problems involving bad loans that they refuse to write off and carry on their books to make their balance sheets look good. There are Federal regulations that try to prevent banks from doing that. I think it would logically follow, because there are these regulations on the banks already, in terms of standard audits and standard procedures, that the banks might be required to follow standard security procedures.

In terms of the inconvenience factors, there are two types. There is the inconvenience factor to the person trying to break the system, and there is the inconvenience factor to the legitimate user. If you lock your house, you must carry your key.

Jon Baumgarten: I think that the bar generally views software duplication and intrusion as two problems. Yet, it seems we have heard a lot about one aspect of computer system intrusion, particularly on the bulletin boards, leading to software duplication. . . . Has the intrusion problem been included in the Association of Data Processing Service Organizations (ADAPSO) inquiry or have they been viewed as two separate problems?

Neil Iscoe: I think the ethical argument is the same. Certain things are wrong, and people must come to realize this. However, the means of telling people that and the means of keeping people on the right track are different. The ADAPSO effort is directed toward single-user microcomputers and local area networks, not the larger systems that typically have data bases and a large number of dial-in ports.

Jon Baumgarten: Apparently, some of the copy protection breaking codes are available on the bulletin boards. In some cases, the software itself can be downloaded.

John Maxfield: You can get programs off the bulletin boards. A lot of hackers started off as software crackers. They started out playing with their home computer, doing everything they could to it and breaking the software. They got bored with it . . . so they got a modem and went exploring on the networks. They were not satisfied with the United States so they went on to the rest of the world, and so on. It just keeps escalating, but it often starts with piracy.

Neil Iscoe: There are a lot of similarities between the technical protection schemes for intrusion in terms of encryption and port protection and the technical protection schemes that are used to keep a piece of software from being stolen.

Michael Tyler: I agree that both ethically and sociologically both problems come from the same mind set. To a large extent, the base of operations is these underground clubs. There you have a peer-to-peer network, and there is a total absence of any kind of governing force—a club adviser who says that they better be careful, this may not be legal.

In my paper I mentioned two different teenagers who made comments on piracy. I'm going to read their comments as piracy, but listen to it as hacking and you will see that it is exactly the same idea. One of them said, "It's fun to break programs. Some groups promote. What happens is one person in the group gets a package and then everybody else goes after it." The second teenager, who went to a computer club, said,

"This is illegal, but we're basically honest people, and I don't know anyone else who doesn't pirate software."

I think that the issue that we must address here . . . is what can the legislators, the vendors, the legitimate users, the managers, and especially the teachers do to change that mind set. I think that it is a psychological or a sociological problem that we must solve.

John Maxfield: Each fall a new class enters high school, and I see an immediate upswing in bulletin board activity and an increase in new names among the bulletin board messages. New handles appear as new teenagers become introduced by the older teenagers and the adults to the phreaking, hacking, and pirating scenes.

It is a self-perpetuating cycle. . . . Now we almost have a complete generation that has been exposed to at least mainframe hacking at the college level. These people are out there in industry now. That is definitely a sociological problem.

I did a talk for some computer science teachers for one of the local school districts in the Detroit area. I asked them that as educators, wasn't there something they could do in their computer classes to teach the ethical operation of computers. One gentleman, a high school principal, said that they had been trying to teach morality to the kids for 50 years, and look where they are today.

So, I didn't see too much help coming from that sector. The educators feel that they are up against a brick wall. It goes back to the fact that many of these kids get into what they are doing because they have the tacit approval, and in some cases the active approval, and encouragement of their parents.

Donn Parker: These kids, through this activity, are establishing values very early in their computer education that it is acceptable practice to violate the law and to engage in this kind of activity.

I've been working with some high school computer technology instructors, who although they are among the worst offenders in this whole area, are starting to realize what they have been doing and are starting to try to give some application of ethics to these young people. But these kids are going to be programming our banking systems in another 10 years, and what kind of values do they take with them if they are learning to break the law in these ways in fourth, fifth, and sixth grades?

Linda Garcia: I'm struck by the ethical issues, or let's say the educational issues. What seems to me to be the dilemma is if you look toward educational institutions which teach the values at the same time that there's an accusatory sense toward teachers as being thieves, I don't know how you're going to get a cooperative mode without some kind of dialog about those underlying values.

I hear both themes expressed. The teachers are the enforcers; at the same time we're accusing them of being pirates. I wonder if there is something that must be done first to get them involved by recognizing their legitimate needs as educators.

Rick Giardina: I would like to address that. I do a lot of lecturing on this subject and I have always visualized a three-pronged approach to the problem, with the major one always being education. It includes a development of the values, but it is even more than that, and I think industry is addressing it. We have developed programs in which schools can get massive amounts of software for an incredibly small amount of money.

We have an entire education endowment program in my corporation, and I know that Ashton-Tate has a similar program and MicroSoft is doing the same thing. But it is more than just the values. There is a basic misconception in this country on the part of educators and users as to what their rights and responsibilities are under the Copyright Act and the other laws.

I absolutely trust the basic American sense of fair play. I just do not believe that the number of people in this country who are making illegal copies would make them if they knew they were doing something that is as improper and dangerous as they, in fact, are doing.

It is that message that I think needs to be gotten across, and that may be the approach with which we need to deal with the teachers so that they understand their rights and responsibilities. Then they can pass those values on to their students while they are teaching them computers in general.

John Maxfield: We're talking about educating the purchasers of software and the teachers. The thing I run into constantly is that law enforcement officials do not understand computers. We need to have some kind of training program set up for law enforcement.

Our legislators, in turn, need to be brought up to date on the issues so that they can draft these laws properly. . . . So there are several areas of education and . . . no one area is going to solve the problem.

BIBLIOGRAPHY

Air Force Communications Command. *A Small Computer Security Handbook,* p. 16. Gunter Air Force Station, Alabama: Data Systems Design Center, July 21, 1983.

American National Standards Institute. *Financial Institutions Message Authentication Standard.* American National Standards Institute, 1982.

Department of Defense. *Department of Defense Trusted Computer System Evaluation Criteria.* Fort George G. Meade, Maryland: Department of Defense Computer Security Center, August 15, 1983.

Edwards, Robert W., and Lynda E. Edwards. "Unauthorized Entry." *ICP Interface-Administrative and Accounting,* Winter (1982): 22–26.

Hansen, James V. "Audit Considerations in Distributed Processing Systems." *Communications of the ACM* August (1983): 562–569.

Murray, William H. "Good Security Practices for Personal Computers." *Computer Security Journal* Fall/Winter (1983): 77–83.

Murray, William H. "Good Security Practices for Dial-Up Systems." *Computer Security Journal* Fall/Winter (1983): 83–88.

National Bureau of Standards. *Guidelines for Automatic Data Processing Physical Security and Risk Management.* Washington, D.C.: National Bureau of Standards, February 1974.

National Bureau of Standards. *Glossary for Computer Systems Security.* Washington, D.C.: National Bureau of Standards, February 1976.

National Bureau of Standards. *Data Encryption Standard.* Washington, D.C.: National Bureau of Standards, January 1977.

National Bureau of Standards. *Guidelines for Automatic Data Processing Risk Analysis.* Washington, D.C.: National Bureau of Standards, August 1979.

National Bureau of Standards. *Guidelines for Security of Computer Applications.* Washington, D.C.: National Bureau of Standards, June 1980.

National Bureau of Standards. *Guideline for User Authentication Techniques for Computer Network Access Control.* Washington, D.C.: National Bureau of Standards, September 1980.

National Bureau of Standards. *Guideline on Integrity Assurance and Control in Database Administration.* Washington, D.C.: National Bureau of Standards, August 1981.

National Bureau of Standards. *Guideline for Computer Security Certification and Accreditation.* Washington, D.C.: National Bureau of Standards, September 1983.

Smith, Jim. "Call-Back Security System Prevents Unauthorized Computer Access." *Mini-Micro Systems* July (1984): 257–265.

Steinauer, Dennis D. *Security in Small Computer Systems.* Auerbach Publishers, Inc., 1984.

Steinauer, Dennis D. "Security of Personal Computers: A Growing Concern." *Computer Security Journal* (1984).

Troy, Eugene F. "Thwarting the Hackers." *Datamation* July (1984): 117–128.

Troy, Eugene F. "A Guide to Dial-Up Port Protection Products." *Computer Security Newsletter* July/August (1984): 4–5.

Von Glahm, Peter G., David J. Farber, and Stephen T. Walker. *The Trusted Office of the Future.* Newark, Delaware: The University of Delaware, October 24, 1983.

—————— eight ——————
SUMMARY AND CONCLUSIONS

Frank L. Huband

I. PERSPECTIVES ON THE PROBLEM

In the chapters by Michael Tyler and by Donn Parker and John Maxfield, the extent of unauthorized software duplication and computer system intrusion is examined. Although more detailed knowledge of the scope of the problems is needed, the authors of both papers conclude that unauthorized use—both duplication and intrusion—is substantial and increasing. One reviewer feels that a more searching examination of costs arising from unauthorized duplication is necessary before accurate conclusions can be drawn. One software vendor representative indicates that his company's policy toward software protection has changed from no protection to sophisticated protection as a result of losses attributable to piracy. Conversely, other vendors have changed their products from highly protected to unprotected. A complicating factor in identifying the extent of computer crime is that related activities range from those that are apparently benign (hobbyists having fun, professionals duplicating purchased software within the fair-use allowance) to those that are clearly criminal or subversive (changing numbers in bank computers, manipulating credit card account records, attempting to gain access to government computers). It is sometimes difficult to separate criminal activities from the noncriminal.

Although the general public views the plight of the software vendors with at most sympathy and concern, the threat of intrusion into sensitive computer databases evokes images of a criminal element causing potentially disastrous consequences. David Burnham of the *New York Times* has presented an interesting thesis: We tend to view computer crime in the context of the impact that the individual has on an institution; but we should also concern ourselves with the impact that abuse of computerized systems in institutions can have on individuals and traditional democratic values. For example, an individual whose computerized credit card or banking records have been tampered with could be greatly harmed.

Several authors express the belief that the root of both unauthorized software duplication and computer system intrusion lies in the mores and attitudes of the perpetrators, based in turn on societal attitudes. There is a lack of understanding among many computer users as to their rights and responsibilities under the law. Unauthorized software duplication and computer system intrusion are sometimes called "piracy," which can cloak illicit activities with an exciting aura. Thus for society to develop an attitude that computer crime is wrong, it must first overcome a current positive image of the activity.

2. LEGAL APPROACHES

The legal approaches to deterrence of illicit software use and intrusion into software databases are discussed in the chapters by Jon Baumgarten and by Susan Nycum and Daniel Appelman. They indicate that, although existing Federal statutes in the area of unauthorized duplication and existing State computer crime statutes in the area of intrusion proscribe these actions in principle and provide a basis for law enforcement action, both types of statutes may require adjustments and clarifications. The existing copyright law, for example, may not draw properly the line between legitimate backup copies and inappropriate duplication. There may be a need in particular to deal with the issue of rental of software, discriminating between legitimate needs for preview copies and inappropriate opportunities for unauthorized copying of software.

The existing patchwork of State legislation with respect to intrusion into computer databases may provide an inadequate legal framework for deterring such intrusion. Establishment of a uniform set of State laws or enactment of Federal statutes in this area are alternative approaches suggested by the authors. Current Federal law is limited to jurisdiction over national security data and over Federal and financial computer systems. If encouraging legislative guidance were provided, Federal law enforcement agencies could become partners with the States in the formulation of coherent, consistent policies regarding computer crime. The fact that computer crimes often take place across state lines argues strongly for the pursuit of such a coordinated effort among states and with Federal participation.

Authors discussing both unauthorized duplication and computer intrusion, however, appear to agree that there are limits to the role of legal process in dealing with these problems. Many investigators believe that the overwhelming percentage of such activities is undetected. Even the most coordinated and comprehensive laws are impotent against undetected crime. Substantial improvements in the levels of technical security may be necessary to surface the existence of illicit activity.

3. TECHNICAL APPROACHES

Much effort has been put into development of technical tools to use as deterrents to unauthorized use of computer software and to unauthorized intrusion into databases. Deterrents to unauthorized use include more sophisticated protection against disk duplication; external hardware devices, such as serial and parallel port boxes, for authorizations; keyboards and other externally connected hardware; cryptoprocessors; and other boards and special chips to be installed inside the computer.

Several categories of controls can provide protection against computer system intrusion. The physical equipment and its operating environment can be protected, emanations control can suppress or shield compromising electronic emanations, security-related events in the system and its environment can be monitored, system and data access control determine which users have access to individual system resources, port protection devices can be added to existing systems to discourage unauthorized access to communication ports, and finally, cryptography can transform data into an unintelligible form for transmission or storage. The effectiveness, cost, and complexity of these protection schemes vary tremendously. The appropriate deterrent device is the one providing the best trade-off between user friendliness and the risk of intrusion.

Establishment of a mandated minimal standard of protection against penetration for all commercial databases could substantially reduce the risk of penetration by amateur "hackers" of limited skill. Some experts, however, argue that amateur penetrations actually provide a beneficial early warning of system vulnerabilities to large potential losses by professionals.

There are systems—Honeywell Multics for example—that are relatively secure. However, the Multics system has been available for a decade, and it has not significantly penetrated the market, perhaps because users of other systems are committed to existing systems, and software conversion is very expensive. A technical solution must be easy enough to use that people will be willing to cooperate. One company that purchased the Multics system, because of the unfriendliness caused by the security features, reportedly removed over a period of time all the control mechanisms until there was no security at all. The result was that everybody was pleased. The Board of Directors were happy because they thought they had a perfectly secure computer system. The users were happy because they had a user-friendly (although completely unprotected) system. Any individuals desiring to penetrate the system would also, presumably, be happy.

Another reason for the relative lack of user demand for strongly security-oriented products is that many people do not want to admit that they have a problem with computer system intrusion. For example, in banks, data processing managers do not want to reveal, by requesting a more secure computer system, that they may be losing money through their existing computer systems. Management also does not want to publicize possible losses for competitive purposes.

4. COMBINATION OF APPROACHES

A combination of legal, technical, and educational approaches will probably be necessary to reduce the impact of illicit software use and database intrusion. Technical and legal approaches are complementary, in that a legal prohibition not only justifies private action or prosecution, but also renders technical approaches socially acceptable. Strictly legal solutions might be premature if people put too much reliance on them and thereby impede the development of technical solutions. The coexistence of educational programs can facilitate the successful implementation of technical and legal solutions. Trade associations, professional societies, and manufacturers can provide educational materials that inform the public about the potential societal harm from illicit computer activities.

As new inventions are introduced into society, standards of ethical behavior for their use are developed. For example, when telephone communications used party lines, "listening in" was a standard practice. Everyone listened to each other's telephone calls, and it was considered to be mere mischief. As more people began to use the telephone for conversations that required more privacy, "listening in" became ethically wrong as well as illegal. Similarly, for unauthorized software duplication and computer system intrusion the main problem may be that society does not understand the issues well enough to determine what is right—computer users remain unconvinced when they are told that unauthorized duplication and intrusion are wrong. Technical protection devices can be ways of putting up "no trespassing" signs that tell intruders that what they are doing is wrong. Moral values associated with unauthorized duplication and intrusion will evolve, and this evolution will influence both the need for and the acceptance of legislative and technical protections.

5. RECENT DEVELOPMENTS

While this book was being edited, additional information became available on some of the issues discussed in the previous chapters. A report of the survey on the extent of piracy of business software by Future Computing, Inc. was released in January 1985.[1] Its results are based on 45,000 responses to a questionnaire mailed to 70,000 households. The report authors estimate that about half of the copies of the twelve surveyed personal-computer business packages were illicitly copied. A most interesting survey result is that copy-protected software is pirated at about the same rate as unprotected software. The authors estimate that about $800 million in additional sales would be made in the United States in 1985 if all possessors of illicit copies of software were to buy that software. To discourage illegal copying of software, vendors and their trade association, the Association of Data Processing Service Organization (ADAPSO), have begun an aggressive program to enforce their rights under the Copyright Act. Micropro International filed suit in February 1985 against a Fortune 500 firm, the Wilson Jones subsidiary of American Brands, alleging illicit copying of several products including Wordstar. Earlier suits against smaller companies have been pursued by Micropro and by Lotus Development Corporation. The publicity from these suits seems to have encouraged more firms to adopt policies against copying of proprietary software, but ADAPSO plans to propose additional legislation to strengthen the rights of vendors.[2]

---

1 Press release from Future Computing, Inc., Dallas, TX, January 17, 1985.

2 *Infoworld,* Feb. 4, 1985, p. 17.

An alternative approach to deter unauthorized copying is a vendor's addition of "worms" or "booby traps" to software so that unauthorized copying will cause an error to be inserted into the user's operating system, causing the computer to malfunction at a later time. Two software protection vendors, Vault Corporation and Defendisk, announced products using this approach in late 1984. The market potential of such products may be in doubt, however, based on the strongly negative response by some prospective users of software protected by such means.[3]

National Security Decision Directive 145 was issued by the White House on September 17, 1984. In it, procedures are established for an increased effort to protect sensitive information and for the National Security Agency (NSA) to exercise a leadership role in defining computer and telecommunications security in all Federal agencies. Some excerpts follow:

Telecommunications and automated information processing systems are highly susceptible to interception, unauthorized electronic access, and related forms of technical exploitation, as well as other dimensions of the hostile intelligence threat. The technology to exploit these electronic systems is widespread and is used extensively by foreign nations and can be employed, as well, by terrorist groups and criminal elements. Government systems as well as those which process the private or proprietary information of U.S. persons and businesses can become targets for foreign exploitation.

The President therefore directed that

a. Systems which generate, store, process, transfer or communicate classified information in electrical form shall be secured by such means as are necessary to prevent compromise or exploitation.

b. Systems handling other sensitive, but unclassified, government or government-derived information, the loss of which could adversely affect the national security interest, shall be protected

---

3 *Infoworld,* Nov. 19, 1984, pp. 45–46.

in proportion to the threat of exploitation and the associated potential damage to the national security.

c. The government shall encourage, advise, and where appropriate, assist the private sector to: identify systems which handle sensitive non-government information, the loss of which could adversely affect the national security; determine the threat to, and vulnerability of, these systems; and formulate strategies and measures for providing protection in proportion to the threat of exploitation and the associated potential damage. Information and advice from the perspective of the private sector will be sought with respect to implementation of this policy. In cases where implementation of security measures to non-governmental systems would be in the national security interest, the private sector shall be encouraged, advised, and where appropriate, assisted in undertaking the application of such measures.[4]

This action by the Executive Branch complements the recent efforts of Congress to deter computer abuse. The Hughes Bill (HR 5616) is cited in Chapter 6 as being in the process of being approved. At this writing, the Bill has been enacted as the Counterfeit Access Device and Computer Fraud and Abuse Act of 1984 (18 U. S. Code 1030). In the Act, felony penalties are established for unauthorized access to computers to obtain information that could compromise national security. Misdemeanor penalties are established for intrusions into computers operated on behalf of the Federal Government or into other computers to obtain financial information from financial institutions, or credit information on consumers. Early in 1985 the first indictment under the Act was reported of a 26-year-old California computer operator who allegedly broke into a U.S. Department of Agriculture computer in Colorado. The American Civil Liberties Union and others have expressed concern that the Act might have undesirable social consequences by being used, for example, to discourage whistleblowers. Others feel that the Act did not go far enough in defining, for example, the legality of wiretap interception of digital data. Late in the 98th

---

4 National Security Decision Directive 145, Executive Office of the President, September 17, 1984.

Congress the Department of Justice submitted an alternate (S 940) to the Hughes Bill that was described as defining but limiting Federal jurisdiction. The House Crime Subcommittee and the Senate Subcommittee on Criminal Law held hearings in the summer and fall of 1985 to assess whether further legislation is necessary.

6. CONCLUSIONS

Effective solutions to the problems of unauthorized software duplication and computer system intrusion will be difficult to discover and implement. The problem is compounded by the fact that we are in an age of ubiquitous information-based services that require computers at all levels of society. It will first be necessary to obtain more empirical data to establish and convince policymakers and the citizens that action needs to be taken. Second, the Federal Government, vendors, and the institutions being injured have a role in educating students, parents, teachers, law enforcement officials, and legislators as to the consequence of illegal computer-related activities. Third, establishment of a minimal security control standard for all commercial systems may deter amateur offenders, and perhaps make for easier apprehension of professional criminals. Finally, improved technical methods to resist unauthorized software duplication and computer system intrusion could be developed and implemented.

INDEX

A

U

U.S. Copyright Office, 4, 36
U.S. Department of Justice, 124
Unauthorized access, 148
Unauthorized copying, 42
Unauthorized duplication, 11
Unauthorized User Access, 181
United Computer Corp., 20
Universal Copyright Convention, 66
UNIX, 228
Unsavory hackers, 126
User friendliness, 244

V

Variance detection, 185
Vault Corporation, 247
Venture capitalists, 32
Verbatim, 57
VisiCalc, 23, 98, 119
VisiCorp, 23, 29, 118
VisiFile, 119
VisiTrend, 119

W

Wargames, 137
White-collar crime, 1
Wildcard, 118
Wilson Jones, 246
Winchester hard disk, 22
Wire Fraud Statute, 163
WordStar, 24
Worms, 247

Y

Yates Ventures, 29